Fallible
Forms and Symbols

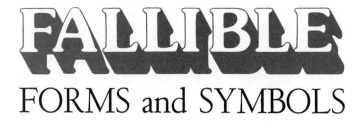

# FORMS and SYMBOLS

*Discourses on Method in a Theology of Culture*

Bernard E. Meland

FORTRESS PRESS   Philadelphia

*Library of Congress Catalog Card Number 76–007868*

*ISBN 0–8006–0453–9*

5775E76     Printed in U.S.A.     1–453

# Contents

# Acknowledgments

The concern with an elemental sense of creaturehood which runs
through all that I have written suggests affinities with the spirit of inquiry
that was initially projected by Schleiermacher, and continued by Rudolf
Otto and Paul Tillich, with revisions and variations expressive of their
own distinctive, phenomenological bent of mind. The affinities here, however, are in the stance rather than in method; for it is my concern to pursue the import of ultimacy within experience as an efficacy within the
lived event, in contrast to their appeal to the *numinis*. This is why William James's view of relations and Alfred North Whitehead's formulation
of causal efficacy loom so prominently in my use of process thought.
Nevertheless, the stimulus and lure of all of these seminal thinkers are
implicit in what I have projected; and for this I express gratitude.

Discussion of method in theological inquiry has long been a concern to
theologians at the University of Chicago, and I have benefited both from
the criticism and the encouragement of former teachers, colleagues, and
students. The persisting stimulus of the early Chicago school as represented by Shailer Mathews and Gerald Birney Smith perennially surfaces,
often to my surprise, in the way that imagery of thought and its historical
development appear important to me in understanding any contemporary
stance. Similarly, the influence of Henry Nelson Wieman is indelibly
upon me, though as much in the way I have resisted or countered his insistence on restricting inquiry to what is manageable, as in the way I have
continued to explore areas of undefined awareness and "the rich fullness
of experience" which were first opened up to me through the stimulus of
his early thought. I am indebted also to Wilhelm Pauck, Bernard M.
Loomer, Daniel Day Williams, and Charles Hartshorne for their stimulus

and encouragement during our years as colleagues in the theological field of the University of Chicago. Our camaraderie of thought, enabling us to confront our affinities and differences with candor and with mutual concern for what each of us was about, even as we pursued common ends as a field, created a situation of criticism and rapport which was unique in its stimulus and in its encouragement of creative effort. Theological method at Chicago during earlier years often appeared to outsiders as being one thing, centering in what has been loosely described as empirical. Yet, to those of us who worked together in pursuing various trails within that common orientation, our occasions of divergence became stimulating, not only in defining our identities within such an orientation, but in opening up dimensions we had missed while pursuing our individual bent of interest. For these memorable experiences and their legacy, I express my gratitude and affection to these former colleagues.

This experience of rapport and mutual criticism has persisted in my relations with younger colleagues, now established in various institutions as theologians, who were formerly students in my classes: notably John Cobb, Schubert Ogden, and Clark Williamson; and, more recently, Edgar Towne, Larry Greenfield, and Philip Hefner, to whom I am also indebted for suggestions and criticism in editing and revising portions of this manuscript. What I have written in these pages will, I venture to say, interest each of them, but will as readily evoke their critical response on various issues. To each of them I express gratitude.

Many of the themes explored in this book will be familiar to many former students of mine in the Divinity School of the University of Chicago as well as to students who were in my seminars at Union Theological Seminary, New York, during the year I was a visiting professor. For their stimulus and continuing friendship I am grateful.

I wish to express gratitude also to Mrs. Delores Smith, administrative assistant in Dean Joseph Mitsuo Kitagawa's office, and to Mrs. Rehova Arthur, faculty secretaries supervisor in the Divinity School, and her associates for their generous help in facilitating the preparation of the manuscript.

Some of the essays in this volume are revised and elaborated versions of articles which were previously published in various journals. I am grateful to the editors and publishers of these journals for permission to reprint material as indicated: "The Structure of Christian Faith," *Religion in Life* 37, no. 4 (Winter 1968–69); "The New Realism in Religious Inquiry," *Encounter* 31, no. 4 (Autumn 1970); "Language and Reality in the Christian Faith," *Encounter* 34, no. 4 (Autumn 1973); "The Mystery of Existing and Not Existing," *Union Seminary Quarterly Review* 30, nos. 2–4 (Winter–Summer 1975).

I am indebted to the following publishers for permission to quote from works published by them: Harper & Row Publishers, Inc., New York, for quotations from Edwin A. Burtt, *Types of Religious Philosophy* (1939); Macmillan Publishing Company, Inc., New York, for quotations from Alfred North Whitehead, *Symbolism, Its Meaning and Effect* (copyright Macmillan, 1927, renewed 1955 by Evelyn Whitehead), *Process and Reality* (copyright Macmillan, 1929, renewed 1957 by Evelyn Whitehead), and *Adventures of Ideas* (copyright Macmillan, 1933, renewed 1961 by Evelyn Whitehead); Macmillan, London and Basingstoke, Ltd., for quotation from Dorothy Emmet, *The Nature of Metaphysical Thinking* (1945); SPCK, London, for quotation from the essay by Rudolf Bultmann in *Kerygma and Myth,* edited by H. W. Bartsch and translated by R. H. Fuller (1953); T. & T. Clark, Ltd., for quotation from H. Wheeler Robinson, *The Christian Doctrine of Man* (1911, 3d ed. 1926); Southern Illinois University Press and Mrs. Henry Nelson Wieman for quotations from Henry Nelson Wieman, *Religious Experience and Scientific Method* (copyright Macmillan, 1926, renewed 1954 by Henry Nelson Wieman) and *The Source of Human Good* (copyright University of Chicago Press, 1946, renewed by Henry Nelson Wieman); and the University of Chicago Press for quotation from Paul Tillich, *The Protestant Era* (1948).

B.E.M.

# Introduction

The theme "Fallible Forms and Symbols" would seem to convey something so self-evident as to appear tautological. Certainly language, in whatever form, by virtue of being human is liable to error. My justification for risking redundancy here is the loss of perspective upon the limitations of language in technical discourse, notably in theology and philosophy of religion, where the precise word or the chiseled belief in expressing doctrine is often zealously sought. The lapse here takes on particular significance because of the nature and scope of inquiry. For, to the degree that a discourse addresses inquiries that look beyond the commonplace concerns of experience to a range of apprehensions dimly in focus, as suggested, for example, by terms like "ultimate reality," "ultimate concern," or "ultimate commitment," the texture of possible meaning both enlarges and intensifies, with nuances only slightly intimated. Among elemental folk a language presumed to be suitable to contemplating such textured meaning was seized upon in the form of myth and pantomime, designed to articulate in graphic, though indirect, language and act, what was dimly apprehended. In being reduced to strict directives in later cultic contexts, these "playful" expressions of apprehension gained in intensity of meaning what they lost in range and sensibility. And this process has been in evidence all along among historical religions where the seriousness of piety and belief impelled rigor in formulating and authenticating expressions of belief. Hence, the creating and employing of forms and symbols in religious thought with a view to achieving precision and propriety of meaning in the exercise and presentation of the faith have run into problems of another sort, such as questioning whether such forms and symbols expressed adequately or even reliably what inhered in the reality apprehended, experienced, or lived.

This problem has been especially acute in Western thinking, notably among Christian theologians and churchmen; for here the demand for meticulousness of belief or the concern for "right belief" has loomed large. Interestingly enough, the subsiding of church authority among Protestants, which removed the pressure of adhering to an authorized system of correct belief, did not alter this emphasis significantly. The so-called free churches, and later, liberal Christians, for whom individual assent supplanted church authority, continued to press for the authentic way of expressing the terms of Christian faith. For the former, "right belief" continued to be a haunting imperative. Among the latter, especially where the legacy of Christian faith as expressed through Scripture or church doctrine seemed unavailable, the appeal to religious experience, to science, to philosophy, even sociology and psychology, became ways of attaining security in belief. The lure of certainty has been perennially with us, either in the form of an appeal to the biblical or creedal word, or to the reasoned word as informed by science or philosophy. In all of these efforts at attaining security, or even certainty in belief, the issue of form and symbol has emerged, though it has not always been in focus, and certainly not always to the fore. It has come to the fore with particular urgency in recent years, and I mean to participate in that effort not simply as an historical inquiry, but as one that is being fruitfully addressed within various disciplines where the dimensional and contextual character of our knowing and our experiencing is being seriously attended.

# I

In these discourses I confine myself to the use of the terms form and symbol in the sense in which they relate to the process of abstraction, much in the manner described by Suzanne Langer in *Philosophical Sketches* (1962) when she writes, "The perception of form arises from the process of symbolization. And the perception of form is abstraction."[1] In technical discourse this would mean the envisagement of whatever is available to awareness through technical terms designed to address its reality abstractly. It is not my intention in these discourses to belittle or to

1. Suzanne Langer, *Philosophical Sketches* (Baltimore: Johns Hopkins Press, 1962), p. 59 (paperback, New York: Mentor Books, 1964).

dismiss this abstracting procedure, in the manner commonly attributed to Bergson; though the insistence with which I stress the fallibility of our forms and symbols may be construed in that way. Rather, I am concerned to assess that procedure critically as it pertains to theological inquiry. And I do so in the light of insight which a process orientation of inquiry, looking to the lived experience, brings to awareness and understanding. The word "process" has never seemed to me adequate to convey what is implied in this orientation; for it singles out the one theme, process, whereas other themes, possibly more important than "process," are involved, themes such as "dimensional meaning," "contextual relations," and "emergent events." In this work I use the words "empirical realism" to express this process orientation in its broader perspective. Here the primacy of experience as lived is emphasized, giving to the notion of reality the connotation of a Creative Passage in which all life is lived. In this mode of thought, it is assumed that our immediacies occur and participate in a dimension of ultimacy, however vaguely attended or unattended. Ultimacy in this context is not a nebulous term. It connotes a continuous thrust of the Creative Passage, and is thus simultaneously the present, inclusive of the legacy of the past inherent in its structure of experience, together with what is prescient of its future range. In the immediacies of experience, ultimacy can be conceived of under the aegis of "importance"; that is, as a dimension of the relational ground of every existent event, having serious import as offering it potential fulfillment of its intention, or what, in the nature of its continuing concretion, persists as a concrete destiny. This penumbra of ultimate intention attending every existent event gives to it dimensional meaning that is at once consonant with what is concretely existent, yet offering as a horizon of emergent meaning what in the nature of the case is consistent with its actualized concretion and "More." The More inheres in the efficacy of the communal ground of every actualized event, and the latter's responsiveness or openness to it.

The mystery of existing thus inheres in this dimensional character of every actualized event, and what that depth of becoming brings to its individuated intentionality.

An underlying thesis of this work is that an efficacy persists within the structure of experience, and within each participant in it, impelling responsiveness to redemptive energies within the Creative Passage. And it is the function of the response of faith to open the creature, elementally as well as critically, to its resources, and thus to avail it of a good not its

own inherent in the Creative Passage which cradles and recreates all existent events.

In this context, the imaginative mode of inquiry is reactivated, supple-
menting and offering to abstractive inquiry resources of a kind that give
entry to a more sensitive mode of awareness and reflection than abstract
thought is equipped to initiate. To a degree the two modes of reflection
may interact insofar as definitive, abstract inquiry can assimilate to its
own reflection nuances and intimations of the surplusage of experience
made available through such sensitive awareness as the imaginative and
creative talent can provide.

These essays, while concerned with a common theme, address various
issues bearing upon theological method. For, underlying the discussion
of symbolization is the concern to point up a mode of theological inquiry
which concurs with judgments relating to the limited character of language. At the same time there is implicit in the procedure proposed to
extend the scope of theological inquiry to include the cultural along with
the cultic import of the legacy of faith. This mode of inquiry is commonly designated *constructive theology,* implying a focusing of theological interest upon immediate demands and concerns of living as these
evoke and convey the realities of faith. The assumption underlying this
procedure is that faith is to be understood not simply as a legacy of belief
inherited from the past, but as a vital response to realities inhering within
the immediacies of experience as a resource of grace and judgment.
Since the dynamics of the lived experience involve a larger orbit of
relationships than is commonly defined or addressed by the cultus, constructive theology tends to embrace a format of inquiry which, in effect,
assumes proportions of a theology of culture. Such theological inquiry,
however, is not dissociated from the cultic legacy, or restricted to a contemporary ethos in the manner commonly pursued by what sociologists
have designated "culture" or "civil religion." Culture or civil religion, as
currently conceived and pursued, presupposes the dissolution of the historic faiths and the evolvement of a fund of values expressive of a cultural consensus dissociated from a religious history. I mean to reverse
this procedure by conveying the persistence of the historical legacy of faith
as a *mythos* within the cultural experience, both by way of informing its
identity and in pointing up depths of its experiences which persist as
resources of judgment and renewal. Basic to the constructive method implied in such a theology of culture is a lifting up of the creatural stance

as being at once more elemental and ultimate than any cultural orientation or perspective contrived out of a pooling of contemporary, sophisticated sentiments and lore.

It may be commonplace to observe that reflection upon method often follows most productively upon engagement with an undertaking. There is a minimal amount of conscious design in what one undertakes initially in one's theological inquiry: enough, that is, to chart one's course of inquiry at that particular stage and to define one's procedure; but maturity in becoming self-conscious about what one has been doing generally follows as a view in retrospect. At least seasoned judgments must wait upon such a view. And once the overall assessment of what one has done has been undertaken, the partial surmises and exploratory ventures fall into a kind of pattern of inquiry that discloses the essential thrust of one's effort. It is for that reason that I am recording in this volume reflections which might well have preceded my previous volumes, notably *Faith and Culture* and *The Realities of Faith*. For what is set down in the various essays that make up the present volume is clearly contributive to a design of inquiry that runs through the two previous books. The three volumes, in fact, form a trilogy intent on presenting a theology of culture. What is insistent throughout all three works is the concern to see religious inquiry as being oriented simultaneously to the cultic and the cultural experiences of a people, rather than being exclusively centered in the cultus of the historic church. Although this insistence runs through all three volumes, it is only in the present work that I address that concern explicitly, and deal with it as a methodological premise.

In a variety of ways I have sought to point up the cultural orientation of every expression of faith, and to see the cultic formulation of it, however basic and primordial, as being but one, albeit by force of historical circumstances the initial and, in certain respects, the central medium of its expression. This is as true of Christian faith as it is of Hindu, Buddhist, Moslem, or any other of the historic religions. In the way we approach the study of other religions the cultural orbit of meaning expressed through the historic experience is made more apparent. On the basis of such historical study of religions, some theologians, by way of providing special leverage for Christian faith, have argued that other historic faiths are to be considered *religions,* involved in a cultural history, as contrasted with Christian faith, which is expressive of a faith that is beyond culture and history. This, in my judgment, is a spurious argument that will not hold up under careful scrutiny. Every religion or expression of faith, in its way, has been expressive simultaneously of a mode of witness partaking of the cultural orbit of meaning and experience in which it has arisen and of a sense of an ultimate witness to what is beyond any human experience or condition. In this context, all of them have addressed themselves to a reality, or realities, beyond the immediacies of experience, even as they have been deeply and decisively involved in them.

The neglect of the cultural conditioning of the Christian witness of faith, on the other hand, following from an attempt to extricate it from such conditioning, has had the effect of understating the real power and persistence of the Christian faith as a cultural energy within the cultural history. As a result, it has been readily assumed that, with the collapse of Christendom, or of the formal appeal of Christian doctrine and history as a cultic legacy, the Judaic-Christian faith is itself destined to extinction. The argument I seek to set forth in this volume is to the effect that all religious faith, and specifically Christian faith, invades and pervades a larger orbit of meaning than is implied in that assumption. For, as cultural anthropologists have been disclosing to us for some time now, every culture partakes of its religious legacy in ways that shape its ethos and sensibilities; and thus gives rise to its cultural identity. Disregard of this basic, historic shaping of peoples is undoubtedly at the root of much of the confusion in relating one culture to another; or of the impasse between them when rapport or negotiation fails.

Fallible
Forms and Symbols

We do not start from projecting modes of our consciousness or analogies of our own activities, on to a world beyond us. We start from consciousness of ourselves as arising out of rapport, interconnection and participation in processes reaching beyond ourselves. Such feeling is a precondition of self-conscious experience. Both Whitehead and Heidegger are trying in their respective ways in their epistemology to go behind the explicit Subject-Object type of thinking and express this basic stage out of which the possibility of thought grows.

—Dorothy Emmet
*The Nature of Metaphysical Thinking*

I suggest that the development of systematic theology should be accompanied by a critical understanding of the relation of linguistic expression to our deeper and most persistent intuitions. Language was developed in response to the excitement of practical actions. It is concerned with the prominent facts. . . . But the prominent facts are the superficial facts. They vary because they are superficial; and they enter into conscious discrimination because they vary. There are other elements in our experience, on the fringe of consciousness, and yet massively qualifying our experience.

—Alfred North Whitehead
*Adventures of Ideas*

Part One

Chapter One

# The New Realism in
# Religious Inquiry

With the death of Karl Barth, Emil Brunner, Paul Tillich, Reinhold Niebuhr, and Richard Niebuhr, an impressive and possibly unprecedented theological renaissance can be said to have passed into history. Intimations of this occurrence had already been given as early as 1957 when Gabriel Vahanian[1] and others began speaking of the death of God and of the fact that we had entered upon the culture of a post-Christian era. For the voices being heard in this vein in the late fifties and early sixties were those of young theologians steeped in the lore of the theological renaissance that had only recently ended. They were the former students and followers of Karl Barth, Reinhold Niebuhr, and Paul Tillich; and in a way, still responsive to them.

## I

Now that a new Christian mind appears to be forming, turning back in major respects upon the theological renaissance of a generation ago, this may be the time to discern the true character of the new Reformation of recent years. If we were to view this historic, theological renaissance simply in terms of its spirited, often unbalanced and polemical, reaction against historical liberalism and its seeming intent upon reestablishing Reformation insights, we would miss the point of its significance as a cultural and religious development within the wider context of Western intellectual history. Within that context, it was much more than a quarrel with evangelical liberalism, or a belated form of neo-orthodoxy. Intellec-

1. Gabriel Vahanian, *The Death of God: The Culture of Our Post-Christian Era* (New York: George Braziller, 1957).

3

tually it participated, however indirectly, in currents of thought that were to effect a revolution in fundamental notions as these bear upon every form of disciplined thought.

The surprising thing is that the theologians within the neo-Reformation reaction, with the possible exception of Tillich, seemed only mildly aware of, or concerned with, this wider intellectual upheaval that was manifesting itself in the sciences and in new expressions of metaphysics. Reinhold and Richard Niebuhr had been attentive to certain of Bergson's writings, notably his *Introduction to Metaphysics* and *Creative Evolution*. All of them had been alerted to the phenomenology of Husserl and to existential developments stemming from a phenomenological orientation as well as from the stimulus of Kierkegaard and Buber. Tillich, in addition, was interested in many new incursions that altered the stance of critical thought in the current period such as Gestalt psychology and later, depth psychology, as well as intimations of new developments in the sciences, notably those relating to the work of Einstein and the new physics. He was responsive also to the new ethos of modern art in various forms, and to a more limited degree, to developments in cosmology and aesthetics leading to the new metaphysics of process thought. Tillich was not really conversant with process thought. However, having mingled with many who were familiar with it and, having discussed with them issues common to process and phenomenological as well as existentialist thinking, he was perceptive of the concerns that motivated process thinking. Furthermore, Tillich's own revisions of Kant and Hegel, following from his intimate and long-standing concern with Schelling's philosophy, prepared him to be sympathetic toward the intentions of process metaphysics, except for one thing: his insistence that the language of religious discourse in approaching ultimates could only be symbolic, never literal in meaning, allied him with a numinous tradition of thought stemming from Schleiermacher and continuing through Rudolf Otto.[2] Tillich, up to a point, could be open to the new metaphysics because, in effect, the cause was his own, or akin to his own. Yet he chose to remain apart from it except as he was lured into discussing its issues in relation to his own by those who

2. Rudolf Otto, too, had been attentive to emergent evolutionists in Britain, notably Lloyd Morgan, earlier in the century, and his book *Naturalism and Religion* (London: Williams & Norgate, 1907) carries echoes of this interest. Emergent evolution, with its anticipation of the novel and the unexpected within the matrix of every occurrence, lent a depth and attending mystery to the natural which tentatively intrigued Otto as a possible alternative to the *numinis*.

were concerned to bring him and Charles Hartshorne into conversation with each other.

Nevertheless I would insist that the full measure of this theological renaissance as pursued by Barth and Tillich may not be realized or appreciated until it has been seen within a context of intellectual upheaval in Western thinking that embraced both its own neo-Reformation thinking, fortified by phenomenology and existentialism, and process philosophy. I would put it this way: A line of protest and inquiry, extending from Barth, Tillich, and Niebuhr to Whitehead and Wieman in the nineteen twenties formed a new frontier of realism, breaking free of the enclosure of mentalism which had engulfed philosophical thinking in the West for more than three hundred years and which had shaped the imagery of theological liberalism since the time of Kant. There were marked differences of theological judgment along this new frontier; but, after all the differences have been taken into account, this widespread reaction against the overreaching rationality of the Enlightenment and modern idealism and of the liberal-modernist theology which presupposed its epistemology may be compared to the rediscovery of the *sensus numinis* among the Reformers that broke through scholasticism in the sixteenth century. It is time that we establish the true character of the new Reformation of recent years, with its openness to *otherness* and its conception of the dynamic character of judgment and grace, as being of a piece with the nontheological rendering of these themes and emphases in the empirical realism of process thought. Unless we assess the turn of recent theological and philosophical developments in this bold and comprehensive manner, we shall overlook the magnitude of what has been happening.

Once we perceive this line of protest and inquiry, which formed a new frontier of realism in Christian thought, we will see also that the significant issues in theological study that were posed are not to be stated as issues between liberalism and neo-orthodoxy, as this has been commonly conceived. That was a false issue from the start, for it assumed, on the one hand, that participating in the protest of the new realism in theology meant the relinquishment of the disciplines of liberal scholarship when, actually, it implied becoming self-critical within that heritage. It assumed, on the other hand, that liberalism, as then currently represented, was to be identified with the defensive and resistant turn of mind that saw no need for a change in a time when the most decisive changes within the liberal inheritance were occurring. Unaware of the creative currents at work within the new realism, this defensive stand among many contemporary liberals took what was actually innovation to be wholly reactionary and accordingly sought to stem its tide. This hardly sounds like the liberal heritage at its height. Actually, these islands of defensive resistance to the self-critical process within liberalism are the clearest evidence that the enclosure within idealistic and rationalistic premises had led liberalism into a series of dead ends. The disciplines of liberal scholarship had all but spent themselves, and would have done so had it not been for the vitality of the new Reformation which, in subtle ways as well as with bold iconoclasm, worked to restore cultural and intellectual change. Any sensible comparison of these two stands would have to conclude that they who presumed to speak for liberalism in a defensive role reflected the temper of a closed orthodoxy, and in fact turned the liberal heritage into an orthodoxy, while the restive and liberating dynamic of Protestantism that once spoke through historic liberalism was now speaking through innovating, at times reactionary, voices of protest, even as it sought new vantage ground beyond the historic site of liberal-modernist theology to cope with the issue of man in the face of new evidence, new intellectual resources, and new cultural responsibilities.

There was an issue between right and left that does have significance for modern Protestant theology; but it was an issue between theologians who stood along this new frontier of Christian realism, yet who saw the meaning of this reorientation differently. Within the prophetic stage of protest and reaction, they formed a consensus in modern Protestantism. It was when each one turned to the constructive task of theological interpretation that differences among them emerged, one turning toward a restatement of Christian doctrine in a pattern continuous with traditional Christian imagery however reformulated and the other to a reconception of the meaning of religion, itself, as in the early writings of Henry Nelson Wieman.

Wieman's first book (*Religious Experience and Scientific Method,* 1926), in which he proposed a wholly new format for inquiring into the meaning of God, prompted certain liberals in this country, who had become awakened to the new theological mind then emerging, to look upon Wieman as the American counterpart of Barth. This judgment, in retrospect, was based almost exclusively on the ardent, outspoken manner in which each of these theologians affirmed the reality of

God at a time when few within the liberal community could use this word confidently or meaningfully. Nevertheless, the perception of a shift in imagery and orientation, breaking free of the mental enclosure of liberal theology that had led to humanism, was sound. Wieman at the time was too readily assimilated to the liberal-modernist format of inquiry, even by his colleagues at Chicago, largely, I think, because he spoke within a nontheological idiom. The empirical bent of his mind concealed his radical divergence from the conceptualism which had shaped the thinking of the early Chicago school of Shailer Mathews, Shirley Jackson Case, Edward Scribner Ames, and others. Ames detected the shift in what Wieman proposed as a way of redefining the term "God," calling it a throwback to a substantive mode of thinking, and on that basis veered away from Wieman's new realism.

Wieman's later writing, notably that which followed *The Source of Human Good* (1946), could more readily be allied with what had been projected at Chicago under the stimulus of John Dewey's pragmatism. And in recent years, Wieman frequently remarked that, in retrospect, the philosopher with whom he had had most in common through the years was John Dewey. Throughout the nineteen twenties and early thirties, however, Wieman's writings would not bear that out. For during those years he reflected a vital interest in the new vision of the sciences, particularly as it had been conveyed in Whitehead's earlier works, and the impact of emergent thinking which had initially stemmed from Bergson's influence. Wieman, in fact, was a lone voice among American theologians and philosophers of religion during that time, conveying the import of the new revolution in the sciences for religious thinking.

In this situation, the apprehension of *otherness* in speaking of God not only was possible, but inescapable. For some who were to respond to this new realism, many of the old words of Christian faith came trooping back with startling new imagery and insistent meaning: words such as grace, judgment, sin, redemption, and many more. These were seen to be transcendent meanings which had been lost to the Christian vocabulary, both consciously and inadvertently, through the psychologizing of theological concepts. The recovery of these Christian words in contemporary theology proved to be a stumbling block to many people within the liberal tradition. They had no other word for it than "neo-orthodoxy." But this was clearly "guilt by association," and a reluctance to inquire into the revolution in conceptual forms that was then afoot, not only in theology and philosophy, but in the sciences as well.

I should say at this point that Wieman did not take readily to the word "transcendent," as it was being used by Niebuhr, Barth, and others. In fact it was not until 1943 that he openly used the term, and then it was "functional transcendence" as he pointed out, implying a distinction between the work God does, and that which human beings do.

The recovery of an historic, Christian vocabulary within the new realism came about readily among European theologians representative of the new shift in imagery. Wieman, however, resisted employing such words throughout the nineteen twenties and early thirties on the grounds that they lent themselves to an evocative usage which readily obscured the critical thrust of the new orientation of religious thought. His resistance to using Christian words stemmed also from a more basic consideration: Christian faith, he argued, had reached a point of dis-illusionment because of a collapse of confidence in the formative notions of its intellectual structure. Its restoration, he insisted, could come about only through searching, critical inquiry into fundamental notions im-plicit in its affirmation of faith in the hope that confidence in its intel-lectual structure might be restored. As set forth in *The Wrestle of Religion with Truth*,[3] and later in "The Need of Philosophy of Religion,"[4] he urged a moratorium on theological inquiry as such until this more basic mode of structural inquiry in philosophy of religion could be accomplished. In this he was not alone, even among American theo-logians during those years.

Wieman was to modify his stance in 1939, however, in a stirring article entitled, "Some Blind Spots Removed,"[5] in which he affirmed his rapport with the thrust of the Continental theologians, notably that of Karl Barth, though he interpreted these grounds of rapport in terms consistent with his own empirical stance. He was to relent a bit also on opposing the use of Christian words; for he had come to see within his own new realistic stance the pertinence of such historic, Christian words as grace, sin, judgment, and forgiveness.[6]

3. Henry Nelson Wieman, *The Wrestle of Religion with Truth* (New York: Macmillan, 1927).
4. Wieman, "The Need of Philosophy of Religion," *Journal of Religion*, 14 (October 1934).
5. Wieman, "Some Blind Spots Removed," *The Christian Century*, 56 (January 27, 1939), pp. 116–18.
6. Henry N. Wieman, "On Using Christian Words," *Journal of Religion*, 20:3 (July 1940), pp. 257–69.

## II

We need now to give closer attention to the nature of the realistic orientation in the era of theological and philosophical thought extending from Barth to Whitehead which we have defined as a new frontier.

One of the most helpful discussions of the new realism that altered the orientation of theological inquiry in recent years may be found in Tillich's *The Protestant Era,* where he is analyzing the various kinds of realism which have appeared in Christian history and the forms in which it now appears. Generally speaking, he writes, realism tends to concern itself simply with the really real in any concrete situation without pressing beyond the historical or even the empirical data, as in positivism or even historical realism. But, he adds,

> the really real is not reached until the unconditioned ground of everything real, or the unconditioned power of being is reached. Historical realism remains on a comparatively unrealistic level if it does not grasp that depth of reality in which its divine foundation and meaning become visible.[7]

Tillich's own preference was for what he called "belief-ful realism" or "self-transcending realism." In these terms he meant to combine two elements which he believed are generally wide apart—namely, "a realistic and a belief-ful attitude."[8]

What is decisive here, as over against the idealism that underlay liberal-modernist theology,[9] is its clear sense of *otherness* beyond the human world. One could speak of this movement of mind as a concerted effort

7. Paul Tillich, *The Protestant Era* (Chicago: University of Chicago Press, 1948), p. 76.
8. Ibid., p. 67.
9. I mean to designate here the explicitly liberal or modernist theologies of the nineteenth century through the nineteen twenties. This would include pragmatic liberals and modernists of the early Chicago school, as well as Continental and American Ritschlians, personalists, and religious humanists. For, despite their objections to certain expressions of philosophical idealism, especially to absolute idealism, all of these theologies shared and participated in the imagery and fundamental notions of idealism, either in the form of a moral idealism in which "self-experience" was made the normative base (Ritschlianism, personalism, religious humanism), or of a conceptualism or a conceptual theism (as in Shailer Mathews and Edward Scribner Ames). In all of these theologies, one could say that the logic of their position led to humanism, though, with the exception of the religious humanists, the sensibilities of faith restrained them and held them within the bounds of some form of theism. I think a careful reading of these representative systems of liberal thought, with particular attention to the problems of God in liberal theologies, cannot fail to bring one to this judgment. I find the one exception to be that of Schleiermacher, who, in a remarkably perceptive way, was able to convey in his notion of "absolute dependence" the sense of otherness that seemed to escape the enclosure of both intellectualism and moralism. Rudolf Otto has noted this point in saying that it was Schleiermacher who rediscovered "the *Sensus Numinis*" (cf. *Religious Essays: A Sequel to the Idea of the Holy* [London: Oxford, 1931], pp. 68 ff.).

to break free of the enclosure of mentalism or of self-experience by which idealism circumscribed every meaning, including the meaning of God. Barth voiced this new freedom from enclosure within human categories for theology in his bold declaration of contrasts between the *Word of God* and the *word of man,* between *God's righteousness* and *man's ideals.* In more abstract terms, the new realism of Wieman announced the *creativity of God* as over against the *ideals and values of man.* One will get a vivid impression of the affinity between these two wings of the new realism by reading Barth's *The Word of God and the Word of Man,* along with Wieman's first book, *Religious Experience and Scientific Method,* particularly the section where Wieman is distilling from Whitehead's earlier scientific work, *The Concept of Nature*[10] the sense of God's otherness as an experienceable datum,[11] as well as those chapters in which man's ideals are sharply differentiated from the good which is of God.[12] It is true that Wieman's language in isolating the datum of the sovereign God appears to be nearer to that of Schleiermacher than that of Barth; yet the insistence upon God's otherness as standing in judgment of man's good, his ideals and values, clearly partakes of the newer realism and its protest. Barth's emphasis was the more decisive and radical, repossessing the rigor of Calvin. In Wieman's later distinction between *creative good* and *created goods,* however, something of the same decisiveness and Calvinistic rigor appeared.

In a similar manner, one should compare Reinhold Niebuhr's *Does Civilization Need Religion*[13] with Wieman's *Religious Experience and Scientific Method.* Both books reveal a transitional character—a transition from an idealistic imagery and valuation to a realism concerning man and God. Niebuhr's concern in this earlier book will be seen to have more affinity with liberal valuations than Wieman's initial book. For there still persisted in Niebuhr at this time some semblance of his Kantian and Ritschlian moorings, as reflected in his ardent concern for personal value, despite his critique of liberalism. And this implied also a certain devaluation of nature and of natural structures insofar as they constituted a threat to personal values. Hence the skepticism which was to seize him, once he became convinced of the relativity of cultural

10. Alfred North Whitehead, *The Concept of Nature* (Cambridge: Cambridge University Press, 1920).
11. Henry Nelson Wieman, *Religious Experience and Scientific Method* (New York: Macmillan, 1926), pp. 176 ff.
12. Ibid. See especially chap. X.
13. Reinhold Niebuhr, *Does Civilization Need Religion?* (New York: Macmillan, 1928).

values, impelled Niebuhr to a swift formulation of a theory of an absolute beyond history with its corollary of self-transcendence.[14]

Wieman, on the other hand, partaking of a radical empiricism, initiated by James and Bergson and modified by Dewey and Whitehead, retained more of an immanent metaphysics even though he had come to a decisive critique of the human structure itself. Wieman's thought was moving toward a "functional transcendence," as he later termed it, which envisaged discontinuities within the continuity of experience. The sharpest discontinuity to which he was to give emphasis was the contrast between the work that God did and the values he created, as over against the work man did and the values he tended to affirm and to cherish. Here Wieman definitely departed from the liberal-modernist milieu and in effect joined with the challenge implicit in the new Reformation then dawning. It could be said, perhaps, that Wieman remained ambivalent in his affinities. In the prophetic aspect of his thought, wherein he openly protested against the idolatry of human values and ideals, he clearly participated in the new age; but by persisting within the categories of a sharply delineated religious naturalism he chose to hold, conceptually at least, to a modernist base. But then one is led to wonder, was Wieman's religious naturalism so different, after all, from Tillich's "ecstatic naturalism"? To be sure, there was an ontology implied in Tillich's language with which Wieman would have no part. But how much more was this language of ontology than a symbolic reference to denote a dimension of depth in speaking of concrete events? Wieman, too, spoke of such depth in empirical events; which is why Dewey was unable to see any similarity between Wieman's empiricism and his own thought, even though Wieman had assumed that there was.[15] It could be argued that Wieman, too, was pressing for a "belief-ful realism," pointing to an ultimate reference within the passage of concrete events, insisting that one cannot be realistic in attending to such events except as one takes this dimension of ultimacy into account. In this respect his religious naturalism appears to have been reaching for the same dimension of realism that Tillich described as being self-transcending. Differences appeared, of course, when Wieman pressed

14. Cf. Reinhold Niebuhr, "What the War Did to My Mind," *The Christian Century*, 45 (September 27, 1928), pp. 1161–63. See also his article "Barth—Apostle of the Absolute," *The Christian Century*, 45 (December 13, 1928), pp. 1523–24.

15. Henry Nelson Wieman, "Religion in John Dewey's Philosophy," *Journal of Religion*, 11 (January 1931), pp. 1–19; Henry Nelson Wieman, with E. E. Aubrey and John Dewey, "Is John Dewey a Theist?" *Christian Century*, 51 (December 5, 1934), pp. 1550–51.

for some definitive criteria by which the dimension of depth could, in some measure, be made descriptively articulate. It was not that Wieman expected to lift the whole of this dimension to the level of empirical description; but only a minimum degree of it in order to acknowledge that, to some extent, it is perceptible in experience and thus empirically verifiable. Here there was disclosed a radical difference between Wieman and Tillich in their doctrine of God. And this difference implied other differences which could not be reconciled, either in their sensibilities or method. Wieman's empirical method, within Tillich's understanding of the nature of God, clearly appeared to be an improper overreaching of human inquiry. While Tillich's ontological method within Wieman's understanding of the nature of man clearly appeared to be an unwarranted overreaching of human inquiry.

It is instructive, again, to compare the imagery which one finds in Bultmann's later writings, especially in his discussion of demythologizing the New Testament, with that of William James, Whitehead, or Wieman. When Bultmann was attempting to point up the meaning of faith or the nature of the imperative which the Gospels lay upon every man, his key phrase is "openness to the future" or "freedom of the future," to which he ascribes the Christian understanding of forgiveness. Following is a representative statement of such expressions:

### The Life of Faith

The authentic life . . . would be a life based on unseen, intangible realities. Such a life means the abandonment of all self-contrived security. This is what the New Testament means by "life after the Spirit," or "life in faith."

For this life we must have faith in the *grace of God*. It means faith that the unseen, intangible reality actually confronts us as love, opening up our future and signifying not death but life.

The grace of God means *the forgiveness of sin,* and brings deliverance from the bondage of the past. The old quest for visible security, the hankering after tangible realities, and the clinging to transitory objects, is sin, for by it we shut out invisible reality from our lives and refuse God's future which comes to us as a gift. But once we open our hearts to the grace of God, our sins are forgiven; we are released from the past. This is what is meant by "faith": to open ourselves freely to the future. But at the same time faith involves obedience, for faith means turning our backs on self and abandoning all security. It means giving up every attempt to carve out a niche in life for ourselves, surrendering all our self-confidence, and resolving to trust in God alone, in the God who raises the dead (2 Cor. 1:9) and who calls the things that are not into being (Rom. 4:17). It means radical self-commitment to God in the expectation that everything will come from him and nothing from ourselves. Such a life spells deliverance from all worldly, tangible objects, leading to complete detachment from the world, and thus to freedom.[16]

Now this is setting the New Testament injunction "Have no thought of the morrow" specifically in a context of *living forward,* not with reckless, romantic abandon, as is often the interpretation given, but with trust in God who fashions the creative opportunities for new life. Here Bultmann is adding the reassurance of Christian faith to the existentialist analysis of the human situation that sees man shorn of the supports of the past or of any other structured value, save his own courage as a human being. Through this promise, Bultmann sees the existentialist act of courage transmuted into an act of faith; or perhaps we should say that he declares that the Christian existentialist is inspired with the kind of courage that can assume the character of faith.

When one places this existentialist view of "openness to the future" alongside of the notion of living and understanding *forward,* as both Bergson and James developed it,[17] one sees both similarities and differences, to be sure; but the affinity in orientation and outlook is unmistakable. Bultmann is concerned here with the redemptive act in self-understanding, while Bergson and James concerned themselves with transformations that alter the way one approaches the epistemological problem in such a reorientation of mind and experience; but the same kind of existential decisions are present in both instances.

The same mood of living and understanding *forward* permeated Whitehead's thought, though with a difference that seemed to make him less existential than Bergson, James, or Bultmann. It was the organismic quality of Whitehead's philosophy which brought to his trust in the future a certain increment of value and support out of past attainment which comes into the present and passes into future events as a qualifying good, providing both limitation and opportunity. In the final analysis, Whitehead was no less insistent upon openness to the future than the others. His conviction concerning how the future is made, how the creativity of God is faithful in a measure to the structured experi-

16. Rudolf Bultmann, *Kerygma and Myth,* ed. H. W. Bartsch, trans. R. H. Fuller (London: SPCK, 1953), pp. 19–20.
17. Cf. Henri Bergson, *Creative Evolution* (New York: Holt, 1911); William James, *Essays in Radical Empiricism* (New York: Longmans, 1912), esp. pp. 238 ff.

ence of past occurrences, led him to define his trust in God as being, not simply a faith in the One *who maketh all things new,* but in One who, in making things new, gathers the achieved values of the past into the creative matrix out of which novelty occurs, thus offering a certain immortality of meaning to every passing event and to the burden of past values which it carries.[18]

Bultmann's formulation of the Christian existentialist's faith is nearer to Wieman's philosophy of the Creative Event, after certain differences in method and concern have been taken into account. In fact, the affinities between these two formulations make clear, it seems to me, how marked the convergence of the two strands of new realism can be when in each instance relinquishment of past supports is merged with a faith that leaps beyond the despair created by its iconoclasm to a trust in the creative venture of God, as being simultaneously a creative act and an act of forgiveness. Compare, for example, the following passage from Wieman's *Source of Human Good* with the statement quoted from Bultmann earlier:

> Despair is the state of mind ensuing when the good to which one clings as source and sustainer of all other good has been taken away. When that to which one clings is not truly the source and sustainer, its removal and the consequent despair open the way for the real source to enter. The real source, however, does not always enter when despair opens the way. But in the case of the disciples it did with the Resurrection, because at that time the creative interchange, held subject to the Hebrew hope while Jesus lived and seeming to disappear with the Hebrew hope when Jesus was crucified, rose from the dead. This creative power could now dominate over all else as it could not before and could penetrate beneath every obstruction raised against it in the persons of the disciples, because there was nothing else to which they clung for security that was more important than it.[19]

Wieman then relates this commitment to the Creative good, as did Bultmann, to the forgiveness of sins:

> This domination over and penetration beneath every obstruction in the life of a man constitute forgiveness of sin. Sin is anything and everything in one's personality which is obstructive to creative transformation, so far as one is responsible for the obstruction. Forgiveness of sin is accomplished by the creative power itself when it dominates over and pene-

18. *The Philosophy of Alfred North Whitehead,* ed. Paul A. Schilpp (New York: Tudor, 1951), p. 684.
19. H. N. Wieman, *The Source of Human Good* (Chicago: University of Chicago Press, 1946), pp. 277–78.

trates beneath the obstructions to its own working within the personality concerned. . . .

But this forgiveness and consequent radical transformation cannot occur without despair if by despair is meant the removal of every other good to which one clings as ultimate source and sustainer. If one clings to something as though it were the source of all good when it is not, then the true source cannot dominate and penetrate and so cannot do what is called "the forgiving of sin". . . .

Without difficulty, danger, and loss a man will scarcely seek his security in the true source of human good. Always he will seek it in some created good, if not the Hebrew Law, then American democracy or scientific method or his health and popularity or his past record or whatever else it may be. These other grounds of security must be seriously threatened or taken away before any man will seek and find his strength, his hope, and his courage in the creative power which generates all value. In this sense, perhaps despair and recurrent despair alone can open the passage into the ways of forgiveness and salvation.[20]

## III

In pointing up affinities between these two wings of a new realism in theology and philosophy of religion during recent years I have had no intention of arguing that they come to the same thing, or of pressing toward a syncretism of insights. What I have been concerned to bring about is the recognition of rapport in orientation between these two seemingly dissociated modes of inquiry in Christian theology that had gone through liberalism and beyond it. Despite all their diversities and special preoccupations, they who had broken free of the conceptual bounds which the era of liberalism imposed moved in a common imagery of dynamic meaning and creative event however differently they may have worded it. Within that imagery the biblical language of revelation, crisis, judgment, grace, forgiveness, and redemption became at once both natural and insistent. It literally projected a new age of reformation in which to repossess the vitality and realism of Christian faith as a living word and witness. In this open world of concreteness, mystery, and revelation, words like "new creation," "new being," "spirit," "spontaneity," "immediacy," "happening," "event or dynamic event," "witnessing," "pointing," "proclaiming," and many more tumbled forth as a fresh and suggestive language of faith.

The scope of the change in theological climate indicated by these new

20. Ibid., pp. 278–79.

terms is sobering. To gather in the full force of its meaning one has
to realize that what had occurred within the three or four decades in
which the new realism had been emerging was a turning back upon
three centuries of theological development in the West. Between
Descartes and Barth, one might say, the drama of Christian thought
passed through three stages: the first stage, through the years of the
Enlightenment, the new appreciation of the power and role of reason
brought into question the meaning and relevance of the notion of
revelation. Typical of the period was the statement attributed to
Spinoza:

> If man's clear intuition of truth is trustworthy in its disclosure, his com-
> petence is equal to that of a divine intuition; if it is not trustworthy, then
> it is just as likely to be mistaken in believing that there exists a super-
> human intelligence able and willing to supplement his apprehensions as it
> is in any other of its beliefs. In the former case it will need no supple-
> mentation; in the latter it can draw no conclusions whatever, even about
> God, with any confidence.[21]

In this turn of mind one might say theology saw the displacement of
the notion of revelation by reason. The second stage came with Kant's
elevation of moral faith to a dominance that was to continue throughout
the remaining years of the liberal period. And in this development,
theology was to see the notion of redemption displaced by the pursuit of
religious and moral ideals. The third and final stage of the liberal-
modernist era came about with the emphasis upon experience as a controlling concept in all modes of inquiry. Though there are antecedent
developments in this direction going back to Schleiermacher, I should
place the serious beginning of this stage in 1860 with the publication of
Tylor's *Primitive Culture,* wherein, one might say, anthropology laid
the ground for a new approach to an understanding of religion. Here
impetus was given to the psychological study of religion and the translation of conventional theological doctrines into their psychological meaning. A tendency already begun in philosophical idealism was thereby
stepped up to a concerted movement among religious scholars, displacing
the normativeness of the Bible in theology with an appeal to experience.
The relinquishment of biblical authority in theology gave rise to various
alternative norms such as religious experience, psychologically inter-

---

21. E. A. Burtt's paraphrase of Spinoza in *Types of Religious Philosophy* (New York:
Harper, 1939), p. 185.

preted;[22] self-experience, philosophically elaborated;[23] and social experience, historically and sociologically interpreted.[24]

The arresting fact is that in the recent redirection of religious inquiry every one of these turns of thought was reversed: revelation, redemption, and biblical faith were each to be reinstated as formative notions in theology. It is understandable, therefore, that many were to interpret these recent developments to be a return to orthodoxy and a complete relinquishment of the liberal heritage. It is my considered opinion that this is a superficial and shortsighted judgment. Rather than being a return to orthodoxy or a relinquishment of the liberal heritage it was a reconception of the liberal understanding of Christian faith at a level of inquiry that enabled it to correct and to overcome the iconoclasm of the Enlightenment and of the modernist era and thus to repossess within the disciplines of liberal scholarship the full range of the Christian witness of faith.

## IV

Even as the theological renaissance which had been projected by Barth, Brunner, Tillich, and Niebuhr was reaching the height of its fulfillment, its formidable impact reasserting transcendence was breeding its own catalyst. For it was among younger men who had been influenced by these theologians that the "reluctant revolution,"[25] forming the initial strands of "the death of God theology," erupted.[26] The significance of that episodic reaction, as Langdon Gilkey has pointed out in *Naming the Whirlwind*,[27] was that it pointed up for many of this recent period the insistent problem of using God-language in a secular age. One would

22. Cf. G. Stanley Hall, Editorial, *Journal of Religious Psychology*, 1 (Mar. 1904–Aug. 1905): 1–6; Edwin D. Starbuck, *The Psychology of Religion* (New York: Scribner's, 1899); William James, *The Varieties of Religious Experience* (London: Longmans, Green & Co., 1902); George A. Coe, *The Spiritual Life* (New York: Eaton & Mains, 1900); Edward Scribner Ames, *The Psychology of Religious Experience* (Boston & New York: Houghton Mifflin Co., 1910). These were some of the early and important works during this period of transition.

23. Cf. Borden P. Bowne, *The Philosophy of Theism* (New York: Harper, 1887) and Josiah Royce, *The World and the Individual* (New York: Macmillan, 1900).

24. See the writings of Shailer Mathews, Gerald Birney Smith, Shirley Jackson Case, et al.

25. John A. T. Robinson, *Honest to God* (Philadelphia: Westminster Press, 1963); Harvey Cox, *The Secular City* (New York: Macmillan, 1965).

26. Gabriel Vahanian, *The Death of God: The Culture of Our Post-Christian Era* (New York: George Braziller, 1957); William Hamilton, *The New Essence of Christianity* (New York: Association Press, 1961); Thomas Altizer and William Hamilton, *Radical Theology and the Death of God* (Indianapolis: Bobbs-Merrill, 1966).

27. Langdon Gilkey, *Naming the Whirlwind: The Renewal of God Language* (Indianapolis and New York: Bobbs-Merrill, 1969).

exaggerate the import of this characterization if one were to take this statement to imply that, in this radical theology, the theological community was confronted for the first time with the difficulty of using God-language in modern times, and of coming to terms as Christians with the secular mood of our time. I have no doubt but that this was precisely true for many of the theological community, and even more so for many contemporary people within and outside the churches who had not participated in the liberal era, or who had no awareness of it. For those who had, the death-of-God upheaval of the sixties was not so much an innovation as a reassertion of immanence in radical form. In this respect it reechoed what liberalism had declared a generation or more ago, and openly drew upon its resources, though more in the literary and philosophical vein of that heritage than in its theological idiom. Actually it had little in common with liberal theology as such; for, insofar as liberalism had deprived the christological figure of its mystique, rendering it wholly in historical terms, the ethical archetype it offered could hardly assume a stature to compare with the fallen God of radical theology who had emptied himself into human nature. The death-of-God simulated or aspired to a mythological imagery in theological discourse to which no historical liberal could attain, or, for that matter, would have resorted. In this its discourse was of a piece with the dialectical theology despite its rejection of transcendence.

At the very time that the death-of-God theology was in progress, a resurgence of process thought, stemming from the influence of Alfred North Whitehead, was becoming evident in many areas of this country as well as in England and Scotland. Initially this resurgence of interest in Whitehead's thought appeared mainly among philosophers; but it was to become even more assertive as a theological movement in the sixties, following publications by John Cobb[28] and Schubert Ogden[29] both of whom were attracted to the work of Charles Hartshorne as a way of pursuing and assessing the legacy of Whitehead. Ogden, more than any other process theologian, has sought to inform his empirical realism with a rigorous encounter with existentialist thinking as encountered, for example, in Bultmann's project in demythologizing New Testament insights.

28. John Cobb, *A Christian Natural Theology* (Philadelphia: Westminster Press, 1965); *The Structure of Christian Experience* (Philadelphia: Westminster Press, 1967).
29. Schubert Ogden, *Christ without Myth* (New York: Harper and Row, 1961); *The Reality of God and Other Essays* (New York: Harper and Row, 1966).

Later he gave considerable attention to Heidegger and Sartre, initially with the expectation of relating Heidegger's ontology and Whitehead's cosmology. Although the project did not prove as profitable as Ogden had hoped, the effort in pursuing the interchange has given special insight to his pursuit of reformulating the theological task. With the inauguration of the journal *Process Studies* in 1971 by John Cobb and John Ford, and the establishment of a Center for Process Studies in Claremont, California, this renewal of interest in process thought has become a concerted movement. During the same year there appeared an anthology of essays in the process mode under the title *Process Philosophy and Christian Thought,* edited by Delwin Brown, Ralph E. James, Jr., and Gene Reeves. This work, in effect, pointed up the thrust of the new era in process studies, citing Charles Hartshorne as its primary stimulus and Schubert Ogden and John Cobb as its principal theological exponents.

Much of the attention given to process thought in recent years has come from a younger generation of Roman Catholic theologians and teachers of religious studies. Disenchantment with scholastic and neoscholastic modes of interpreting Christian thought has led to a concern with viable, modern alternatives, among which are phenomenology, the philosophy of Teilhard de Chardin, and process thought. Since process thought in the tradition of William James, Henri Bergson, S. Alexander, and Alfred North Whitehead, and the thought of Teilhard de Chardin stem from similar historical developments in science and metaphysics, Roman Catholic scholars and students attracted to the writings of Chardin tend to be alert as well to writings in process thought, with concern for both their affinities and their differences. Thus, in a recent work entitled *Process Theology,* Ewert H. Cousins brings together writings by process theologians and philosophers principally oriented toward Whitehead and writings based on the thought of Teilhard de Chardin.[30]

Post-liberal theology thus appears to be moving into fruitful paths of inquiry along several fronts. The situation at present seems so much in flux that one would be wise not to generalize upon the outcome. The promising lines of inquiry seem to be those which have become alerted to the complexity of theological discourse itself, and which strive to differen-

30. Ewert H. Cousins, ed., *Process Theology* (New York: Newman Press, 1971). Cf. also David Tracy's recent work, *Blessed Rage for Order: The New Pluralism in Theology* (New York: The Seabury Press, 1975), which devotes considerable attention to process thought in the context of alternative contemporary theologies.

tiate between modes of inquiry that can pursue different levels of apprehension and understanding.   And in this there is a paradox.   For in
becoming more sophisticated in theological inquiry, we may become more
attentive to elemental religious concerns as these are made evident in
myth and symbol.

Chapter Two

# Language and Reality in
# Christian Faith

Despite dissimilarities between various modes of post-liberal theology, stemming either from a phenomenological orientation of thought or from that of a process metaphysics, an underlying ground of new realism pervades them. This new orientation has enabled religious thinking to break free of the enclosures of mentalism and personalism which had shaped the imagery of theological liberalism since the time of Kant. Whether one pursues a line of inquiry within the dynamic and relational ground of Whitehead's reformed principle of subjectivity, or in that of the phenomenologist's revised notion of *intentionality,* as formulated by Merleau-Ponty, or as expressed by Martin Buber in his notion of the *I-Thou-encounter,* something more contextual connoting a sense of otherness is conveyed than had been possible within an earlier liberalism. That earlier liberalism had been shaped within the imagery of Kant's transcendental ego and the dominance of the notion of personality as being the criterion of ultimate value. In both wings of the new realism ultimacy is seen to inhere in a ground of otherness to which man, in his subjectivity, relates himself. The thrust of the argument here, however, is to indicate that, in going beyond historical liberalism in these respects, post-liberal theologies are not abandoning the critical, post-orthodox or post-authoritative stance which liberalism initiated. Hence their concern with *otherness* in designating or defining ultimate reality represents, as we have said, a radically reformed rendering of the liberal heritage designed to repossess, within the disciplines of liberal scholarship, the full range of the Christian legacy of faith.

## I

The realism in this post-liberal orientation has been, in part, a reaction against all forms of idealism, in part a fresh start toward recovering an objective stance in religious inquiry. The realism implicit in the dialectical theologies within the phenomenological orientation was muted, except for its insistence on *otherness* in speaking of God. Here the word "transcendent" was preferred, which had the effect of accommodating this mode of new realism readily to earlier legacies of Christian thought. For the new realists of the process mode of thought, *otherness* is incorporated in the notion of *withness,* implying distinctions, radical distinctions, between individual entities, community, and God; yet, with all its sharpening of distinct, concrete entities, there is introduced the notion of prehension, implying that each entity, including God, prehends every other entity with varying degrees of relevance. No sheer immanence here, as in earlier idealistic or romanticist philosophies. Transcendence? Yes, though integrated with this pervading notion of prehension. In *Faith and Culture*[1] I spoke of this correlation of otherness and withness as being a reconstructed notion of immanence.

Now what all this technical talk comes to is that affinities between reality and modes of expressing reality are acknowledged, but in a way in which language and reality, while related, do not coalesce. Yet, neither are they dissociated. The language of any people is a formulation out of their structure of existence; yet their structured existence participates as bodily event, and possibly much more, in the Creative Passage which connotes the whole of the ongoing reality.

This, then, is not the old distinction between appearances and reality, but one of accounting for individuated, creatural differences along with designating identity both with the community of creatures and the ultimate Creative Passage in which reality as ultimacy inheres.

## II

But the language people employ in speaking of reality may not necessarily speak *for* reality. The limitations of the human structure are in focus here—structural limitations, creatural limitations. Our language,

---

1. Bernard E. Meland, *Faith and Culture* (New York: Oxford University Press, 1953; paperback: Carbondale, Ill.: Southern Illinois University Press, 1972), pp. 32 ff.

in other words, is inevitably, and of necessity, made up of fallible forms and symbols. And while the disciplining of language and our use of it may clarify communication between us, they do not and will not set aside, break through, or overcome this inherent fallibility of our human forms and symbols. We may overlook it, ignore the primal disparity between language and reality. This, in fact, is our most common form of hubris among disciplined thinkers in the intellectual community. Realities in such disciplined efforts are, in effect, reduced to the measure of our specific modes of thought by way of rendering them intelligible, meaningful. Only as they are rendered meaningful and manageable within that restrictive, disciplined, discourse, will we acknowledge them to be real. This is a grave problem which has given me a good deal of anguish in recent years.

In certain areas of religious inquiry, especially among younger historians of religion, I sense some hint of revolt against this restrictive use of disciplined inquiry, suggesting a reechoing of Rudolf Otto's *mysterium tremendum*. There is implicit in process thought, too, wherever the note of dissonance is taken seriously, a similar uneasiness or distrust of adhering rigorously to an accepted mode of disciplined inquiry without taking note of these overtones of judgment and prophetic anguish in addressing the realities of faith. It must be said, however, that in the current rendering of Whitehead, in which Charles Hartshorne's influence is dominant, this harsher, more agonizing aspect of the new realism tends to be muted. Hartshorne, himself, has expressed indifference as to whether he is characterized as an idealistic realist or a realistic idealist.[2] And this, I think, says a great deal about the temper and prevailing mood of process thought insofar as his influence is in dominance. My own mood, while not disclaiming the concern expressed in this realistic-idealistic temper of mind, partakes of a darker vein precisely because of the emphasis I have been impelled to give to the notion of dissonance in recent years, at least as a correlate with that of coherence, which appears to be the prevailing mood in process thought at the moment.

This stark contrast between the language we use in attending the religious realities, of whatever faith, and the realities themselves should not strike one as strange. Simple acknowledgment of the fallibility of our human forms and symbols should offer precedent enough for insisting that every creature, however elevated or humble, however committed in

2. Charles Hartshorne, *Reality as Social Process* (New York: Free Press, 1953).

his heart and mind to the truth of the faith, stands under the judgment of reality as lived; of reality as encountered in experience. With the use of language, man may appropriately grope toward understanding and toward some degree of intelligibility in responding to what meets us in these lived experiences. But, since we live more deeply than we can think, no formulation of truth out of the language we use can be adequate for expressing what is really real, fully available, fully experienced, within this mystery of existing, in the mystery of dying, or in whatever surpasses these creatural occurrences of such urgent moment to each of us.

We live by trust, in part by hope, in part by inquiry, patiently and humbly pursued. And to the degree that these sensibilities of our creaturehood are observed, the pursuit of intelligibility and understanding in the life of faith is a creative adventure full of promise in expanding, sensitizing, illumining, and hopefully fulfilling this pilgrimage of existing. Every other mode of seeking to wrest the fire and efficacy of reality, either by way of sanctioning those who presume to believe, or as grounds for registering reality's curse upon those who presume not to believe in accordance with the prescribed language of human forms and symbols, is blasphemous, and carries within its own degree of dementia. And this, I submit, is the judgment of reality itself; not of any human formulation dependent upon the language of our fallible forms and symbols.

## III

The stress upon right language in creed and confession has had its counterpart in the writing of dogmatics and systematic theology, for these have been regarded the critical tools of institutional expression for declaring and controlling the cultic witness to the faith. And I think it must be said that there runs through the history of theology an underlying assumption that *the word's the thing*—the *right* word, else the realities of faith elude us.

The change that came in the Enlightenment during the seventeenth century implied no marked deviation from this basic premise concerning language and reality. It implied, instead, a vigorous and decisive rejection of the institutional control of language in defining and conveying the realities of faith. *Right reason* still prevailed as a guarantee of reality discerned; only right reason was proclaimed as a gift or possible gift within every man. The more cautious and discerning among these "enlightened"

Protestants insisted upon disciplining reasoning in coming to appropriate statements of personal conviction, or to a common witness of faith. Thus reason within every man held a priority that authority in church belief had previously held. The most winsome appeal to "right reason" among these seventeenth century rationalists appears in the writings of the Cambridge Platonist, John Smith.[3] Here it is acknowledged that, although reason in every man is a precious gift of the Almighty, and the sole means of access to the wisdom and directives of a loving God, every man's reason is caught and entangled within a web of sensory deflection and distortion which must be dispelled before the reasoning of any individual man can be expressive of what is consistent with that God-given legacy, namely, the mind of God speaking through the mind of individual man. Discipline in sensibilities and judgment, therefore, was made imperative in John Smith's mode of rationalism in attaining or in releasing "right reason" within any man. Not all rationalists were that sensitive to the moral or psychical pathologies of men. And when early deism gave way to a more assertive and impassioned rationalism, wherein "reason alone," as employed in any mode of discourse, was adjudged "right reason" if it prevailed against its opposition, the deeper vein of these seventeenth century reforms was displaced by a more arrogant and self-assured mode of rationalism.

The eras following the earlier period of the Enlightenment, up to and throughout the period of the nineteenth century, persisted in distinctive ways in perpetuating this basic assumption of correlating language and reality, though with checks and balances consonant with their particular assessment of reason.

## IV

What marks the contrast between the new realism in religious inquiry, notably that in process thought, and the eras preceding our own, about which we have just commented, is the recognition of the structural limitation of the human organism, including that of mind and feeling, and a correspondingly new awareness of the complexity of the vast realm of reality in which our lives are cast. The decisive turn of thought bearing upon this new sense of complexity and unpredictability in comparing our language with reality came, not in the areas of theology or philosophy,

3. John Smith, *Select Discourses*, 1660 (published after his death).

but in the field of physics, dating possibly from the discovery of radium in 1898 by Marie and Pierre Curie, which was to set in motion a whole series of discoveries and reformulations of physical theory leading to what was termed "the new vision in science." The sure sense of a natural order measurable and describable by the synthesis of the natural sciences in accordance with the Newtonian vision gave way to a more modest understanding of the nature and scope of scientific inquiry, and of the complexity of this elusive notion of reality.

The shorthand way of stating this judgment is the now well-known distinction between "picture models" and "disclosure models," as phrased by the British language philosopher, Ian Ramsay.[4] The "picture model" he ascribed to that mode of thinking within the era of Newtonian science that assumed that scientific discoveries progressively contributed to a picture of the natural order; hence the sum of the sciences provided a picture of nature as a whole. The "disclosure model" applied to intermittent discoveries through scientific inquiry and experimentation. Many, many formulae were projected for experimentation; but only occasionally did one succeed, and this among scientists was a time of great rejoicing. At times the successes were overwhelming, as in discoveries leading to the release of atomic energy, or to flights to the moon. Even so, physicists of stature, among the most humble of human inquirers in my judgment, insisted that there can be no direct application of laboratory findings in venturing a total cosmology in the manner of the Newtonian world order. Even the notion of order was, in a way, tentatively tabled. The *assumption* of order, as both Einstein[5] and Whitehead[6] had stated, is acknowledged to be a function of scientific inquiry, and may be employed as a venture of faith for purposes of inquiry. Hence, every act of inquiry, scientific, philosophical, or religious, presupposing coherence on a cosmic scale, or the notion of order as an ultimate picture of reality, is asserted as an act of faith, not as a proven fact of science or philosophy.

## V

Given this understanding of its relation to reality in the present mode, the use of language in theology is of a tentative, explorative, or questing

4. Ian Ramsay, *Models and Mystery* (London: Oxford University Press, 1964).
5. Cf. Albert W. Levi's account of Einstein's thinking on this point in *Philosophy and the Modern World* (Indianapolis: Indiana University Press, 1959), p. 265.
6. Cf. Alfred North Whitehead, *The Principle of Relativity* (Cambridge: Cambridge University Press, 1922), pp. 29–30; cf. also *Modes of Thought* (New York: Macmillan, 1938).

nature; not definitive, restrictive, or compulsive. With this understanding of the use of language, pursuing religious inquiry implies, in part, clarifying the terms of thought we mean to employ, but recognizing this critical effort as being preliminary to a more profoundly sensitive effort: namely, that of attending the penumbra of meaning which, in Wieman's words, "is more than we can think." Now this sounds nonsensical, but it makes great sense when it is understood to mean addressing thought, religious ideas, doctrines, themes of the faith, within the living context in which these realities of faith transpire as energies of the spirit, of the human spirit as manifest in human relationships, a spirit beyond these communal relationships insofar as it conveys to us resources of creaturehood within the mystery of existing which both judges and redeems our human ways.

Faith, Christian faith, is not a matter of words only; it is energy: social, psychical, redemptive energy within individual human beings, within corporate action among groups, within the culture, expressing this grace and judgment of relationships in terms of the resources that heal and redeem our ways.

I am trying to express here an age-old point made in many ways, but pointed up sharply by William James, in saying that language is instrumental to attending the realities of living, of action, of being. Language is no substitute for this faith that issues in lived experiences. Thus theology must understand itself to be not an enterprise of words for their own sake or even for purposes of verbal confession and acclamation; rather a discipline in course with these lived experiences, sensitive to the depth of meaning they body forth in every moment of living; sobered and heightened, both with anxiety and anticipation by the very mystery of existing in which we are involved; and forever open to the intimations of reality as they come into focus through the structured thought we may tentatively formulate; through the sense of wonder and apprehension that may seize us when, in our solitary moments, or in common deliberation we ponder the mystery of existing, the mystery of being and becoming.

Language is an indispensable tool of thought and inquiry. But it is a limited tool, expressive both of the heightened powers of our human creativity, and of the fallible character of our forms and symbols. Reality in all its vastness meets us in each and every succeeding present moment of lived experience, and much more within the purview of our several acts of perception, cognition, and reflection. The whole of the Creative Passage of events in all of its immediacies, and in its thrust toward an inconceivable ultimacy, is in each of these encounters, with varying degrees of relevance and awareness. It is my conviction, and in this I think I concur with both James and Whitehead, that we participate in this Creative Passage as bodily event at a depth and fullness not manageable at the cognitive level; for in the conceptual act, the limiting purview of our own fallible human structure intrudes with a sharper focus and assertiveness than occurs simply in the act of living. In a word, again, we live more deeply than we can think. Yet thinking is our indispensable need for expressing, affirming, and clarifying our individuated identity, in concourse with all other entities, within this vast Creative Passage in which inheres that sensitive working and efficacy to which some have applied the word God, the Holy One. Schleiermacher referred to it as "God-consciousness." In the words of Rudolf Otto, it is to be as creatures. "In the presence of—Whom, or What?" he asks; and then replies, "In the presence of that which is a Mystery inexpressible and above all creatures."[7]

Process thought in its deepest vein acknowledges this that Schleiermacher and Otto have designated the Ultimate Mystery. Its venture in formulating terms expressive of it is in the mood of experimenting with the use of language for acknowledging and attending this that is more than we can think. Whitehead entitled one of his books *Adventures of Ideas*. All of his works are in the nature of such an adventure, and his *Process and Reality* is his most ambitious one. Yet it remains an adventure of ideas, a kind of empirical realism, an outreach of the human structure with all the sensitive awareness at its command to discern in experience, and thus to express in language, some hint of the fullness and depth of experience as lived within this Creative Passage: experiences in which ultimacy and immediacies traffic together; for ultimacy inheres in every act of our immediacies.

## VI

Language, then, is expressiveness, conveying the fact and reality of existence from creature to creature. Creatures, by reason of their separate languages, are divided among themselves in their expressiveness—nonhuman as well as human. Because of this differentiation in language it would seem that much of the reality of existing is denied to them. Yet there is a bond of existing that exceeds, and in some ways, transcends

7. Rudolf Otto, *The Idea of the Holy* (London: Oxford University Press, 1928 edition), pp. 12–13.

this differentiation in language and the separations it imposes. That bond is the fact of creaturehood evidenced simply in the act of existing. The sheer act of existing, however differentiated linguistically, culturally, or by reason of any other circumstances, affords common participation in these creatural depths of existing; hence the grounds for awareness, common awareness, of the realities to which we seek to give recognition through language precede our speaking, our expressiveness through language. Thus there are depths of awareness accompanying the bodily event of living and experiencing that yield conditions of knowing what language may not convey, or, perhaps, *cannot* convey.

I have been speaking of this dimensional character of knowing and awareness with specific reference to our creaturehood. The same phenomenon of participating awareness occurs within the commonplaces of our everyday living, within the family or community, and with those with whom we relate intimately under other circumstances. In all of these instances there are depths of awareness accompanying the bodily event of living and experience that yield conditions of knowing which language may not convey; or, for that matter, cannot convey. Whitehead expressed this point in those memorable words, "Mothers can ponder many things in their hearts which their lips cannot express." Similarly, fathers ponder many things in their hearts, in their acts, in what they convey or exemplify in their crafts, their disciplined labors, which their lips may seem helpless to express.

I speak here out of personal reminiscences which offer some illumination of the point I am making. My father was a cabinetmaker; the best I have ever known. As to words to describe his craft, or to offer instructions for performing it, he was hesitant, even inept. Yet his very stance in approaching the sawing of a board or in fitting a joint, or just his manner of handling tools in performing any single act, bespoke the talent and craftsmanship which he possessed and exhibited. I do not recall our exchanging any words concerning the use of tools or the exercise of his craft; yet, to my surprise in later years, I found I had acquired something of his skill, even to the extent of designing and building a house.

Children and youth, too, ponder things in their hearts that their lips cannot express. In recent years, many of them have become demonstrably eloquent, in expressing with their lips and through their acts what they have long pondered in their hearts. And this, too, is relevant, terribly relevant, to the theme we are discussing. Through these unrestrained declarations and acts we are witnessing eruptions of the lived experience long dormant and smoldering, awaiting a time of release and expressiveness.

It does not follow, however, that the realities of these lived experiences lay dormant or unexpressed, except as they can break forth verbally in language. Nor is living with integrity, with style and beauty always, or necessarily, the fruition of language employed instructively, testimonially, or with moral direction or insistence. *Presence,* sheer presence in and of itself, is a mode of communicating. In the West we have possibly accented the use of words more than other cultures, other religions, in reaching for or giving expression to the realities to which we stand committed; or to the legacy of faith which underlies and nurtures our mode of living, and bequeathes to us our cultural identity.

What we are acknowledging here, echoing what many before us have said, is that there is language in silences; and in the spaces between words. Reality is not absent because of the silences, any more than when words are used. There is an alternating and intermingling here of the modes of language in expressing and enjoying, or in simply enduring reality. Our language is rarely of a depth to apprehend, least of all to comprehend, the realities of which our lives are made, and within whose context they exist. Yet, when we speak, we speak out of a depth of existing; and, to a degree, in terms of it. And that may be the best we can hope for. But awareness of *that,* sheer appreciative awareness of that depth of our existing, is a gain in stature as a human being, and possibly in communicating as a human being.

So it is with the legacy of faith that inheres within the structured experience of any people. Words upon words may be piled upon one another, or alternate with one another, in successive efforts to bear witness to the faith. And restless and zealous advocates of the faith will contrive special means for expanding and extending it. But again, the witness of faith and its survival, or its persistence from age to age, may depend but slightly, if at all, upon this organized zeal to spread the word.

## VII

Now lest my words be misunderstood as defending or pleading for a nonintellectual approach to religion, let me hasten to say that the intellectual dimension of faith is really not at issue here. For the tendency to confuse reality with language about reality, doctrines for the realities of faith, zealous use of words, pious or otherwise, with the experiencing of reality as lived, is common at all levels of the human community: among nonintellectuals as well as sophisticated people of learning; among pious evangelicals as well as among secularists and liberals. The point toward which we have been steering in our remarks thus far is that reality is in the immediacies of these lived experiences which are of a piece with and participate in dimensions of ultimacy within the Creative Passage. Language may illuminate and significantly inform our participation in this depth of reality which exceeds, or may even elude, our forms and symbols; yet its formulations in words or doctrines, in myths or metaphysics, are not to be made coterminous, in the sense of "picture models," with this reality as lived; or with the realities of faith as experienced. Yet they may serve as disclosures, momentary or even enduring disclosures, of what is real and reassuring in these experiences as lived.

While the realities of faith with which we are concerned in living are energies within experiences that are now immediately upon us, it is nevertheless true that awareness of this inherent efficacy within the structure of experience among any people rests back upon, or in some subtle way issues from, a cultic or cultural legacy of long-standing which may best be expressed in terms of themes or motifs of the faith. I have come to regard these primal themes or motifs as the enduring basis of our Christian legacy, rather than any formulated doctrines or creeds; for the latter, while they have their claim to importance for specific purposes, cultic or otherwise, must be regarded as various renderings of this primal legacy. Doctrines have proven expendable; yet the legacy of faith persists.

These elemental themes of faith, conveyed in thematic form as a drama of redemption, constitute a language so expressive of the primal events of creature experience that they readily coalesce with the sensibilities and outreach of a people, and thus become symbols ready at hand in times of duress or exhilaration to give voice to what transpires within the structure of experience within any given time of history. When they so erupt to give voice to deeply felt experiences of the culture, they convey less of a doctrinal connotation than of an expression of human outreach—in some instances as agony, in others, as exhilaration or ecstasy, consonant with what inheres as a legacy of faith, latent or otherwise, within the ongoing structure of experience.

Thus there is a silent working within the historic structure of experience that carries its own efficacy, and which, in a way, persists more in the guise of sensibilities and feelings, apprehensions and appreciations, than in the codified words of creeds and moral directives. That is why the rhetorical expression of faith can wane, seemingly subside, give way to secular ends devoid of any directives out of the legacy of faith; yet, in a time of crisis, or in penitent years following from a drought in human sensitivity, or from blatant evil within the whole of society, sobering even the most secular of taste, something out of the depths of human awareness seems to erupt to bear witness to that legacy long dormant, a legacy presumed to be merely cultic in import, yet suddenly assuming the proportions of a cultural witness to what in the depths of their anguish, or in their mood of renascence, looms as the living reality of their faith as a people. Insofar as the words of our mouths illumine this creaturely participation they enhance, and may encourage, the elemental trust that holds us in existence. Yet the process of living out the demands of ultimacy within these vital immediacies through negotiable acts that are put upon us is the very core of what fortifies us in daily living, and most assuredly so in times of duress or crisis when our fallible forms are most likely to fail us or to seem unequal to the impact of reality itself.

The import of these remarks is not to discount rationality in the understanding of faith, but to identify it in its most adequate sense, and thus to understand the role of critical inquiry in achieving, not certainty, but reassurance, confidence in a response of trust. Theology, when it is adequately exercised, is a contrapuntal mode of inquiry in which themes distilled as motifs of faith from the living structure of experience are in concourse with analogical notions provided by conceptual visions of thought. In this understanding of existence and inquiry we are made attentive not just to a reasonable explication of things, but to the surprises, the intimations of wonder and novelty in these lived experiences; yes, and to the judgments upon our limited responses, or overt acts of evil and folly when we act wrongly, insensitively, even destructively.

The constructive use of reason in theology is not that of bringing life and faith into a domesticated situation of reasonableness; but to provide us with vistas of the mind by which we can best apprehend and be responsive to what really constitutes the circumstances of reality as lived;

to provide an orientation, as it were, within which we can respond to these immediacies with a sense of their depth and ultimate import, as being constituent of the Creative Passage, which in religious language is to speak of our life in God.

Because theology deals with issues of such dimensions as having immediate and ultimate import, its problems can never be resolved other than as tentative solutions or resolutions to a complex of queries, the answers to which elude final or absolute formulation. They will always remain, as Whitehead has phrased it, *adventures of ideas.* Yet the truth of the faith, I repeat, lies not in these formulations as such, or in any word or symbol pointing up their meaning, but in the actualities themselves, in the realities of grace and judgment of which these formulations speak, and toward which they direct concern and reflection.

Chapter Three

# Language and History

The language of any culture tends to record the rhythms of reaction and release as these come to fruition at various junctures of its history. In this sense language is at once a depository of a culture's dramatic occurrences and their perpetual medium of expression. Language and history, therefore, are organically interrelated. This insight is more apt to be evident in momentous breaks in the rhythms of historical action than in the continuous flow of events or experiences; as in intermittent periods of special note evoking reaction, or when rare instances of expressiveness will intrude upon the regular flow of events with dramatic effect.

I

The words of Scripture arising from Judaic-Christian history, for example, often speak out of situations of extremity: situations of great joy as when "the cup runneth over," or of dire import, as when, by the waters of Babylon, dislocated and despairing Jews sat down and wept. And these words out of the biblical heritage acquire pertinence and precision whenever such dire occasions or times of wonder and joy recur in our history or in individual experiences. This would suggest that precision of meaning is not always a matter of definition, but of historical relevance, enabling realities to find voice within an adequate and appropriate idiom in the language we employ. It is this coherence of events with human utterances appropriate to them that has periodically put to rout coherences preestablished through thought and custom, when they, in turn, have been inadequate to historical experiences or even indifferent toward them.

I am speaking here somewhat reminiscently out of personal history, reflecting upon the years spanning the forties and early fifties, a time when the culture of the West appeared to be in jeopardy, more seriously so perhaps than is true of it today. During those years peoples of the Far East and Southeast Asia spoke of the lights going out in Europe and America. Words are strange creations of the mind. They have a way of being born out of an historical situation. They are formed out of a concern to designate what is seen or heard, felt or experienced. What is most obvious and commonplace rarely requires definition. Thus when they cohere with historical events they will be employed freely without thought of definition. But words fall into disuse, as many Christian words did, say from the close of the seventeenth century onward: words like revelation, judgment, redemption, and grace. These words were retained, as liturgical terms, suitable for expressing cultic beliefs in ceremonials and confessional; the culture at large did not evoke their usage nor did the imagery of thought arising from the disciplines of inquiry in the sciences, in the reflections of philosophy and religious study, or even in the language of poetry. So these words lay interred in the ceremonials of churches bent on sustaining the tradition within a persisting orthodoxy.

Then it happened! The revolution in the sciences that was to inaugurate a new stage of the modern consciousness with new realism during the earlier years of the current century broke upon us. It was as if a change in the wind had occurred. The down pressure of fixed forms of thought lifted. Intellectually we seemed to breathe more freely. The spaces of the mind seemed to expand with the distance which new dimensions of thought and imagination brought to the sciences, and which was to have ramifications in philosophical and religious studies as well. I am speaking, of course, of circumstances relating to the rise of a new realism in Western thinking following upon developments in some of the basic sciences and related modes of study.

This heightening of the imagery of thought in the sciences was to be accompanied a few years later by similar eruptions in the historical experiences of the West, ranging over two or more decades. Amidst these shifting winds of doctrine and historical cavalcades, vocabularies underwent radical change. It was not so much a new vocabulary that was being initiated; though something of this was occurring also, notably in the sciences. More amazingly, however, were changes in the culture at large, among sophisticates in literature and critical commentary as well as in common talk. Older vocabularies began appearing in fresh guise. Words which had lain dormant for centuries became as current as new words, charged with fresh power and meaning. Formerly identified with cultic beliefs of an older Christian vocabulary, they now seemed coherent, both with the spatial dimensions of thought and with the intensities of anguish within the immediate historical experience.

Much of this renascence of Christian language dated from World War II. My own *Seeds of Redemption,* written and delivered in 1945 just before the first atomic bombs had been dropped, but published in 1947, and *The Reawakening of Christian Faith* (1949) were somewhat in the nature of testaments to this renascent occurrence. But the literature that most readily reflected this linguistic awakening was not specifically theological. Much of it came from addresses by atomic scientists, reported in the press and journals; for, following Hiroshima and Nagasaki, atomic scientists, many of whom had resisted the use of the bomb, became as a band of prophets, appearing in churches and public assemblies on weekends to warn communities of the impending peril in turning atomic power into instruments of destruction. War novels and poetry, following from this traumatic period of guilt and confession, were among the first to restore these cultic terms to their secular usage, although they had been employed this way in accounts of the devastating experiences of war and dislocation and in concentration camps, as the memorable little book, *Dying We Live,* and Bonhoeffer's *Letters from Prison* disclose. And then these cultic words began to appear in common speech wherever the tragedy of modern times was being talked about. Words like sin and redemption, grace and judgment, demonic forces and the Kingdom of God, death and transfiguration, or even resurrection, took on a vitality and relevance they had not had in three hundred years.

The situations of history just seemed to lift these words and phrases out of their cultic forms in which they had been interred, and appropriated them as words for those troubled times. Whether secular or sacred made no difference. For a time, at least, following the dropping of the bombs, when as President Robert Maynard Hutchins said we had but five years to ponder the good news of damnation, the words of the Gospels took on the relevance of atomic science itself.

Now in part this renascence of a sense of reality in the language of faith was a direct response to the crises of the period. Catastrophe upon catastrophe had brought our dreams of progress and our illusions of Western idealism to a startling halt. They had evoked in us as a people elemental feelings of extremity, feelings which were both humbling and leveling in a way that awakened us to our common state as being fallible human beings. The facades of sophistication and class distinctions seemed to slough off, or melt away, as this mood of our primordial humanity asserted itself. The only way that seemed open to us for restoring our sense of human dignity, or the likelihood of survival, was that of repentance, confession, and the consolation of judgment. Judgment in a time of stress and remorse is not the harsh note of negation we commonly ascribe to it. It is, as it were, a note of restoration: a cleansing and clarifying word that somehow prepares the human spirit to receive the grace that is given or can be given, the forgiveness that awaits the repentant one.

As a theologian, however, I sensed that there was something more in this traumatic response than a falling back upon sacred stereotypes. To some extent, especially among discerning and critical minds of the period, these words of Scripture, now resonant with new tones, strikingly contemporary, seemed to accord with the new imagery of thought that was now informing and shaping our secular speech insofar as it had become truly modern. The fruition of scientific labors which had begun at the turn of the century was now full upon us. The effect of these labors had been to rend the enclosures of the mind which nineteenth century positivism had provided and in fact imposed. And it also disrupted the surety of the life of reason which various forms of modern idealism had established. Yet the consequences of this breakthrough in the imagery of thought and in the use of reason were bewildering and threatening, even as they offered release from older fixations of mind. And the promise of incredible advances in the creation of power and its technological uses, along with the new potential of demonry implied in its usage, added to this bewilderment.

Once again, insofar as it partook of this scientific revolution in thought and experimentation, the Western world experienced a widening and heightening of the world of space along with an acceleration in time that seemed to restore a sense of mystery and misgiving which ancient worlds had experienced. In fact, the nineteen forties and fifties present in retrospect our nearest parallel in Western history to the fifteenth century sense of dislocation and troubled anticipation: an era in which invention and travel radically extended the bounds of thought and experience.

## II

With the settling of scientific research into an orderly program of technological advance, applied to industrial and other civilian ends, something of an earlier aplomb and confidence in science and industry seemed to be restored; sufficiently, at least, to reinstate a mood of complacency concerning the new age of power, now in full operation. And as this sense of assurance gathered momentum, one could detect a return to a kind of stolid mood of settling into the cultural benefits of mechanization, and an economy of mass production. More seriously and menacing, our mania for marketing American democracy abroad returned, displacing our penitent mood with a return to the doctrine of our *manifest destiny*, making other people and cultures over in the image of ourselves. The spontaneity and expectancy of the new vision of science, which gave rise to a new realism with its possibilities of openness and wonder in thought, seemed to subside as scientific energy and insight were channeled once again into orderly and routine paths of mechanization.

A striking shift in theological awareness could be detected in response to this restored sense of assurance in the sciences, and the accompanying acquiescence to mechanization as a mode of existence. It was an uneasy awareness, recognizing, on the one hand, the primacy of the scientific outlook in its new phase, yet noting as well a creeping subservience of this scientific vision to the demands of industry and the dominance of governmental designs in the use of power. In this puzzled response to the momentum of secular forces, the Christian legacy as a cultural witness which had enlivened earlier years with the promise of a renascence in sensibilities continuous with that legacy was to be replaced by an overt secularism within the churches and among theologians bent on getting new leverage and a sense of relevance. Issues and motives here are by no means clear. And I do not presume to be able to clarify them fully. One observation is pertinent, however; namely, that *relevance* in our ministry and church life, except as it exhibits and expresses some coherence between language and reality in its witness, can be a false allure.

By contrast, I find the witness of faith, or whatever it is we have been hearing from a younger generation (witness of protest is probably the appropriate caption), rings truer to the realities of the human situation, and to what, in truth, inheres in the legacy of faith to which our Christian words and other religious words bear witness. For the words of protest, insofar as they are something more than a reckless revolt for revolt's sake, seem to speak out of anguish over our return to a mechanizing and dehumanizing secularization of life. Language and reality seem to cohere in this expression of anguish and despair over what is imminently inhuman in design and objective. By contrast, the language of complacent compliance with established dehumanizing designs, consistent with our conscious intent as a people and as a culture, inside as well as outside the churches, has a ring of unreality and obscures or evades the signs of an impending peril.

These contrasting occurrences present instances within our lived experiences and our cultural history in which a disparity between language and reality has been evident and instances in which they appear to have been vividly in accord. And they direct attention as well to the realities of these lived experiences within the depth of the Creative Passage wherein a sense of ultimacy is apprehended, and our sense of creaturehood is reaffirmed. In that context the realities of faith, as conveyed in our Christian legacy, are seen to be energies of grace and judgment experienced through our relationships with one another and within the cultural community of events. And their truth, yea their meaning, is in the actualities of these lived experiences, however worded, however construed or misconstrued in the language we employ to express them or to explicate their meaning.

Concepts, visions, and formulated theories have their day, and then give way to more appropriate images of thought. But the death of language need not imply the dissolution of the realities of which they speak or have spoken. Reality as lived, wherein the Creative Passage of events endures with unmistakable identity, is neither so vulnerable nor so fallible as language itself. It is, in fact, the fecund source of new language when old ones become impotent of meaning, as legacies of past experiences subtly interweave as a structure of experience with an innovating present.

In short, our securities are not in language, or in any formulation or theory projecting our possibilities, or envisaging our destiny. Our security is in the living nexus of events that has brought forth life and faith, and in which we participate at great depth in our creaturely relationships as we respond to and partake of the grace and judgment within our human associations.

Chapter Four

# Fallible Forms and
# the Mystery of Existing

A dilemma confronts every serious scholar or scientist concerned with exploring the nature of the world or of human existence, or some definitive aspect of it. It is that the very act of undertaking disciplined inquiry requires that one adhere to a manageable course. In doing so one must intrude the limited forms and symbols of human understanding to such a degree as to risk enclosing the data of experience within those intelligible forms to the exclusion of what, in reality, may elude them, or be inadequately addressed by them. One need not resort to some esoteric view of reality or experience to acknowledge this fact. It is written in the daily work of the laboratory, as modern physicists have acknowledged; and in the frustrations of any serious kind of inquiry into man's ultimate or immediate meaning, as philosophers, psychologists, or theologians might pursue such inquiry. The impatient effort to get on with the business of establishing a disciplined mode of inquiry and to arrive at usable insights bearing upon the general welfare or well-being of the human community impels earnest men and women among various disciplines to bracket out this penumbra of unmanageable realities, or simply to ignore it, and to get on with formulating the terms of understanding as well as the bounds of legitimate inquiry. Speaking and writing within such a recognizable and shared mode of discourse are acknowledged to be disciplined inquiry. Not to speak *beyond* the bounds of controlled inquiry so understood has come to be the mark of scholarly and scientific sensibilities and learning.

I

As long as one could assume that what was so ventured on a tentative and highly guarded basis was fully coherent with what persisted in nature or reality in general and therefore a direct accounting of it, there seemed no need for serious misgivings concerning the mode of inquiry itself. To be sure, the tentativeness of every judgment, however confident one might be of momentary results on a provisional basis, assured openness to new data, new circumstances within experience. Yet the reliance on forms and symbols employed, in fact on conceptualization, itself, was such as to enable one to assume that any discrepancy between what had been critically observed or interpreted, on the one hand, and the reality or actuality of what was being experienced or encountered, on the other, was simply a matter of further observation or reflection within the accepted rules of logic, testing, and speculative inference. The hard truth that has pressed to the fore in recent years among knowledgeable scientists and philosophers is that such assumptions can no longer be sustained in so sanguine a manner, given the current understanding of all acts of human inquiry whether scientific, philosophical, religious, or aesthetic. Nevertheless, critical and disciplined inquiry must persist. There is no discontinuing such inquiry, however marginal its purpose or results; for the margin of intelligibility it affords makes all the difference between there being some degree of responsible judgments and acts within the human community, with a funded reserve of accumulative wisdom, however tentative, and there being but a potpourri of impulsive and contradictory suppositions and opinions.

However, in the context of human inquiry made imperative by our understanding of the limited function of our forms and symbols, a horizon of incalculable data looms as a relevant dimension of experience. In that context, the mystery of existing, as an inescapable depth and overtone of our understanding, intrudes a persisting horizon of awareness which somehow gives new dimension to understanding, itself, along with intimations of resources which cannot readily be dismissed or ignored wherever critical inquiry is ventured. In the early twenties, before these complexities of scientific and philosophical inquiry were generally noted, it was commonplace among social scientists and natural scientists to dismiss such undefined areas of experience or awareness as being irrelevant to disciplined inquiry. During my student days in the University of Chicago the refrain "We know nothing of beginnings or endings" echoed throughout the quadrangles as a glib retort to any suggestion of taking account of such dimensions beyond observable events. The import of that comment was to assume that what was of ultimate concern lay either at the beginning or the end of time. In between these mythical poles of beginnings and endings lay the vast expanse of knowable data where available tools of inquiry could readily apply. That retort, "We know nothing of beginnings or endings," expresses the contrast between the inquiry of an earlier era and the one which engages us now insofar as the new vision of science and modes of inquiry related to it shape our thinking. For where the event of existing embraces depths of ultimacy or of reality within the very *immediacies* of experience being lived and observed, literally as a dimension of what is observable and knowable, however elusive or unmanageable, the arbitrary act of ignoring that dimension, or of bracketing it out of awareness or reflection, will not do.

The word "depth" in this context is not intended as an evocative term; in fact it becomes misleading when it is so understood. That it has evocative power may not be denied, especially when the force of its epistemological import is made clear. What is basic in this notion of depth as I mean to use it is the recognition that relations are experienceable and are actually experienced, forming a substantive part of the continuum of experience as lived, a point initially made by William James in his *Psychology*[1] as against the sensationalist view of Hume. An accompanying insight, which James made insistent in his later writings on radical empiricism, is that perceptual experience is a richer event than conception can possibly be, providing every occurrence of awareness with a "fringe," implying a "More," much of which persistently evades conceptualization. These insights were to be given more explicit formulation as abstract notions in Whitehead's philosophy of organism in which "concrescence," or the textured character of experience, was advanced as a key notion. Within that perspective, every event, including every person, was to be envisioned simultaneously in terms of its individuated concretion as a novel event and the communal ground in which the individuation occurred. "Individual in community" thus became Whitehead's formula for expressing the nature of each

1. Cf. William James, *Psychology*, vol. 1 (New York: Henry Holt & Co., 1890), pp. 243 ff.

concrete event, including each person. But this textured character of every event, including every person, carried with it overtones of a prescient awareness of a future thrust of occurrences already implicit in the existing structure. This was the emergent theme in this philosophy of organism. Thus every person was seen as holding in tension within one's immediate existence a persisting structure of experience bearing past valuations along with a restless bent toward novelty as a futuristic motif.

Depth, in this sense, then, is contextual, relational, and simultaneously so in a spatial and a temporal sense. The relational or contextual ground of all existence is dynamic, ongoing. The notion of depth thus provides a perspective upon every single or individuated event or person that illumines the context in which each "lived experience" takes place. That perspective, in turn, provides a resource within and beyond what each individual in himself or herself initiates or represents, as well as a source of judgment or caution toward what is individually enacted with indifference toward that relational ground. Yet a valid correlation of each centered existence and its communal ground is simultaneously one of individuation along with being communal, implying an appropriate degree of dissonance along with a communal response. Sheer subservience of the individual entity to its communal ground is thus viewed as a breach of the contextual occurrence; for any resolution that implies relinquishment of the authentic, novel concretion of the individual within community would be false to what is crucial in the creative event itself.

Similarly, in speaking of the mystery of existing, I mean to do more than to evoke a mood of wonderment or apprehension about that event, though both responses are appropriate. I mean, rather, to lift up implications of the dimensional character of each concrete occurrence as this applies to each human experience, particularly the depth of immediacy in each such experience.

The mystery of existing, with its experiences of joy and sorrow, fulfillment or defeat, is the vivid empirical datum which evokes inquiry. The bare event of existing is the most immediate and enduring fact of experience, and thus the most immediate empirical datum; yet, this bare event of existing rarely, if ever, presents itself to our conscious awareness. For the sensory responses in each individual, and the quickening of conscious meaning that follows from such psychical and conceptual interaction, clothes each life-span with a plethora of images, giving to each moment of existing its own self-conscious experience. And this can be a complex of feelings and valuations expressing intermittently a heightened awareness of the joy of living or an aggravating sense of anguish, anxiety, and despair; or, possibly, a persisting experience of ennui in response to its deadly routine and futility. Normally an intermingling of these moods and valuations characterizes human existence.

The sheer event of existing, however, is deeper than consciousness, and deeper than anyone's sensory awareness of it. It opens into an ongoing stream of interrelated events simultaneously enjoying or enduring this fact of existing.

Each event, as we have said, at whatever level, appears to be held in existence through a structure of relationships that is integral to its own act of existing and to circumstances creative and supportive of its existing. The history of natural structures is thus a serial accounting of the various nexus of relationships that have accompanied this "coming into being and perishing" of the many existing events throughout nature. Our human existence in each instance subsumes much that has preceded man in this emergence of natural structures; and it contains within its own structural emergence tendencies and sensibilities that are responsive to this depth of relationships which supervenes it, and more. The More, in this instance, is not just this sequence of subhuman structures, but the ever-present interplay of *creativity, sensitivity,* and *negotiability* that gives dynamic possibilities to each nexus of relationships imparting to each event a creative intent, enabling it to live forward and to participate in the élan of existing.

The limits of our human structure preclude our having full understanding or steady awareness of this depth of mystery that has brought us into existence and, for a time, holds us in existence as humanly conscious beings. Thus our existing as immediate occurrences takes place with but marginal awareness, and often with relative indifference, to the penumbral occurrences that carry and give intimation of the Ultimate Efficacy attending all existence.

All existing, as we have implied, is fraught with peril as well as with possibility and promise. The peril of existing derives in large measure from the surd of insensitivity that intrudes upon all relationships with varying degrees of defeat and destructiveness, ranging from the anguish and evil of isolated existences among individuals to explosive encounters between individuals and groups. As an empirical datum, this surd of insensitivity appears to derive from pathological conditions within the human structure itself and, conceivably, among other structures within nature. There is no assurance, however, so it would seem to me, that this surd of insensitivity is confined to conditions within these created structures. Speculatively speaking, there is the possibility that it may extend to conditions accompanying creativity itself, that it impairs the creative process, or, in any case, sets obstacles to the creative act, thus persistently offering a threat to that act and to conditions consonant with it as implied in the terms sensitivity and negotiability.

To the degree that this peril assumes ontological proportions, say as an abyss of disorder and irrationality, or as an aggressive distaste for or disregard of creativity, it becomes a threat to the Ultimate Efficacy attending existence as well as to existence itself. I see no way of affirming or disavowing such an ontological peril categorically; but the tendency of my thought is to assume its possibility to the extent, at least, of acknowledging that the creativity, sensitivity, and negotiability that bring meaningful and redemptive events into existence do so at a price—at the price of an ultimate encounter with suffering and anguish, consonant with qualitative attainment. Thus our anguish and suffering, while pertinent to the conditions that attend our structure of existence, may not be peculiar to our situations as created human beings. It may be analogous to, if not a counterpart of, the strain attending creativity itself in its encounter with an ultimate surd of insensitivity.

So much, then, for a minimal sketching of the mystery of existing as an empirical datum.

## II

Now the problem that has perplexed empirical thinkers since the time of William James, and which, I confess, has been a persisting problem for me, is, how are we to attend this most immediate empirical datum, the bare event of existing, in a way that can take account of its multidimensional realities as experienced, as lived, as they bear upon disciplined inquiry? Critical reflection, even when it presumed to be empirical, has consistently veered from the stance of attending that bare, empirical datum of existing, preferring rather, to assemble a fund of abstract symbols, presumably identifiable as pointers to the concrete occurrences, but which lend themselves to being employed logically with a facility not possible in attending concrete data. Such abstractive extension of the perceptual event has had the effect of rendering the mystery of existing relatively clarified within the forms and symbols of abstraction. Yet one is not able to suppress the suspicion that such extensions of the perceptual act into vivid and logically responsive structures of meaning have been but a ballooning of minimal perceptions into formidable systems of ideas which, in effect, may convey more of our abstractive genius in exercising our fallible forms and symbols than of the realities experienced. And an overconcern for precision and clarity in the use of these abstract forms and symbols has led us by default to relinquish the empirical data to occult interpretations, or visionary ventures and explorations.

Concern for a judicious use of intellect, I am persuaded, does not warrant its abdication when confronted by the dimension of depth just described, thereby abandoning it to the lead of the psyche in this esoteric sense. That, in my judgment, was the unnecessary assumption that misled previous generations of discerning scientists, philosophers, and religious inquirers, positing either a firm rationality, or commitment to the nonrational, in unrestrained recourse to psychical or mystical domains of experience.

Historically speaking, it would seem that we need to cut a path between what Bergson and what both James and Whitehead, each in his own way, sought to achieve (possibly between phenomenology and process thought, whatever that might be). William James was simultaneously scientist and philosopher (initially artist) in his approach to any inquiry. Yet he brought to each of these efforts a schedule of demands issuing from experience lived at various levels of the human community, and pulsating with anguish, even despair, and much searching, as various kinds of people would communicate them to him. James was keenly aware of the dilemma that confronted critical inquiry in any effort to wrest from these immediacies of experience as lived some orderly judgment or conception that could be simultaneously clarifying and continuous with the actualities of experience.

Whitehead, too, from the very beginning of his career as mathematician, seems to have been primarily the scientist, concerned with establishing the grounds of inquiry amidst a vast array of unmanageable data that simply would not yield to the measure of precise inquiry. His reference to aesthetics, as being the more primary and appropriate means of achieving an adequate vision of the whole of reality, was his astute way (possibly his mathematical way) of acknowledging the intricate, subtle, and elusive character of the interplay between manageable and unmanageable data and of pointing up a disciplined mode of inquiry that could accommodate itself simultaneously to the structural character of events and to their feeling context. By implication, Whitehead seemed to be saying that science and philosophy as well as theology in their usual mode of inquiry tend to be too flat-footed in their approach to such data to be sensitively informing as to what actually transpires.

It is common among recent process thinkers, committed to the metaphysics of Whitehead, to assume that everything of importance in process philosophy that began with James and Bergson was assimilated by Whitehead and given a more systematic formulation in his thought. This I have regarded as being but partially true, and possibly misleading. For while Whitehead was deeply appreciative of James, and responsive to him at various critical junctures, he was intent upon giving structural form to empirical insights which had been less formally addressed by James and Bergson. And in this effort it must be said that Whitehead was unable to sustain James's acute and persistent sensitivity to the issue concerning the use of language or abstractive forms in addressing the import of this depth and surplusage of experience in understanding the act of existing. Numerous references to it appear in various writings by Whitehead, indicating his awareness of the issue and his concern with it as a sensibility of thought; but these appear mainly in his secondary writings, and less vividly or continuously in his major, methodological work *Process and Reality,* which has been the basic text for much of process theology in recent years.

James's radical openness to the More of reality confronting one in experience stemmed from the seriousness with which he took the perceptual flux as the living nexus of what is really real. Concepts played their role in James's empiricism; but they were instrumental in a limited and controlled sort of way. They served, on the one hand, to extend the vision beyond individual tracks of perception, relating one track of experience to another, or posing questions which enabled one to probe and contrast these various tracks of experience. And they provided swift and economical ways of surveying experiences in acquiring some generalized view of existence, a view which would be unavailable concretely, except as one might live through each and every track of perceptual experience that had ever occurred. The latter being impossible, conceptual knowledge, abstracted from the perceptual flux, served for James an indispensable function, but was to be justified only on grounds of economy and practical concerns.

What James recoiled from was the assumption that one could extend this abstract conceptual knowledge indefinitely, or speculatively, into a total vision of reality, as if this that was encountered in experience *could* be grasped summarily or as if a conceptual vision so projected could be considered in any way adequate to or expressive of the total import of this living nexus of events which was ever growing, changing, developing, and erupting in new and unexpected ways. And his restraint here was motivated by a vivid sense of the mysterious depth that moved out from each individuated experience into associated levels of consciousness. This, James felt, must be taken into account as a dimension of depth or heightening supervening experience; but it could not be attended in any direct mode of inquiry. Nevertheless, this mysterious depth or heightening of experience functioned in James's thought as a significantly creative More in experience that could take over when human creativity faltered or as saving energy that could come to the aid of an individual under extreme conditions of need or despair. James had only the crudest kinds of imagery as were offered by testimonies of mystical experiences, psychical research, and studies in the unconscious in addressing this More in existence. In our own time, having passed through developments in emergent theories of evolution, Gestalt psychology, field theory in modern physics, and many other changes in imagery of human life and thought, we are better prepared to see in technical ways what James was acknowledging and toward which he was reaching.

## III

In pursuing the problem which plagued both James and Whitehead, I wish to focus first of all upon the limitations of our human forms and symbols for conceiving and expressing ideas pertinent to the mystery of existing and note also the subtle tendencies within the human structure which give promise of a mode of response within human inquiry which, conceivably, might mitigate those limitations.

In assessing those forms and symbols, I avail myself of the judgment which has been with us for at least half a century, dating from a time when, as a result of various inquiries into the sciences of man, the limitations of the human structure as a level of emergence were noted and seriously taken into account. Not all that was put forth under emergent theories in the early twenties has been sustained by subsequent inquiries in biological studies; but the notion that does persist with increasing clarity is that human facilities of thought and reflection partake of an organic structure that is expressive and representative of its distinctive, and thereby limited, level of emergence. In Whitehead's words, "We think with our bodies." Mind is an emergent within nature; and human mind represents a distinctive level of that natural history, expressive through the bodily facilities available to such a structure. Yet its awareness and reflection are not wholly enclosed within that definitive, humanly structured existence. Mind carries within its facilities, not as a representative feature of its level of emergence, but as a restive, anticipatory surge within its structure, what S. Alexander identified as a *nisus* toward a further level of sensitive awareness.[2] Thus every natural structure exhibits its own representative character as an explicit level of life, together with a restive and prescient thrust toward a higher degree of sensitivity and awareness.

The forms and symbols which the human being employs in its representative mode as a natural structure at the level of human emergence, therefore, are expressive of that mode of existence in its definitive, yet limited, structural occurrence. Nevertheless, it appears to have tenuous access to what is more than this structural occurrence through prescient tendencies that are implicit in it. The antennae for that kind of participation are not necessarily intellectual in the typically rational or discursive sense, consonant with the forms and symbols devised for communication in that mode. Insofar as they can be designated mental, they are expressive of the human mind in its most sensitive outreach, as in open awareness or discerning waiting, in the mood of being responsive or receptive to dimensions of the lived experience which deeply nurture and sustain the creatural stance. Where this can occur in the human being, the More of existence can have access to its structured life, and possibly evoke awareness or intimations of what exceeds its creaturely life in the deeper concourse with that which is expressive of the Creative Passage.

---

2. Cf. S. Alexander, *Space, Time and Deity* (London: Macmillan Co., 1920; reprinted, New York: The Humanities Press, 1950), vol. II, book IV, esp. pp. 353 ff.

Because of the subtlety and unassertiveness of this prescient aspect of the human structure, manifest more through qualities of awareness and sensibility than through overt acts of intellection, it rarely appears dominant in the human structure and is more apt to be obscured by assertive drives and capacities. But even when acknowledged and valued, these prescient qualities of human spirit tend to be identified as unique instances of human expressiveness, discernible only in rare human beings[3] rather than as being expressive of a dimension of potential response in the human structure itself. In isolating this prescient quality as a rarity, instead of acknowledging it to be potentially expressive within every human structure, and conceivably pervasive within the human community, one sees this outreach of the human spirit toward a good not its own, potential in every human organism, as tending to be muted. This muting, in effect, is to nullify it as a resource for human motivation or for serious consideration in sensitizing and fructifying intellectual inquiry.

These observations raise troublesome questions bearing upon the central theme of the chapter: the use of disciplined inquiry in attending, if not addressing, the most immediate empirical datum, the sheer event of existing. For they thrust the creatural stance to the fore as being indispensable to such inquiry, however difficult its assimilation to critical methods may be. This was a problem that continually haunted Schleiermacher, as it did Rudolf Otto and Paul Tillich in later years. It was implicit in both James and Whitehead; however, in process theologies stemming from Whitehead's influence, that implicit note tends to be assimilated to the abstractive task in ways that nullify the impact of the query upon the methodological task.

In raising the question of the bearing of the creatural stance upon critical inquiry one is literally opening a Pandora's box. Instantly one is aware of hornets flying about one's head. For creatural awareness, commonly understood, means piety. And that, so it is widely assumed, stands over against *critical* inquiry. For many in the university community, including the theological community, piety represents a stance that subsided when intellectual inquiry took over. And I must confess that where it persists in our intellectual communities, it seems to imply little more than a sentimental softening of the critical edge of thought.

3. Cf. Henri Bergson, *Two Sources of Morality and Religion* (New York: Holt, 1935), and Rudolf Otto, *The Kingdom of God and Son of Man,* new and rev. ed. (London: Lutterworth, 1951).

Hence, I have noted that, where piety intrudes with any visible effect, the rigor of inquiry lessens. But that is precisely where rigor is needed; rigor, not so much in the use of concepts as in the restraint with which we use them, recognizing the critical limits of their usefulness, even as we cherish the margin of intelligibility they afford. "For the depths, there is no language," one poet has said. Yet there is a kind of awareness that may accompany our use of language to give it proportion and the readiness to be judged, or simply confronted, by the realities of which it presumes to speak.

What is being insinuated here is that mind, in and of itself, functioning as a finely tuned mechanism, is not to be regarded the summit of the human outreach or its expressiveness. Conceivably it is the summit as far as it is expressive of the representative human structure. Yet, by itself, functioning critically and designedly, it falls short of attending or expressing that dimension of the human spirit in which concourse with the Creative Passage is somehow attended. We are back again to the observation that the creatural stance, that is, the stance oriented toward the depth of the lived experience, is to be reckoned potentially more profound and discerning than that of the technical, critical, intellectual one. To be sure, the legacy of piety hardly gives encouragement to such a generalization. Nevertheless, however one assesses specific acts of piety or its exemplifications in human cultures, the significance of the creatural stance for enhancing our humanness beyond its structured limits as a level of emergence assumes a primacy that can be attributed to no other function of our humanity.

One may make the point that the trivializing of the creatural stance is at the root of our disparaging of it. One could argue that the initial folly was in setting up the creatural response as a special, cultic act, thereby tending to dissociate creatural awareness from other modes of human expressiveness such as critical reflection and inquiry, creative literature and the arts, and the vast domain of human activity bent on exercising and sustaining the common life of communities. In making creatural awareness a special act of piety dissociated from these lived experiences, one cuts the vital nerve of creaturehood, rendering the creatural response little more than sheer religiosity. In effect, this was to represent creaturely awareness as optional, and, to many discerning human beings, expendable, if not, in fact, an offense to the sensibilities of the human spirit. And, sad to say, in one community after another, it became and has become just that.

To speak of creaturehood as a *religious* fact is to *under*state the import of its meaning, and possibly to misconstrue its meaning. To speak of it as a *religious* fact, thereby implying it to be optional, or worse, inappropriate to the language and stance of critical inquiry, is to render critical inquiry, itself, uncritical in the basic, human sense of our existing. Creaturehood is not simply a *religious* fact; it is a *human* fact, a human fact having cosmic importance. And to speak of the human reality without cognizance of that fact is to diminish the seriousness and the magnitude of the human reality.

## IV

Thus far we have been concerned to point up dimensions which at once afford depth and nuance to every immediate moment of our existing, yet, in subtle but significant ways, elude our conceptual awareness. The mystery of existing in large measure inheres in this dimensional aspect. The impulse to vivify this that eludes us, or to clarify its meaning, if not its import, is understandable. And much of our religious discourse is bent on accomplishing such clarification. To the extent that such efforts offer only pointing directives, content to evoke a sense of wonder in contemplating or in being aware of the depths of our existing, these discourses can be a stimulus to inquiry, if not illumining of it. To the extent that they aspire to more definitive ends, especially when they presume to dispel the mystery of existing through facile clarifications or occult explanations ready at hand, they actually profane what evokes wonder. The art of thought in attending to that which eludes definitive thinking is to be receptive as well as directive; or better, to be receptive in a mood of waiting even as one attends critically and intelligibly to what can be reflected upon. This is a quality of perception, observation, and reflection that is found in discerning scientists, poets, artists, and scholars, or simply sensitive observers of whatever bent of mind or purpose. It may be but the initial act of observation and inquiry; but, except as it does initiate the effort to inquire, or simply to reflect, what follows under the guise of discovery or knowing can be simply a projection of our fallible forms and symbols upon that which

is "more than we can think." The realities of the lived experience awaiting recognition and response may thus elude us. This leads to the
suggestion that the stance that has been assumed throughout this discussion of the mystery of existing will become increasingly recognizable
to the extent that the focus is seen to be upon experience as lived.

"Experience as lived" is a phrase that has been made familiar in
philosophies of phenomenology and existentialism; but the notion implied
in the phrase belongs to the vocabulary of process thinkers as well, insofar as they are concerned with empiricism in its post-positivistic sense as
connoting a context of living rather than simply the conceptual track of
knowing and meaning. In process thought lived experience takes on a
holistic character, implying not just the discernible and describable
datum available to any mode of empirical inquiry, but that discernible
datum in the full, ongoing context of whatever is involved, whether
discernible or not. As a total datum of reality, it is inclusive of whatever is to be apprehended, embracing an ultimate reference along with
the immediacies of recognizable occurrences. The scope, in a word, is
as inclusive as the datum that would designate all that is.

The notion "lived experience," as employed in empirical realism, embraces then, the full range of immediacy as it applies to individual life-
spans, families, or communities of people, of whatever scope. It is the
living nexus of human activities and relationships at any given point in
the life-span of a people. It is the concrete datum within which the
thrust of an historical lineage takes on actuality as event, happening, or
occurrence, or simply as a vital process of existing.

In depicting the structure of experience in *Faith and Culture,* I stressed
the transmission of the inherited legacy within each life-span and within
each family or group experience, and suggested how past valuations and
decisions are insinuated into every emerging event, and thus into every
instance of individuated or communal life. Here the moving edge of
history as stark residue was silhouetted, and its role as causal efficacy
was highlighted in contrast to, or simply in comparison with, memory,
reminiscence, or recorded history. In speaking now of the lived experience in any instant of immediacy, I wish to point up in a similar
manner the stark, innovating occurrence of any moment of immediacy
within a life-span. or within any communal experience, in contrast to, or
in comparison with, anticipation, hope, expectation, or even forecast.
Here the dynamics of immediacy as they front a further range of occurrences, while bodying forth an inherited shaping, are in focus. The

concern here is not to belabor the issue of determinism and freedom. I would settle for deciding that there is probably more determinism and more freedom involved in the dynamics of every immediacy than discussions of this issue have contended. Anticipation or hope, like memory or reminiscence, tends to intrude an abstractive note, impelled by wishfulness or idealization, which may or may not coincide with what is concretely imminent or implied.

The datum that is in focus in discussing lived experience within the perspective process philosophy, or empirical realism, differs in one major respect from that envisaged in an existentialist or phenomenological analysis. In the latter, the self as a willing being is in large measure what is in focus. Thus the intentionality of the self as expressed in conscious design and purpose is what is deemed creative of whatever occurs within any immediacy, shaping the emerging self. The perspective of empirical realism views the self more contextually as being simultaneously self and not-self. Whitehead's doctrine of prehension, as we noted earlier, has been largely influential here, wherein each emerging event has been described as prehending every other event with varying degrees of relevance even as it bodies forth within its own concretion its distinctive and unique emergence. Process thought, in other words, intrudes into the discussion of every emerging selfhood a vast fund of *relata* which need not, or at least does not, concern phenomenology or existentialism. For Whitehead, both the uniqueness of each concrete occasion and the relational ground of each such instance of concretion register a priority, though it would appear that the concrete occasion carries a primacy in every instance of creative advance which cannot be shared by the contextual ground. The thrust of creativity, in other words, is discernible in each individuated event. Presumably one could argue that this concession brings the process mode of conceiving the emergence of the self strikingly close to that of existentialism. The difference, however, is equally decisive. For while initiative is ascribed to the individuated event in both modes of thought, the prehending occurrence accompanying such initiative alters the circumstance qualitatively and substantively. For concrescence then is viewed as interlacing the primary thrust of creativity with a vast array of attending and relevant relationships. "We are made for ourselves, for others, and for God" is one way of focusing this communal dimension of every concretion.

Given this relational character of every instance of intentionality in the process perspective, the notion of lived experience takes on comparable dimensions. Lived experience is simultaneously a patterned occurrence exemplifying and bodying forth the stream of ever recurring concretions as a communal event and an intensified channeling of that stream into individuated life-spans, each with its own legacy of inherited possibilities as given in the structure of experience and with its unique fund of possibilities as an emerging event.

The insistent note in conceiving of experience as lived within the process perspective, other than its relational aspect, is the realism of its occurrence: its structured and immediate character as each moment of spanned existence "gnaws" its way forward. I am meaning to focus here upon the actuality of occurrences as lived events rather than upon some generalized view of experience as perceived or conceptualized. Thus the language employed here is not so much designative or descriptive as directive: pointing to a depth of happening that will not be segregated or projected as data—only lived! Thus all particularizing or projecting, like conceptualizing itself, is a remote and reflective route to what cannot in actuality be thought apart from existing. And immediately the dimension of existing eludes the act of thought, or so exceeds it that it is uncontainable within it. This is so not only because of the complexity and fluidity of the living act itself, but because of what inheres in such a dimension as ultimacy, which traffics with every instance of immediacy.

Where the contextual or relational ground of any event is seen to be a datum in its own right, to be understood, or at least attended, configuratively, something more than analytical thinking and the clarity or simplicity distilled from such inquiry is needed. And here the imaginative mode becomes peculiarly relevant. Imagination has been referred to as a mode of "extended meaning" (Ricoeur); that is, imagination is meaning that extends beyond the discernible range of vision or experience to apprehend what exceeds the manageable stance. From within the orientation of empirical realism, understanding imagination as providing "extended meaning" is certainly pertinent, but partial in what it conveys of the imaginative act. For within that perspective, depth, as well as range, is significant. For depth of meaning, implied in the ultimate reference, interpenetrating the immediacies of experience, gives to each moment of it a textured quality which, in large measure, eludes our common perceptual mode of awareness, as well as the more definitive, conceptual modes of abstraction. Here subtleties, nuances, intimations suggestive of the More abound, compounding the complexity of the perceptual and conceptual acts. For the most part, both in commonplace and technically critical inquiry of an abstractive sort, these qualitative depths of experience will be unattended, and, for the most part, they are assumed to be irrelevant, if not nonexistent. The significance of the imaginative mode, as employed by the poet, the artist, or by anyone concerned with sensitive inquiry attentive to the penumbra of experienceable meaning of events, is that it both enlarges the range of awareness and discerns its subtle, qualitative depths. Imagination employed in this disciplined and creative sense, I would argue, is an indispensable accompaniment of critical abstraction, rather than merely its antithesis. It becomes an appreciative mode of inquiry and reflection, extending, deepening, sensitizing the range of apprehension and awareness from within the margin of intelligibility available to technical modes of abstract reflection and inquiry.

It is in this mode of inquiry that one would expect awareness responsive to the prescient dimension of the human structure to bear fruit. In any case, it could be counted on to advance creatural awareness beyond its customary form of sentiment and piety. And that, in itself, could help to make it available to disciplined inquiry. In correlating inquiry with sensibilities attentive to, and, in a measure, expressive of the prescient outreach of the human structure, reflection in the imaginative mode may enable thought to be discerning or even expressive beyond these fallible forms.

Distinguishing between the imaginative and the analytical modes of inquiry or reflection as a concern with "extended" or textured meaning and that of abstractive reflection states the contrast methodologically. When one considers the *intention* of inquiry or reflection in each instance, the terms would seem to reverse themselves: abstractive, analytical inquiry is seen as simulating an "overview" and its reflection directed toward creating the grounds for such a view as contrasted with the "narrative vision" of the more concretely oriented mode of imaginative reflection.[4] Yet, while the overview of abstractive reflection presumes to be an "extended" vision of experience, it is so only within the limited or limiting and abstractive terms of a given discipline and its methodology;

4. I am borrowing here terms proposed by William A. Beardslee, "Narrative Form in the New Testament and Process Theology," *Encounter*, 36:4 (Autumn 1975). See also his "Openness to the New in Apocalyptic and in Process Studies," *Process Studies* 3 (1973): 169–78.

while the narrative vision, concretely oriented, becomes an entry into *all there is* as lived experience in any given moment of time within the Creative Passage. However expanded, the abstract vision is limiting in method and terms. However concretely oriented, the narrative vision becomes an opening into depths of the lived experience that are "more than we can think."

Chapter Five

# Fallible Forms and
# the Mystery of Not Existing

The mystery of existing is exceeded only by the mystery of not existing. And this is to confront the inescapable fact of death. Here one comes to a strong sense of the limitations of critical inquiry in the area of theology and philosophy. Except as theology and related disciplined thought can break through its conventional format of critical inquiry to enable the inquirer to assume the stance of a humbled human being confronting the mystery of existing and the more devastating mystery of dying, such inquiry may go far afield, both in what it offers as illuminating that event, or as consolation or support in the experiencing of it.

The task of the constructive theologian in confronting this query is made acute by the very nature of his concern, namely, to address the more elemental question within the legacy of faith which, in effect, underlies the tradition of doctrine to which the systematic theologian speaks. The systematic theologian tends to be concerned mainly with conveying and, possibly, reconceiving the historical legacy of doctrine bearing upon the problem of death and the hope of survival beyond death. This generally takes the form of speaking to the resurrection experience. But, if faith, itself, is problematical for the constructive theologian, the legacy of belief and its various doctrinal interpretations are rendered even more unavailable as a guide or a resource for inquiry. In effect, the mystery of not existing is then full upon him. To be sure, that legacy of belief is not wholly ignored or set aside. In the language of phenomenology, it is "bracketed," or held in abeyance as a witness of belief with an attitude of critical reserve and questioning, as are the legacies of belief of other religious cultures. The stance of the constructive theologian with regard to this issue, however, is not that of the historian of religion, or of the philosopher of religion who may review the legacies of the various faiths comparatively or abstractly, either by way of vivifying the rich texture of religious belief, or of detecting an underlying kinship in response to a basic, human outreach or concern. By contrast, the constructive theologian, while attentive to these other modes of inquiry and research, approaches his inquiry within the legacy of the creatural response that is expressive of his cultural history and witness. In this respect he is like the systematic theologian within "the circle of faith," as it were, though the circle has widened to include the larger orbit of meaning which speaks through his own lived experiences.

Both existentialism, speaking out of a phenomenological inquiry, and empirical realism, speaking within a process imagery, address the issue in this manner. Yet both are attentive in their way to the witness of faith that speaks out of other cultural orbits of meaning, insofar as they are critically or even existentially or empirically available to them. At no point is the elemental stance of the creature lost sight of. Such flights into abstract reflection which simulate an overview, extricated from creatural existence, can be helpful only as a vision upon experience imaginatively projected; but its value is visionary only until it is brought into some accord with, or subjected to, a critical encounter with experience as lived. The vital stance of creaturehood thus looms large in empirical realism, and all reflection or inquiry that moves abstractly or imaginatively beyond that pivotal stance must be regarded as secondary, though by no means irrelevant, or necessarily misleading.

Where one is thrust back to so elemental a stance, the impulse to keep the issue of the ultimate horizon open may be accentuated. This will be especially true when the shattering experiencing of death is intimately encountered, as in the loss of the one beloved. The sheer fact, for example, that this person, who meant more to one than any other human being, and whose presence was cherished above every other experience, has vanished, will mean to the person surviving either that the past now holds more of the reality of grace and meaningfulness than any future occurrence can provide or that these immediacies now upon one, shattered and desolate though they seem, somehow contain and body forth the meaningful reality of grace and beauty, vigor and strength, that was known and experienced in the living presence of that person, though under circumstances not readily apprehended or imagined by those yet living. To succumb to the first alternative would mean relinquishing meaning in life, if not life, itself. Baffling and incredible though it may seem on first confronting it realistically, the latter opens up possibilities of heightening and of making more vivid a judgment that the immediacies of our experience carry within them depths of ultimacy and import that exceed our conscious awareness. The latter supposition, to be sure, opens the door to all kinds of mythological and mystical mumbojumbo, and would seem to be a turning back upon the stance which can assure critical security of judgment. I regard this, however, not as a collapse of critical judgment, but a tempering of the audacity implied in the willful enclosure of the mind within an assertive system of thought, in humble response to pressures of reality within the lived experience to which such a system may not readily or adequately speak.

The relational ground in existence at once gives more empirical warrant than was hitherto available for attending seriously to the events of our immediacies as being genuinely expressive of the full measure of realities that pervade our existence and for acknowledging at the same time the limited purview of every natural structure, including the structure of man, to attend to those immediacies, accompanied as they are by a depth that cannot readily, if ever, be consciously apprehended or perceived. It is in this sense that we are justified in saying that the lived experience, or experience as lived, is a deeper, richer event than experience as thought or consciously attended. And this limitation of conscious thought is not overcome simply by appealing to disciplined measures of observation and reflection. Nor does it follow from this predicament that what cannot be thought does not exist. That is the illusion, I believe, that has tripped up empiricists and sent them back into the company of rationalists and idealists. The import of taking relations seriously, ontologically or psychologically, theologically or sociologically, requires us to affirm that reality exceeds thought and, to a considerable degree, eludes it.

This is not to revert to supernaturalism in any form, "experimental" or otherwise; it is to accent our empirical realism fully cognizant of its relational ground. It is empirical realism, acknowledging that these realities are experienceable, though much that is experienced as lived exceeds the bounds and capacities of thought. Thus reason as we know it is a function of our humanly defined natural structure, with all the potentialities and limitations appropriate to that level of emergence.

Given that emergent and relational quality, naturalism itself, as expressed in empirical realism, becomes multi-dimensional in a way that accords with the various levels of emergence. Accordingly, the human level, though vastly more complex and diversified in its possibilities of expression than other creatural levels, is nevertheless limited in its way to the facilities that are expressive of its emergence as a natural structure. The reality of nature as conveyed through the Creative Passage thus presents a horizon of import and efficacy transcending the human structure, as it transcends all creatural existence, except for the quality of prescience that attends the human level of emergence—an open awareness toward what is "more than we can think" which nevertheless functions as a creative and redemptive efficacy within these lived experiences. Thus to presume to gather the whole of reality within the intelligible forms of the human structure in the manner of positivism or of the nineteenth-century vision of a Newtonian world order would be to presume an ultimacy for our human findings from which the sensibilities of discerning scientists today demur. Reality as lived and experienced within the Creative Passage will not be gathered into the structures and forms of this human level of emergence in so ultimate and definitive a manner.

The alternative, so it seems to me, is to pursue our sciences and our rational inquiries with full attentiveness to their limited purview, and thus with openness to reality as lived, or as it persists within dimensions beyond our present ken or manageability. Many scientists, insofar as they embrace a post-Newtonian vision of the universe and understanding of their discipline, seem to have no hesitancy about pursuing this course. Philosophers and theologians, on the other hand, many of them committed to a universal mode of rationality which they assume speaks through human reason, and thus foretells or forecasts a coherence inherent in man's world of experience which must somehow be found and articulated, seem more resistant to such marginal inquiry, and thus indifferent, often hostile, to the open adventure in thought or experience which appears to be our only critical and disciplined option.

In assuming such a stance in response to death, one must be prepared to endure a great deal of frustration—frustration that arises from the persisting anguish of the situation despite the passage of time, that gnaws at one as he reflects upon what seems a cruel disruption of a life intent on living forward—frustration over the opaqueness of the broken situation that is immediately upon one, with no sure thrust toward its resolution or acceptance.

Yet one learns to live with such anguish, with the sense of being bereft. One may not become reconciled to it, either psychically or theologically. And one may resist such efforts at theological reconciliation either because of their patness, or their utter lack of empathy with what has really happened in such instances of dissolution.

This may in turn lead one to look upon the many historic ventures in contemplating a myth of the eternal return in the form of the resurrection hope with more patience, rapport, and understanding; not that one will be persuaded by them intellectually, or impelled to succumb to their lure on other grounds; but that one will recognize in them an elemental yearning and resistance to what happens in death which concur with one's own experience of its deprivation.

In an effort to evoke serenity and acceptance of the irrevocable fact of death, some have chosen to speak of death as culmination. I, myself, have often spoken of it this way. Yet in many instances, death is not culmination, but disruption—sheer, unexpected intrusion with a tragic sense of a life unfulfilled, and an extended chain of despairing circumstances for those who survive the loss. Where one has finished out one's years and is prepared to relinquish his labors to others better able and suited to pursue them, the event of death is clearly one of culmination, and can be celebrated as such. Yet even in such instances the extinction of an identity so vividly and concretely experienced and enjoyed is at least a surd that will not dissolve readily.

There is, to be sure, what some have spoken of as *the economy of death,* by which is usually meant nature's way of eliminating or disposing of the burden that the prolongation of life would impose, and of providing new configurations of experience for generations that follow. Professor Daniel D. Williams stated this point succinctly in saying, "Even death has its place in the service of God. It is the way life makes way for more life."[1] The social economist will carry the argument still further, pointing out the sheer necessity of death as a way of preserving a livable social economy in any culture. These observations seem highly

1. Daniel D. Williams, *God's Grace and Man's Hope* (New York: Harper, 1949), p. 163. Cf. also William E. Hocking, *Thoughts on Death and Life* (New York: Harper, 1937), pp. 12–26.

acceptable as generalizations upon the phenomenon of death in the abstract. And they will help socially minded human beings to place their own demise in a perspective that enables them the more readily to accept relinquishment. Accepting one's own death on these terms seems to me to present no serious problem. In confronting the death of the one beloved, however, such a perspective is of no more help than theological or philosophical generalizations.

There is also, in some instances, a humane aspect to death. When, for example, the person dying comes to a judgment out of endless cycles of suffering and meaningless persistence that release is imperative, it would seem that he or she should have the right to relinquish life, and thus be released from interminable suffering. Medical ethics, as well as the legal code to date, is, of course, an obstacle to this kind of humane act. Or, again, where the personal presence of an individual has receded, or has dissolved into sheer vegetative existence, with the result that the medical act of keeping the patient alive becomes an incredible burden upon others, death would clearly seem to be an act of release. All such conditions may render the explicit occasion of death acceptable. It does not, however, alter the fact of death inherent in the process of deterioration, and the problem it poses to the one who intimately confronts the loss of that personal presence.

Now one might assume from this stubborn stance of being unreconciled to the fact of death in its intimacy that one might be impelled to attend to various speculative inquiries concerning life beyond death; more specifically, to pursue the Christian doctrine of resurrection more assiduously. The truth is many are not. One can live on in trust, open to possibilities exceeding our rationally or empirically defensible views of existence or nonexistence. To press beyond this elemental stance, so it seems, would be to try to think and to presume beyond our structure of experience. Neither our structure of experience in and of itself nor our imaginings that transcend that structure offer any warrant for speaking definitively or confidently on that issue. It does not follow, however, that one so disposed has only to rest on his oars with a cynical or stoical attitude of "Come what may!" in awaiting his own dissolution. Quite the contrary! The mystery of dying, or of contemplating the death of another intimately cherished, whose very life has been one's own life, may pose an inquiry in one's mind which, though it may never be resolved as a conceptual problem, may be contemplated or envisaged "as through a glass darkly," within the structure of life of our sensory experience.

To come to any such glimpse of what could be, or can be, that could amount to something more than a projection of experience as lived, we must first sense, acknowledge, and take seriously, the limits of our structure as creatures, which is to feel the full, existential depth of what it means to be held in existence. The mystery of that event of existing may then bring to mind a vivid sense of not existing, were it not for what is presently operating as a resource of grace and recreative power within the Creative Passage that sustains life. Such a resource, presumably, could have ways of sustaining further, even beyond the event of death, whatever has been attained within the identity of each such created event, other than that of emptying all created good into "an eternal treasury of good" expressive only through the Creative Event itself, which is God. All possible occurrences of resurrection, transmigration, or other modes of transcending the event of death rest ultimately upon this redemptively creative resource within the Creative Passage and the power it wields in the ultimate passage of events.

It is here that I am led to regard the ultimate issue of existence and nonexistence as being more problematic than Christians, Hindus, Buddhists, and other world faiths have acknowledged or recognized. For invariably within these historic formulations the ultimate act beyond the drama of existence tends to be made consistent with the way existence itself has been understood; hence the episodes or stages of an after-life, following upon any given span of existence, tend either to be reenactments of the life-span as known, or conversely, one posed in sharp contrast to what has been known. Either way there is implied a projecting of what is presently given in history as a measure of what is beyond the given. It has become increasingly insistent in my own reflections during recent years that the creative matrix itself inclines to suggest that coherence, taken by itself or comprehensively, tends to be a false motif; or at least a misleading one when it is employed to project beyond the span of existence we have known, for that is to subsume whatever might emerge beyond death under the structure of meaning of what has been or now is as an available rationality within experience.

This vivid sense of existing and the mystery of its occurrence are the threshold through which all else follows as reflection upon what may or could conceivably extend beyond existence, beyond, that is, each person's existence.  No reflection, it would seem, can be profitable as bearing upon this ultimate issue of life and death except as it stems directly from this immediacy of lived experience.  Efforts to transcend this concrete matrix in ways that ignore its focal role can have only the value of wishful or mythological musing.  What this statement means to affirm is that such redemptive or resurrective power as may bring about drastic, renascent change in the lived situation now entering death is an efficacy within the vital immediacies, themselves, an efficacy that has persisted all along as a depth of those immediacies, however marginally attended.

To "live forward" in death, therefore, is consonant with the act of living forward in life; that is, it is assimilated to the depth of existing in some dimension and with some vivid, concrete effect.  It is to participate as well in the life of God which provides the creative matrix for all lived experience.

Now to speculate beyond that concrete mystery of the Creative Passage, that is, to ask how consciously they who have entered death form the depth of our immediacies, or participate in it, is to reach beyond our structured existence in a way that abandons the focal orientation of the inquiry.  And this is by way of transcending it.  However, insofar as we attribute to this depth of our immediacies the creative and redemptive qualities expressed in the affirmation of a Creative Passage having the tender, negotiable, and redemptive efficacy of a good not our own, an inherent Creative goodness we call God, this depth of ultimacy within our immediacies will itself be the bearer of that concreteness which, as we say, endures or lives forward in death.

This may seem to be but a variation upon Hartshorne's theme of an eternal treasury of good; but I do not mean it precisely in those terms. For the concreteness that lives forward in death is not a deposit of value accrued, but a continuing thrust of concreteness which, in ways we may not surmise, persists within the Creative matrix of our lives in God. The mystery of this concreteness that lives forward in death may be experienced by those who persist within life only as a presence, a depth of memory with hope of "an eternal return."  To be sure, this in itself gives no indication or measure of the depth or reality of such a presence. And to pursue its reality within the terms of our critical disciplines offers no such insight into it, for such disciplines are not formulated or prepared to address so imprecise an inquiry.  The imprecision here is of a piece with the emergent quality of events which, while they participate within the existent structure, at the same time intrude a prescient quality of a not yet that is incipiently present. What is beyond our comprehension may not be made the subject of reflection without inviting deception or fantasy; but this need not imply that it is beyond our awareness, our wonder, and, perchance, our waiting.

Meanwhile, there is a concreteness about the persisting, living presence of the one who has entered death which can be assimilated to the lived experience of those who survive—not simply as a haunting memory, or personal reminder of the desolation this death has wrought, but as a depth of intentionality in individuals or in a community who, as it were, provide in their identification with that life-span as recalled, and their cherishing of it, continuity with the ongoing stream of existence. How to carry this life that has physically ended into the future as a participating presence then becomes an empirical inquiry. An obvious answer to such a query would be along lines of enabling its qualitative attainment to live on as a continuing presence within the enjoyable and decision-making events of one's experience. The fulfillment of any life often awaits such completion beyond its own death, and is beholden to others who survive for the accomplishing of it.

This empirical presence, however, is not to be made a substitute for whatever in the nature of the ongoing stream of lived experience may occur beyond the ken of our awareness. The two may be consonant with each other, though never interpenetrating: being two levels or dimensions of the life-spirit participating simultaneously in different structures of emerging fields of events.

One will see from these remarks that I am struggling to avoid, on the one hand, simply projecting a coherence consonant with our humanly limited structure, and, on the other hand, abandoning all critical control of reflection upon the event of death. What has become insistent for me is the concern to take seriously the persisting dissonance within experience, seemingly defying our efforts at establishing rationality and coherence in living, by recognizing this dissonance to be an accompaniment of and a persistent, even irresolvable surd within our rational experience. Despite all our talk about a critical realism in recent periods of Western history, we as Western people and as scholars have lived out of a bankrupt legacy of idealism which somehow sees the ultimate issue as being resolved in a way that accords with our own rationality and its cherished dreams. This was too easy a reversal of the demonic account of natural man put forth in supernaturalist theories. The critique of supernatural theories must partake as well of a critique of idealism and of the tepid forms of realism which somehow seek to salvage the investment of rationality affirmed in idealism as an eternal treasury of good. Acknowledging, even stressing, the note of dissonance as a qualitative corrective of our rationality achieved through idealization seems to me to offer some leverage for exerting a realistic stance that is not wholly tragic, yet sufficiently sensitive to the tragic sense of life to take account of the surds of insensitivity along with that which is expressive of a good not our own, a good that is beneficent and blessed.

What it comes down to, then, is that one is led to have concern and respect for what simple folk have mythically affirmed, though one will take this to be but a marginal apprehension beyond our own structure of experience. And one will be impelled toward a distrust of any definitive attempt to employ our own structure of rationality too readily for apprehending or systematically formulating what the full truth of experience may be, either as it pertains to our lived experience, or to death, and to what may or may not pertain to what lies beyond death as each of us may encounter it. There will then be more impulse to wonder and to wait, to live expectantly with openness to what can release or transform this limited structure of creatural existence in ways that emulate a New Creation.

Part Two

Chapter Six

# The Structure of Christian Faith

The lure of certainty has been at the root of much of the pathology in empowering fallible forms and symbols with an assumption of authority in the statement of beliefs. But even when such authority has subsided, the lure of certainty has continued to weave its spell, impelling earnest and persistent efforts among philosophers and theologians to recreate in disciplined thought what had been lost to institutional authority.

Given the relativity of perspectives within a pluralistic culture, how much certainty can we have in matters of faith? And an equally relevant question is: How much uncertainty can we live with? The assumption that earlier generations of Christians could affirm the ultimate end of faith as an absolute and thus had no occasion to waver in their commitment to faith is grossly exaggerated. I see far more evidence of insecurity in these earlier writings, and a great deal of evidence of doubt and disbelief. It is easy to be overimpressed by the assurances of the ancients, not realizing that, in an authoritarian era, it would be precisely these documents in positive thinking that would have survived, while the literature of despair and disillusionment might very well have been suppressed or destroyed. Even so, the strains of anxiety and uncertainty do persist in these ancient writings. And when one comes to Reformation literature, particularly the writings of Luther, the note of despair rises at times to pathological heights, and the words of assurance appear to have been said with a tremor, echoing the lines of the distraught father in the Gospel of Mark, "Lord, I believe, help thou my unbelief."

What is often in mind in contrasting the sense of providential care

71

among the ancients with the lack of such certainty and security in the modern world is the strange, new world of man's own making stemming from the Enlightenment period, and its progressive dissociation from any imagery of providential care offering an assured destiny. In viewing the problem in this way, however, one overlooks the fact that the kind of certainty implied in the notion of the Absolute is really more akin to this post-Enlightenment thinking than to periods of Christianity antedating the seventeenth century. It would, in fact, not be amiss to argue that the Absolute was a creation of this modern, liberal period, supplanting the authority of the church and Scriptures. For the Absolute implies a rational certainty established by logical argument out of concern to find points of fixity and ultimate reference in a world of finitude and change.

Isaac Newton was able to provide such imagery for his generation and for generations following his time in a natural philosophy based on the concept of absolute space. Modern idealists in the lineage of Hegel were able to give completion and a sense of ultimacy to every fragmented span of existence in projecting the concept of absolute mind. In our own time, Charles Hartshorne, having assimilated the notion of change as a controlling idea in his philosophy of becoming, nevertheless is impelled to reestablish a sense of absolute assurance concerning the ultimate goodness of God by meticulously developing his logic of perfection. So, while the Absolute has been in dissolution for many years in many areas of our culture, its ghost or some apparition strangely like it keeps haunting these modern scenes. It would seem more to the point, perhaps, to argue that the Absolute dies hard; for the shadow of ultimate certainty, first initiated in the dogma of authority, to be followed by biblical literalism and an appeal to reason, has a strange hold upon the human mind. And conversely, the ability to sustain the venture of faith in the face of uncertainties calls for a childlike trust that is not readily come by in our sophisticated age.

On the other hand, in the face of this persisting concern with absolute certainty, there have been counter developments in the most disciplined areas of experience, in theology as well as in modern science, setting themselves against absolute notions—against Newton's notion of absolute space and against Hegel's absolute mind. But these instances of rejecting the Absolute represent not just a secularizing of life and thought, they express a more serious and sensitive probing of the realities that reach us in concrete experience. In a word, the Absolute has been shown up as being itself a phantom of our conceptual world, and as having little to do with the concrete realities of existence as they are lived. I would say that the Absolute has dissolved all about us not through neglect, but through the most spirited and persistent efforts of sensitive minds of our age, both in religious and scientific studies, aiming not at robbing us of a sense of reality, but at recovering it after centuries of captivity in a wasteland of conceptual abstractions.

It can be argued, I think, that the Christian witness of faith, in its most elemental as well as its most discerning expressions, has never assumed absolute certainty, or relied upon it. It assumed an attitude of *trust*. But this is not the same as absolute certainty. Whenever people of lesser sensibilities with regard to faith have undertaken to depict or to dramatize the Christian faith, they have usually made a mockery of it, parading Christians as impassioned zealots declaring with bombast and fervor the assurances of their beliefs. The movie versions of Christian history usually offend in this way. I am not denying that many Christians do embrace the faith in this way. And it is true that where institutions and the letter of Scripture are placed above the spirit, there develops a fanatical preoccupation with certainties. Not one jot or tittle of the law, ecclesiastical or biblical, is to be overlooked, for they add up in their entirety to a dogma or absolute certainty in faith.

Such a concern with certainty is neither profound nor sensitive in its response to the realities of faith. And ultimately it is dehumanizing of faith itself; for in its zeal for minutiae and exactitude, it is unattuned to the travail of existence, to the cry of the human spirit, to the pain and anguish, joy or ecstasy of fallible man. It is common observation that an inflexible display of certainty invariably tends toward intoleranace in one's witness, arrogance in exercising judgment upon others, and narrowness in one's sympathies or in one's understanding of the human situation.

It can be said too that the dissolution of absolutes has gone hand in hand with a growing realization of the nature of human existence as it is concretely envisaged, and with the growth in sympathies among men, regardless of race, creed, or color. The human reality, seen as a primordial demand upon our thought and beliefs and the bearer of divine grace and judgment as it comes to us in our experience, has steadily shattered these preoccupations with inflexible dogmas of certainty that have no defense or standing, except in our moral pretensions and our intellectual pride. Faith, when it is really faith, assumes a more humble stance.

On the other hand, in assuming such a stance, one need not be indifferent toward efforts to achieve some intellectual purchase upon this unsettling flux of experience, or veer from such efforts as if the very act of exercising intellectual inquiry in matters of faith were a profaning of it. Concern for intelligibility in expressing faith can also assume a humble stance. And this implies retaining, even asserting, the creatural response in the very act of inquiry. Under such circumstances, even the simulation of a total vision of experience, wherein tentative tools of thought in the form of fundamental notions and explicit concepts will be employed by way of offering some explication of judgments traditionally assumed, or of venturing new perspectives upon them, can illumine the experience of faith. It can, in fact, actually fructify the experience in quickening its sense of vision, or by routing a lethargic reliance upon what had become simply a conventional habit of response with no vivid awareness of its wonder or serious import.

But we miss the point of much that transpires under the guise of intellectual inquiry in religious faith if we assume that it is always a shift from a concern with faith to a concern with reason in the sense that the one displaces the other. Often, in fact, the outreach for some intelligible grasp of life's meaning is less an intellectual query than an existential groping, or, as in some instances, an interim of respite from the anguish of contemplating the threats to existence itself. This aspect of the matter may be present at any time, even in the most sophisticated occasions of inquiry; but it tends to be made more explicit in times of war or in similar periods of national crises when the threat to life itself erupts persistently and with such scope as to involve the whole of life within a community.

J. Seelye Bixler, commenting upon his experiences at Harvard in engaging young men in philosophical discussion who were about to be called into action during the Second World War, spoke of the sense of unreality he felt initially about such occasions, knowing how remote the problems must seem to the men at that time. "Yet," he said, "that very remoteness seemed to provide a perspective for confronting concerns too immediate and traumatic to be faced directly." As Bixler talked, I recalled a letter I had received from a former student, writing from "Somewhere in Germany," just as the Third Army was preparing for the winter push. Small tents were all that shielded them from the weather: outside, the rain and mud; inside, the light of a torch and whatever they were able to think about. Sitting there, waiting for the winter drive to begin, he thought back to seminar evenings around our fireplace where we had talked, several of us, about issues that now loomed so real and menacing. This was what sustained him now—"the things we had talked about."

Yet, even apart from such immediate threats, in fact when the intellectual quest itself is one's very life, one's vocation, the existential motivation may figure prominently, if not urgently, in one's intellectual pursuit. A prominent philosopher, on being asked why he persisted in pursuing the logic of theism, replied, "I suppose it's because I would not enjoy being an atheist." To be sure, the motivation may be a blend of the two concerns: to exercise integrity of mind in the act of affirming faith, and vice versa. And there have been times in our intellectual history when the correlating of the two has not been readily at hand. Thus one's motivation can involve a deeply cultural cleavage as well as a personally existential one. And often the former can be the cause of the other without one being fully aware of it.

What surfaces in instances where intellectual inquiry and the urgencies of existence are simultaneously in focus provides a clue to what is most characteristic of the structure of faith itself. I would put it this way: The structure of Christian faith is symphonic rather than logical. There is a logic implicit within its minor themes, but the overall movement of its affirmations presents a dissonant situation in which contraries are simultaneously acknowledged and disavowed, in which resolution and peace are somehow attained, but not without the price of conflict, pain, and suffering; and not without a sense of taking into oneself, of bearing the burden, of that over which one has triumphed.

In short, the resolution of faith is not a logical argument into which everything reasonably fits, but an arduous and long-suffering venture in negotiation in which conflicting claims, reasonable in their own right, are somehow adjudicated, or brought into a livable correlation without achieving full conformity or uniformity of meaning and purpose.

And the outcome of the negotiations, be it conquest over sin or remorse, the transcending of grief, or a total summation of experience against the years of travail and fulfillment, is never one of total victory, and in that sense conclusive. Where the realities of experience are soberly assessed, the outcome is always one of assurance, tempered with restraint and with lingering misgivings. Assurance is sufficient, however, to impel one to move toward a relinquishment of one's own pressing anxieties and distress, not with despairing or with a blandishment of naive hope, but in trust. This I find to be the critical stance of the man of faith who cuts a path between naive hope and despair.

Presumably there is an ultimate resolution of all conflict and striving in the final destiny of God. And the Christian philosopher, eager to anticipate this ultimate resolution, has sought to envision it as a structure of meaning and to designate the logic of its perfection. With the logical assurance of this ultimate destiny established (albeit a destiny in which all persons and events realize their fulfillment in the consciousness and life of God), the Christian philosopher finds the chaos and pain of our present striving, our conflict, bearable, and even justified. This kind of logical demonstration of the vision of faith is more a venture in understanding or anticipating the ultimate outcome of existence than a direct inquiry into the nature and resources of existence itself.

It is apparently felt by the one who undertakes this kind of rational quest that, except as this ultimate vision of God as a guarantee of the final good of existence *is* logically assured, the very effort to negotiate existence with any degree of hope or incentive is in jeopardy, and perhaps futile. Now it should be said that this concern with some demonstration of our final assurance is not so alien to the life of faith as theologians commonly assume. Put in the philosophic mode as a logically demonstrated perfection of good, it seems to the theologian to state the truth of the faith too explicitly as a realized goal. Protestant theologians especially have preferred to emphasize the precariousness of existence with its possibility of despair, and to move toward the assurance of salvation by way of Christology rather than through a logical demonstration of God's goodness. A word about this distinction in a moment.

What the theologian needs to recognize is that such logical demonstration is aimed at providing a reasonable basis for the faith he affirms, not a substitute for that faith. The aim of the philosopher, however, often does go astray, and thus what was initially ventured as a form of inquiry to mitigate "the mind's allegiance to despair," and thus to open the human spirit to the appeal of faith, does result in becoming the mind's answer to despair, and thus in fact a substitute for faith.

The theologian is justified, in my judgment, in resisting this kind of philosophical substitute for faith simply on the grounds that our visions of rationality, when projected toward final meanings, can only be in the form of a venture in understanding, abstractly considered. This venture says, in effect, this is how it could be, given certain presuppositions which we are presently committed to assuming. It thus becomes a bold, though usually a highly disciplined, projection of the lines of continuity, extending out from initial premises, controlled by forms and categories along with conceptual rules designed to guide its long-range reflection. Although such reflection means to be a commentary upon what has been historically and is presently occurring, given the ultimate vision of orderliness, it is really focused upon the ultimate outcome, insofar as it speaks of God and of our life in God. With this vision of what is ultimately real, it is assumed we will then be able to see life in its proper (that is, in its ultimately assured) perspective. Always this vision of God in his ultimate perfection and of life viewed in relation to its ultimate end and purpose remains controlling and normative for judgment.

Christology, on the other hand, is not God in terms of logical perfection, but God in his concreteness, God reconciling the world unto himself, God taking upon himself the form and burden of actuality, God becoming man, enjoying the simple joys of a carpenter's family or the rugged pleasures in the fisherman's community, alternately partaking of the solitude of the open sea or the arduous climb of some steep ascent. But Christology envisages also God in the form of one man enduring commonplace bigotry and smugness of people in authority, or of people in common places possessed and dominated by the canons of their own self-righteousness. Thus Christology envisages deity not in its majesty and power as supreme ruler, but as suffering servant, taking up the cross of humanity that is borne by all who suffer from the insensitivities of creaturely existence, both those of their own making and those of others' with whom their lot is cast.

Christology, precisely because it presents the God-man within perspectives amplifying the imperfections of existence, has posed an insoluble issue for certain philosophical architects of faith who could tolerate only a vision of God resting back ultimately and singularly upon the logic of perfection.

Such truth as is periodically conveyed in the declaration "God is dead"

is in the disavowal of that singular view of perfection in God insofar
as it presents that ultimate and holy reality as being immune to the
joys and pains of existence and in the disavowal of the vision of God
that lends a pale cast of unreality to this veil of tears by way of coming
to a logical solution of contending contraries which would seem to give
the lie to this kind of ultimate unity and peace.

I find the Christian gospel in its starkest and most realistic utterances
coming to terms with these contending contraries that give character
and substance to the events of existence. I find it affirming, on the one
hand, that we are born into a community of love and forgiveness, as
disclosed both in a primordial vision of creativity and in the ultimate
vision of God's perfection, and this affirmation is its key assertion, from
which other constructive assertions follow. But I find it asserting too
that we are born into a world of insensitivity, terror, and cruelty, a world
of narrow loyalties and strife, of bitterness, self-striving, pride, and
competitiveness. In short, we are born into a situation of sickness and
health, of growth and decay, of hope and despair.

Now the impatient resolution of these contraries, either in the
direction of proving a final perfection or in the direction of declaring
an ultimate despair, short-circuits theological inquiry, enabling it to
sublimate the intricacies and inconsistencies of lived experience in the
generalized vision of God, or to capitulate too readily to the slings and
arrows of outrageous fortune on the assumption that this is the way life
is. In the one instance, destiny is too obviously designated and assured;
in the other instance, cruel fate displaces all sense of destiny.

If my remarks so far are not too oblique or elusive, one will see that
I tend to cast my lot as theologian with interpreters of the Christian
faith who see it as a narrow way rather than as a broad way of generalized knowledge. I see it as a disclosure accompanied by discernment that issues forth out of the responses we make in seriously
confronting the demands and opportunities of each moment of living.
And each moment of living is itself an act of living forward.

Seeing experience as an incessant act of living forward carries certain
implications. Each turn of events is in part borne forward by the
momentum of an initial rhythm of living which carries its own implicit
trust in the current of action. So there is, on the one hand, a level of
animal faith, as Santayana once put it, which generates an unreflective
will to live and, on the other hand, a level of conscious decision wherein

these acts of living are negotiated by each of us with the resources for decision and response at hand. Keeping this in mind, one can understand the emphasis given to the immediacy of grace and judgment as energies effecting or conditioning our acts or decisions.

The existentialist's reading of experience, as given, for example, by Jean-Paul Sartre and Simone de Beauvoir, strongly asserts the power and necessity of decision; for in this human act, initiated by each human being on one's own authority, and in response to one's own command, it is claimed, one both declares and attains authenticity as a self. This is but a more explicit way of asserting the perfectibility of the law, of Stoic reason, and of moral idealism. Man wills himself into authenticity. Christian faith, for better or worse, has radically questioned not only the possibility of attaining such virtue, but the wisdom of projecting the venture. It has taken me some time to take a proper measure of this Christian assessment of our human powers and possibilities. Where there is a strong sense of commitment to the dignity of the human spirit one will readily rally to any appeal to the authenticity of the self—even as one resists any indulgence in piety that would obscure or diminish that sense of our human creativity.

Yet part of any repossession of the Christian witness consists in confronting the Christian critique of man wherein his powers and limitations are realistically assessed. On the one hand this Christian interpretation of man sees these human powers to be expressive simultaneously of a level of creativity that is to be cherished and furthered, and of capacities that carry their own inherent bent toward ambiguous good, mounting at times to demonic evil. That our goodness, our ideals, our highest motives and intentions can be sources of demonic power in the form of insensitivity and pride is a truth that has been repeatedly demonstrated in experience. On the other hand, the Christian interpretation of man has maintained with considerable documentary support that the weaknesses and failings of men and women have not invariably issued in defeat; on the contrary, they have actually been the means of opening one's life to resources over which one has no command, except in one's capacity or readiness to receive what they offer and can give. This childlike acknowledgment of dependence is the most difficult act for proud and presumably mature men and women to effect. And it is also the one most readily exploited and sentimentalized by those who recoil from the disciplining of the human spirit. Here, again, one is confronted in the Christian witness with contraries, the resolution of which is neither in the conquest of the one by the other, nor in capitulation to the one rather than to the other, but in the transcendence of both deficiencies in a way that accepts and transmutes what is affirming in each.

Now I have found interpreting the Christian witness to this act of simultaneously affirming dependence and independence of spirit clarified and even enhanced by what process thought contributes to its formulation of creativity and prehension. Within its imagery, we are born into a situation of conflicting demands. Each individual comes into existence with distinctive and characteristic facilities and propensities, the mere fruition of which sets one apart as being peculiarly oneself. Yet every individual is said to prehend (with varying degrees of relevance) every other person, and to stand in a relationship of dependence and responsibility toward them. Here the formula of "individual-in-community,"[1] expressive in modern terms of the covenant relationship, only giving it ontological dimensions, applies. In a remote way it is expressive as well of the familiar theological formula *imago dei,* which was initially intended to focus the relationship between God and man, divinity and humanity, and at the same time to take account of the breach between them.

Where one is fully cognizant of the communal ground of each individual existence and, at the same time, sensitive to the demands of each individualized person as having a career in one's own right, even as one participates in the communal ground, one will have some basis, both for understanding what is implied in the Christian concern with grace and judgment and for developing a full-orbed Christian ethic. Grace and judgment point up resources of what I have chosen to call our second level of freedom, the freedom to acknowledge relationships and to receive the resources and disciplines they offer.[2] It is in this context that such notions as guilt, remorse, contrition, repentance, forgiveness, and redemption take on meaning. Each of these terms has its psychological meaning or implication which usually centers in the state of the individual psyche or in the response that issues from it; but the theological import of these terms carries more objective meaning and implication as well, grow-

---

1. Cf. Alfred North Whitehead, *Religion in the Making* (New York: Macmillan, 1926), p. 88; cf. also *Adventures of Ideas* (New York: Macmillan, 1933), pp. 225 ff.
2. Bernard E. Meland, *The Realities of Faith* (New York: Oxford University Press, 1962; paperback, Chicago: Seminary Cooperative Bookstore, 1970), pp. 236 ff.

ing out of the interplay between the two levels of freedom, or the interchange of demands consonant with the ontological character of existence as defined by the formula, "individual in community."

The Christian ethic, following from this way of responding to the Christian witness, is one that turns upon the competing demands of individuality and its communal relationships, or upon the dissonant claims of the two levels of freedom. In the nature of the case this becomes a "situational ethic" stressing the relativity of circumstances in which these competing demands and claims assert themselves, yet one in which a principle of negotiation is clearly affirmed. One of the weaknesses of situational ethics as it is often advanced under secular auspices is its sheer relativism, leaving to fortuitous values or sentiments of individual circumstances, often in a haphazard way, to provide the tone and mode of ethical judgment. A Christian ethic, participating in such situational analyses, can, in my judgment, contribute some guidelines that take their cue from sources other than sheer traditional authority, or the a priori, centering instead in a correlation of the reasoned view that discloses the complex, contextual character of each individual existence, and attending the peculiarly concrete circumstances and concerns relative to the individual situation under scrutiny.

As one who seeks to interpret the themes of the Christian faith constructively, one will thus move between an ontological vision of God in his ultimacy, and a christological vision of God in his immediacy. And, in employing christological directives, one will tend to correlate eschatology and ethics (which is again a mode of thinking holding together ultimacy and immediacies). The structural or conceptual image that informs and controls this procedure is the juxtaposition and interplay of ultimacy and immediacy; the interplay of the abstract logic of God's ultimate order and perfection, and the travail and ecstasies of creatural existence; of the mystery of the Kingdom and the concrete acts of decision and response; of the More that continually confronts experience, and the visible events in the stream of experience.

But if an emphasis must be declared, it is clear that, while the abstract vision of God in his ultimacy is a kind of lodestar holding inquiry and the act of living forward in their courses, the disclosures of this ultimate vision as a fact of experience in the concrete pathos and promise of existence, as these loom in individual and communal instances, form the burden of inquiry. This is why grace and judgment, sin and forgive-

ness, despair over the magnitude of human evil, anxiety, or absurdity, and
the redemptive life remain the perennial topics of inquiry in pointing
to realities of the human situation for modern, secular human beings, as
they were for archaic and medieval ones.

Much has changed in the way modern men and women formulate
these truths of faith. Nothing has changed, however, so far as I am
able to see, in what ultimately and immediately confronts modern human
beings as the stark truth of existence and the elemental needs that intrude
in the face of any ultimate reckoning, or in the face of any immediate
encounter with events of experience that evoke some kind of reckoning,
both in death and in life.

There remains for me to say a final word about how the words we
form into an interpretation of Christian faith for the modern day
actually speak to the conditions of people wrestling with the realities of
faith as living energies of the social experience. Whatever we may say
about the relevance of Christian words and doctrines to the modern
mind, the realities of spirit and the human spirit to which they bear
witness are inescapably present in our human situation. This expresses
a certain skepticism about the semantic task of conveying Christian
meaning to modern people, but an implicit faith in the persistence of
what was initially designated a New Creation, opening the experiences
of men and women, of whatever age, to the redemptive good offered
through grace and judgment. This view identifies me as an elementalist,
meaning that *we live more profoundly than we can think,* not only when
we are unable or unwilling to think profoundly, but even when we
address ourselves in the profoundest way possible to the issues of our
existence.

Theology, important as it is in dealing with the problematics of faith,
has limited value in clarifying or evoking the faith. It is instrumental,
not substantive, in providing the resources we need for living and for
confronting the inevitable and forever baffling event of dying. Where
the exigencies of existence erupt to press upon one existential demands
of profound moment or to disrupt the web of relations that has formed
the meaningful context of one's existence, the words one has affirmed as
a theology, or even as a credo, assume a strange and detached status,
awaiting their confirmation or disputation in experience. It is not that the
event alters the words one has affirmed; only in the crisis of loss and

deprivation the reality of their meaning is now full upon one and demands something more than reaffirmation or consent to them when they are reasserted by another. What confronts one in the dissolution of tender relationships that have given continual support, incentive, and direction to one's living, not to speak of the tender graces of companionship, is not readily assuaged, either by the philosophical vision or by theological judgments that presume to give form and substance to one's affirmation by faith. Theology is no cure-all for the ills and deprivations that beset us in human living or in human dying. These reasoned views do provide a backdrop to the events that transpire, and to that extent set the stage for reflection upon these events, and in time will offer resources by which reflection and inquiry can be helpfully nourished. But living and dying, and the human responses to these occurrences, are more complex than reflections about them, or than any intellectual query evoked by them.

Here one sees that the truth of the faith as lived experience is mediated to such situations not through words that abstractly state our human situation or that reiterate the vision of our ultimate end. These, in a way, are cold, remote austerities that in that context somehow do violence to the tender feelings and emotions which more accurately convey the tragic sense of separation and loss. They must await their time when the structures of the mind can be received in ways consonant with the bodily feelings. The truth of the faith as lived experience is mediated in such critical situations of grief and deprivation through a vivid uprising within immediate relationships of the very community of love and forgiveness that forms the ultimate ground of man's existence. It is here that we learn what we mean to one another in the ultimate aspect of our existence. We are literally the bearers of grace and redemptive love to one another, and there is no concrete nature of God, no new creation except as it is made incarnate in these relationships that hold us in existence. Conversely, we are also the bearers of demonic evil, transmitting to our fellows whatever is expressed through us of the surd of insensitivity that resists and defiles the communal growth of love and forgiveness.

It is in this sense that I would speak of the energies of grace and judgment as being social energies—real, explicit instances of efficacy carrying forward the creativity, sensitivity, and negotiability within the

Creative Passage, and of the surd of insensitivity being an accumulative psychical barrier to the redemptive good, or a counterforce of demonic magnitude striking at the very core of being and becoming itself.

Because theology deals with issues of such immediate and ultimate import, its problems can never be resolved other than as tentative solutions to a complex of queries whose answers elude any final formulation. But the truth of the faith, I repeat, lies not in these formulations, or in any word or symbol as such, but in the realities of grace and judgment of which they speak, realities that sustain, alter, and ultimately redeem our human ways.

Chapter Seven

# Themes and Motifs of
# the Judaic-Christian Legacy

The enduring legacy of faith in any age inheres in what surfaces
as themes of the faith which, in turn, bear witness to realities, redemptive and judging, within experience itself, transmitted from generation
to generation within the structure of experience as a mythos of sensibilities and hope. Now it is the witness of faith in this broader and deeper
context, as it informs or illumines the immediacies of experience,
presently lived, that forms the area of study pertinent to constructive
theology. And, in this sense, constructive theology, by its very focus
and mode of inquiry, tends toward becoming a theology of culture.

I

Theologians have varied in the degree to which they have acknowledged or attended this larger, cultural orbit of historical experience in
identifying the structure of faith, or its legacy. They have also varied in
the extent to which they have envisaged this structure organically,
psychically, or subconsciously. For the most part, they have preferred to
attend to the overt level of conceptual decisions. Insofar as there has
been awareness of a psychical thrust consonant with a structure of experience, persisting as an ordering event, defined or undefined by
cultic doctrine, it has had the effect, either of evoking distrust and concern, lest it erupt in undisciplined manifestations, or of eliciting religious
zeal and sentiment in defiance of disciplined doctrine as a witness to
individual religious experience. Neither of these responses has attended

to the ordering effect of faith that is lived, or of the persistent shaping effect of such faith within the culture itself. In a way that was unavailable to theological inquiry conceptually as well as experientially. For the most part, in these instances, the culture represented simply a realm of power and practice presumed to be indifferent to the witness of faith, if not consciously opposed to it, or a realm of secular power condescendingly supportive of the cultic faith for reasons of expediency or compromise.

Now the thesis I have come to assert, and for which I have argued through the years, is that faith is a deeper psychical and realistic event within the culture than this cultic experience, defined and conveyed through church doctrine and history, has made evident, and than theologians generally have recognized. Faith is also more pervasive than is generally acknowledged within theological circles. Its apprehensions and sensibilities spread wide and far throughout the social experience. To a considerable extent, much of the contextual spread of its witness throughout culture remains unarticulated and latent, remaining as an overtone of common thought, or an undertow of feeling. But it somehow seems to affect the way articulate speech and action within that cultural history takes shape; for people outside the culture readily detect what they term a biased or inherited way of speaking and acting, which they attribute to our Judaic-Christian origins. Faith also becomes manifest as motifs in the arts and literature of a people, again readily detected by outside observers, but often employed by artists, poets, creative writers, and composers quite unconsciously or subconsciously as being the creative, sensitive, or appropriate symbolism or metaphor for the occasion at hand.

The culture in all its modes of thought, behavior, and creative effort thus becomes a bearer of the witness of faith with varying degrees of relevance and recognition. Liberal theologians, in my judgment, were in a favored position to note this cultural depth and pervasiveness of the Judaic-Christian faith in Western experience, for they had ready access to the cultural disciplines informing critical thinking on this aspect of experience; but, for reasons peculiar to their own bent of mind or interest, most of them bypassed this insight completely. Hence, with some notable exceptions,[1] one finds among liberal theologians, from the

---

1. One finds hints of such an understanding, to be sure, in some of the theological writings of the period, notably those of Schleiermacher and Schelling. And in later liberals like

seventeenth through the nineteenth century and after, a studied avoidance of the mythical or imaginative dimensions of faith, except as a mode to reject or to reconceive. In fairness to liberal theologians of that era, one should recognize that the organic, contextual imagery which has become so prevalent in our time, and which is largely responsible for critical advances in assessing the imaginative idiom, was not available to those earlier modes of discourse.

Meanwhile, various cultural disciplines in recent years have contributed to a concern with the kind of dimensional or contextual thinking that has made for a deeper view of man's existence, enabling theologians of our time, along with depth psychologists and cultural anthropologists, to look at the dynamics of faith with a new seriousness, both in pursuing understanding of the nature of man and in reconceiving the character of cultures. All of these disciplines attest to the complexity of such occurrences, as seen, for example, in the new physics, in the concern with what Jung has called "the collective unconscious," in the configuration of events and feelings in Gestalt psychology, and in similar modes of dimensional inquiry. In effect, they present us with a new stage of the modern consciousness in terms of which one may venture more boldly and fruitfully into the dynamics of faith as a structured event within the culture that is available to one.

My own efforts to take account of these developments as they bear upon theological inquiry began with my *Seeds of Redemption* (1947) and *The Reawakening of Christian Faith* (1949). They took more serious form as a constructive theology in *Faith and Culture* (1953) and in *The Realities of Faith* (1962). Some of the basic, philosophical discussion pertinent to these efforts appeared in *Higher Education and the Human Spirit* (1953), having to do with the concept of *the appreciative consciousness,* and with relations between the perceptual event and conceptualization. I undertook some of these essays simply as tentative efforts in what might be designated "the appreciative mode" in order to point up a different way of envisaging the structural character of

---

Dilthey and Troeltsch, the cultural orbit of meaning begins to loom more prominently as shaping, and in decisive ways determining, the mode of meaning available to any period of history. Considerable attention was given by modernist theologians and church historians, notably of the early Chicago school, to the conceptual influence of the social environment; and, in this way, to the cultural context of Christian origins as well as the growth of its religious ideas and doctrines. Yet, this was not the same thing as detecting the interplay of faith and culture at the deeper, preconscious or preconceptual level. Any dabbling in that area of human response seemed to the modernist to be anti-intellectual in method and concern.

faith. In this mode the intention was to let the formative notions of the cultural history come forth as a holistic pattern of meaning and intention.

It takes no studied deciphering of texts and materials in the Judaic-Christian Scriptures to distill from this recorded history the outlines of a drama of hope and redemption, extending from the pages of the book of Genesis through the book of Revelation. This has been visually dramatized in Christian ceremonials and worship, in art and architecture, from at least the beginning of the Christian era. It lies back of every systematic theology like a kerygmatic witness to a revelatory event that has expressed itself serially and continuously through various episodes. It inheres in the sensibilities and bents of mind of the culture of the West, which has been the culture most intimately and continuously shaped by its ministrations and imaginative force.

## II

Now in expanding the sphere of influence of the Judaic-Christian pattern of meaning from its cultic orbit to that of being formative of the mythos of Western culture, one confronts the question, on what grounds can one assert the seminal and formative influence of that legacy in Western experience? The obvious and simple response is that there has been but one indigenous sacred Scripture in the West that has pervaded the whole of its history, namely, the Judaic-Christian Scriptures, containing the Old Testament of Jewish origin and the New Testament of Christian origin. Other bodies of literature have been venerated in the West as sacred lore, such as the sagas of the Norsemen, the legends of the Druids among the Celts, Greek mythology along with the Iliad and the Odyssey, the accounts of the old Roman religion, the heritage of the Aztecs, and the vast lore of the American Indian. And the listing could go on. In the medieval period of Western history following the Crusades, the influence of the Koran became assertive in the West, notably in Spain; in recent years, stimulated by the proximity of Arab nations bordering upon Western experience and the growing impact of their presence on world affairs, that influence has mounted in significance and pervasiveness within the West. Following the World Parliament of Religions in Chicago at the turn of the century (1904), Hindu and Buddhist writings became known in the West; and in recent years they have been eagerly sought after and read by a younger generation of earnest discontents, distraught over Western mechanization and with dubious turns of the American experience.

Yet, after all this has been taken into account, the judgment of history would seem to be that the impact of these other legacies in the West has been intermittent and regional in significance, as contrasted with the pervasive and persistent influence of the Judaic-Christian Scriptures. At the most, their influence in the West has been cultic rather than cultural. This is not to deny the importance or impressiveness of any of these other legacies within the spheres of influence in which they have been expressive. It is simply to acknowledge the limits of those spheres of influence within Western history as compared with that of the Judaic-Christian legacy. Acknowledging all this, to be sure, one may still observe that the Judaic-Christian legacy of faith and its Scripture are imports from the Near East. It would seem to follow from this judgment that the West, in fact, has no indigenous mythos except these several regional cultic legacies. This, I think, is to make too much of geography in isolation from history. Western culture as a social configuration is a particular historical epoch wrought within Western geography, dating politically from the fourth century A.D. Yet, by virtue of its imported legacies, which were then made indigenous to its life, Western experience assimilated to its own cultural history the Christian era of Southwest Asia along with its Jewish, Egyptian, Assyrian, and Babylonian antecedents.

The church, having been given authorization and power by the Roman Empire in the fourth century A.D., lifted this Judaic-Christian legacy to a level of conscious motivation which it never could have achieved in its most restrictive state as a Palestinian or Alexandrian movement. In doing so, it merged its biblical themes with existing Roman motifs, variously modified by Greek influence, and thus set the stage for a drastic revision of what had been primordially bequeathed to it as a covenant faith with its ensuing redemptive drama. And with the codification of Roman law by Justinian after 526 A.D. the formalizing of the drama to accord with authorized belief and liturgical precedent accelerated.

Given the set of historical circumstances that lifted this mythos to a new stage of self-consciousness within Western history, bequeathing to the Judaic-Christian Scriptures a primacy in the West no other document shared, the impact of this document and its witness of faith upon Western history became formidable and irrepressible, and, in a way, irrevocable.

But there were always two levels at which this formidable witness of faith, emanating from Scripture, was proclaimed: (1) the more immediate and obvious level of the authoritative and institutional consensus; (2) the level of the Word itself, as an historic, primal witness of faith which was persistently being rediscovered or attended to in remote centers by various communities which were to erupt into renascent piety groups.

The historical test as to whether the Judaic-Christian mythos is seminal, and, in that sense, formative of Western culture, rests upon certain judgments concerning (1) its pervasiveness; (2) its durability as a continuing witness of faith; (3) its renewability, or renascent power, in various periods of Western history; and (4) its defensibility—that is, its ability to remain consistently persuasive as true to the exigencies of the lived experience and to reflection within various perspectives that have been brought to bear on it, and within various idioms through which it has been expressed. On all four counts this witness of faith, stemming from the primal mythos is formidable, and for many of the West, commanding as a personal commitment as well.

Having said this, however, one is impelled to recount significant developments within Christian history that would seem to question attributing so singular a role to the *Judaic*-Christian legacy: such as the impact of Greek thought (neo-Platonism) through Clement of Alexandria and Origen in the third century A.D.; the assimilation of Roman forms and symbols in the fourth century A.D. when Christianity became the religion of the empire; the resurgence of Greek influence within this Romanized Christianity when St. Augustine embraced neo-Platonism; the reassertion of Greek influence through the discovery of Aristotle in scholasticism, by way of Moslem influence; and the rediscovery of Greece and Rome in the time of the Renaissance, when neo-Platonism was reaffirmed and Roman studies in literature were discovered afresh. All this would certainly seem to argue for a radical reshaping of the Judaic-Christian legacy, or the replacement of it, in Western experience. Reshaping is the appropriate term if one of them is to be chosen. To be sure any historical study of Christian thought and liturgy or church development would need to give major consideration to these various environmental and structural influences, or to episodic eruptions of their impact as in the time of the Renaissance.

Speaking more generally, the *cultic* history of any religion would need to be attentive to such periodic transformations and metamorphoses of thought and ritual. When, however, one is centering upon the seminal and formative legacy itself as it relates to an historical cultural experience, the problem assumes a different focus. Then the question is not how have thought and practice (liturgy), or institutional development within the church or cultus been affected; but how have the seminal strands of the formative legacy persisted as carriers of the themes and motifs, however reshaped by, or accommodated to, insistent forces of change and reconception. When applied to early periods of transition and environmental change, say through the fourteenth century A.D., there can be little doubt but that these themes and motifs have persisted under various guises, although an imbalance between Scripture and dogma, weighted on the side of dogma, as carriers of the faith is clearly in evidence.

The period of the Renaissance, however, presents a different complex of circumstances. Insofar as the Protestant Reformation is to be viewed in certain respects as being within the context of Renaissance sensibilities (and one must admit that the Reformers, to some degree, did share in them), one may say that the Renaissance in certain respects reasserted the Judaic-Christian legacy, addressing directly the medieval imbalance between Scripture and dogma, with the result, however, that a new mode of Protestant imbalance was effected. Initially it gave Scripture the dominant role, as in Lutheranism and Calvinism in the sixteenth century, and then, in the seventeenth century, it attributed to Scripture singular, if not exclusive, authority in matters of faith, as in the famous utterance of Chillingworth, "The Bible, and *only* the Bible, is the religion of Protestants."

Yet the larger sphere of Renaissance thought presents more radical deviations from the primal legacy, and gives rise to the question of whether an implicit rejection of the Judaic-Christian legacy is indicated in favor of Greek and Roman influences at a higher level of literacy than had been evident in earlier periods of change. For the Renaissance was not only a revival of philosophical (notably Platonic) and literary works, long in obscurity, but a rediscovery of nature in a new context. This projected a new dimension not only of Renaissance influence, but of Grecian influence as it had been historically experienced. For example, the siphoning of Aristotelian influence into Christian reflection among the Scholastics, following from Moslem stimulus, was in itself not in-

novating; nor was the revival of interest in Platonic studies in the
Renaissance period a radical departure. The interplay of these strands of
thought with Christian theology had been in evidence in the early
Councils, though, of course, not with dimensions of reshaping Christian
thought so evident in these later periods. A somewhat different claim
can be made for the impact of early Greek science upon Western
Christian thought in the time of Copernicus and, later, Galileo. This
sphere of influence presents complications not visibly present in relating
philosophy to the biblical legacy. During the Renaissance, the issue
that was implicit here was not really raised, though it was implied in the
church's suppression of Copernicus' work and in its open confrontation
with Galileo. Among theologians of the period generally, however, the
issue was deftly muted in acknowledging, simultaneously, as Herschl
Baker has noted in *The Dignity of Man,* an appeal to the *imago dei*
and to the *imago naturae* in speaking of the nature of man. Thomism, to
be sure, had already reflected this correlation of the two spheres of appeal
in associating the natural and the revelational dimensions of human
nature. And the imagery of this correlation persisted among Roman
Catholic and Protestant philosophies alike throughout the seventeenth
century, though its Scholastic derivation was not explicitly acknowledged among Protestant philosophers and theologians. The *imago
naturae* was an acknowledgment of the creatural dignity of natural man,
and, in effect, released literary and philosophical speculation among
Renaissance writers concerning the creative powers and possibilities of
natural man. Insofar as this became assertive and philosophically elaborated it became an explicit challenge to the medieval conception of
piety, and it was to stand out in contrast to subsequent forms of
Protestant piety as well. It is easy to conclude, then, from this observation, that the Renaissance, by reason of its affinities with classical Greek
and early Roman sensibilities with regard to human nature, had rejected
the Judaic-Christian legacy in favor of the classical legacy of ancient
Greece and Rome.

Another way of interpreting this "humanistic" bent of mind in Renaissance studies, however, is to see it as restoring to the covenant relationship the subtle sense of mutual regard between Creator and creature
which had been all but lost to medieval piety, following from imbalances
in the Justinian code, wherein God the Almighty was represented as the
sovereign power, seemingly indifferent to the earthly plight of his

creatures. The artistry of the period immediately preceding the Renaissance, contrasting the warmth and consoling intercession of the Mother Mary in tenth century cathedrals with the wrathful God and the avenging Christ, gives credence to these characterizations of medieval piety prior to and even beyond the thirteenth century A.D. The assertive affirmation of "natural" man in Renaissance studies can be viewed as an advance beyond Mariolatry as a way of countering the ruthlessness of deity, expressing not pathos and consolation, but resistance to the medieval conception of piety itself. In this respect, the Renaissance theme, accentuating "the dignity of man," was essentially a recovery of the earlier spirit of the covenant in which God and man (viewed in its communal context) stood related. The dignity of man along with the supremacy of God was somehow adjudicated, if not correlated.

Certain strands of the Protestant Reformation may be viewed in this light, though with less assertive claims concerning "the dignity of man." The emphasis there was more upon the dignity and graciousness of a *righteous* God and his requirement for salvation. Protestant sects of the eighteenth century and after, however, were to restore the imagery of the wrathful God and the avenging Christ with no source of respite, such as had been provided by the Mother Mary; thus these sects reached a new low in the perversity of piety. Liberal theologians, intent on countering this imbalance, effected their own imbalance in portraying God in the image of man, even appealing to human ideals as our clearest indices to the nature of God. With the nature of deity so clearly given in human ideals, it was not surprising that the logic of liberalism should lead to a religious humanism. If a decisive break with the themes and motifs of the Judaic-Christian legacy in Western experience can be historically identified, it would appear to surface in instances singularly appealing to nature to the exclusion of either a scriptural or a revelational dimension. But this would seem to correlate the Judaic-Christian legacy too readily with Scholastic imagery, as in seventeenth century rationalism, notably among the Deists, or with particularized forms of theism, as in the death-of-God movement of recent years. As an ethos of thought and experience, the Judaic-Christian legacy transcends all such conceptual formulations. It addresses, instead, the formative level of sensibilities, which may work on hiddenly when the rationale for authorizing such sensibilities as response may have been dissipated.

## III

The defining and formative motif of this Judaic-Christian perspective upon the experiences of human life, as this tends to emerge as a Christian mythos, is expressed in the redemptive theme, a theme that mounts in proportion and detail until finally it is represented as a fully elaborated drama of redemption. This motif has empirical roots in certain historical events of Hebraic-Christian history in which apprehensions of God's efficacy are said to have been recorded, as elemental folk will take note of such things. These apprehensions came to be celebrated in folksong and folklore as a commonly shared "wisdom of the people," to use Dorothy Emmet's phrase.[2] But more than that, they were later given articulate, sophisticated expression in the prophetic sermons and poetry of exceptional seers who saw critical implications of judgment and hope in these events beyond the common celebrations of them.

Folklore, prophetic sermons and poetry, then the law! The law was not contrary to these sensitive apprehensions; it was the systematic codification of them. Yet the law, expressing the accumulative and integrated wisdom of generations of tradition, was as the root and stalk of the flowering that was to break forth as a revelatory disclosure in the person of a Jewish villager, Jesus, who was to be called the Christ. In that person and in events continuous with him, there appeared to emerge a new kind of wisdom, at once more simple and penetrating, correlating judgment and grace, which had a spontaneity of meaning that could not be contained in law or in any similarly measured wisdom. It was "gospel as over against the law," some were moved to say; a creative word as over against a created word; seemingly the Word of God as over against words which men, in collaboration with one another, had fashioned into law or into moral directives. Yet this overstates the contrast, for, as has been noted, the law itself had emerged out of sensitive apprehensions distilled from generations of living, and the gospel, for all its forbearance and openness to the spontaneous and innovating good, subsumed within its gracious acts the integrity of the law as a witness to the role of judgment. Nevertheless, the gospel stood apart, elevating to the stature of God himself him to whom the new wisdom, the new Word, had been attributed. Hero-worship was undoubtedly present here, but that does not obscure, nor need it detract from, the critical fact that

2. Dorothy Emmet, *The Nature of Metaphysical Thinking* (London: Macmillan, 1945).

the reality of a new consciousness, "a new creation," did come into history, giving rise to a "revelation in act," to use Whitehead's phrase, what had been "divined in theory."[3]

The "revelation in act" through the person of Jesus who was to be called the Christ, gave rise to "the gospel," then the community of witnesses, out of which emerged the reality of the church. The community of witness was to the church what the apprehensions of faith had been to the drama of redemption: formative beginnings of a holistic movement that was to assume integration and articulate structure. This community of witness was more than a simple response among people to the person of the Christ and to the gospel. It was a bodying forth of that revelatory act, or event, lifting to communal relationship what had been as a New Creation of individuated consciousness and intention. The subtle process by which the sensitive core of an individuated spirit is insinuated into a corporate movement of faith is one of the mysterious occurrences of human history. And the forming of the communal witness, giving to this nucleus of revelatory being and act carrying power, cultural actuality, and persistence beyond its initial, individuated form, is one of the remarkable instances of that subtle process. The church as the body of Christ has almost a literal connotation when seen in this contextual imagery.

## IV

To lift up this structural character of the faith, the theologian will need to simulate the disciplined imagination of the artist's mind. What the artist does in conveying an appreciative approach to any data is to execute certain broad strokes that give an unmistakable representation of the event or object being presented. This seemingly free execution of broad outlines is anything but a casual conveyance of what is being presented. It follows from a prolonged identification with the subject, an absorbing assimilation of its subtleties and nuances, along with its explicit claims. And, from that internalizing of the lived reality, the artist, poet, creative writer, or musician renders a vivid portrayal of the complex of experiences, a holistic view, however selectively executed. Such utterances employ the parts to convey the whole, or so employ the

3. Alfred North Whitehead, *Adventures of Ideas* (New York: Macmillan, 1933), p. 214.

parts as to convey the whole of their intention. Something of this method of indirection and presentational immediacy is involved in the appreciative method I have employed to evoke and to convey the structure of faith.

The structure combines a series of reiterated themes; but the themes follow, as it were, from a qualitative impact or feeling-tone, conveying the character of apprehension and concern expressive of the cultural outreach. Thus, it is not as if one had first analytically detected the several themes and, in a mechanical way, assembled them into a visible whole; rather, it is as if one had come upon a qualitative response as a mode of "spirituality," a conveyance of grace and discipline which, on examination, was found to consist of various themes, organically related, each of them seeming to be more than itself and pointing to a holistic occurrence.

The root-metaphor of this Judaic-Christian drama is the covenant relationship between God and man; a relationship which one Old Testament scholar has indicated implies "the juxtaposition of faithfulness and freedom."[4] Now it should be noted that, in its more primitive, Hebraic setting, personality was a communal term. The individual acquired and conveyed his distinctive, personal identity and expressiveness through the communal experience and history, and was therefore representative of the community. Thus, in speaking of God and man in this context, one was speaking of God and his people. The entire drama of strain and repentance relating to this relationship of faithfulness and freedom in the Old Testament centers in the encounter between God and his people.

The individuation of this relationship, making it a metaphorical commentary upon the nature of man, is of later origin, and was to become dominant in Christian imagery.[5]

---

4. H. Wheeler Robinson, *The Christian Doctrine of Man* (Edinburgh: T. & T. Clark, 1911; third edition, 1952).

5. Robinson attributes the beginning of a more individualistic consciousness among the Hebrews to the prophetic movement. He writes: "It is clear that primitive morality and religious conceptions based on the idea of corporate personality, were seriously limited by the absence of a fuller recognition of individual rights and needs. The development of Israel's morality and religion involved, as one of its aspects, a new emphasis on the individual person; consequently a full account of the rise of individualism would be the history of the prophetic movement. It would be necessary to begin with Elijah in the ninth century. His protests against Ahab's introduction of foreign worship and against his immoral acquisition of Naboth's vineyard already shew the double line of advance in religion and morality. These protests were continued by the great prophetic group of the eighth century, Amos, Hosea, Isaiah, and Micah. These prophets, it is true, addressed Israel as a nation; but their insistence on moral righteousness as the true bond of connection between

Historically and empirically, following Old Testament scholarship, we have said that the redemptive motif is the prior theme growing out of a covenant relation between the human and the divine, man and God. Creativity, or the notion of creation, is a generalization upon experience and history, based upon empirical events of a redemptive character. In this sense it may be said that the redemptive act is a defining motif in the cultural experience shared by the Judaic-Christian history in a way that creation is not. Creation is a universal myth. But creativity, presupposing a context of the covenant relationship in which the redemptive concern is primordially intended, provides a distinctive setting in which relations between the human and the divine occur.

But the redemptive motif not only gives rise to a particular conception of creativity; it presupposes a condition in man and in the covenant relation that necessitates a redemptive activity which man by himself cannot provide. An implicit brokenness in the communal ground, following the creative act, and a consequent individuated freedom that both imperils and excites human creaturehood ensue. The covenant, the root-metaphor of this Judaic-Christian history, conveys an identification of God with man, and of man with God. "Created in God's image" is a poetic way of expressing this identity, and is meant to imply not only a likeness in form, but a solidarity in intention and self-expression.

But the myth of identity between the human and the divine in this covenant relationship was to be complicated in the Judaic-Christian imagery with the introduction of the note of dissonance in its theme of the fall. Properly speaking, I would think that this notion of the fall derived more directly from the strain implicit in the covenant relationship than in anything inherent in man himself. But once it was asserted, it became a commentary upon man as he is in himself; for then human initiative in the communal act, and later in individuality, loomed as a source of demonic freedom. Thus man, by himself, acting for and by himself, earned the name of sinner, as one who had breached the relationship. A possible contribution toward reinterpreting this basic idea of a breach in the relation between the human and the divine would be to take it out of the traditional setting as a fall in man's nature, and to see it, in part at least, as an inescapable condition of dissonance in

---

man and God already contains the implicit individualistic principle which finds explicit statement in the prophetic lawbook of the seventh century: "The fathers shall not be put to death for the children, neither shall the children be put to death for the fathers; every man shall be put to death for his own sin" (Deut. xxiv. 16)." *Ibid.*, pp. 30–31.

relationships where two or more centers of dignity are involved. Dissonance is the accompaniment of freedom and dignity wherever a qualitative concern exists, whenever perspectives are relative to a given center of dignity. I would be for preserving this fact of dissonance, even though we rise above differences; for the dissolution of differences in the interest of unity may be but the easy way out at the expense of qualitative distinctions.

Both this sense of dissonance in the divine-human relationships and the marked awareness of human freedom which was to become individuality are distinctive in Judaic-Christian history. In Christian history, bearing the imprint of the Judaic myth of the fall, individuality implies a marred freedom that is always ill at ease with itself: rebellious, at times penitent, potentially both demonic and redemptive. The influence of Greek philosophy, particularly as it developed in the city-states, was to lift the notion of human freedom, and the intellectual assertiveness and creativity associated with it, to a new level of dignity. And Christian theology has tended to embrace both of these strands, at times to vacillate between them, or to choose between them. Western philosophy, however, has chosen to follow Greek influence rather than the Judaic myth of the fall. Insofar as the Greek view of man has been pressed without qualification, as in Renaissance humanism and seventeenth century rationalism, the West has approximated the Hindu dictum, *That art Thou.* And this was even more true of nineteenth century idealism as well.

But it would be a mistake to assume that the Western image of man is divided between Judaic and Greek ways of conceiving human nature. For what was explicitly expressed in Greek philosophy, and more vigorously in Western humanism, was implicit in the covenant relationship itself; and finds periodic eruption in Judaic literature, as in the Wisdom literature, particularly in Job.

Certain forms of Christian theology, in formulating the doctrine of *imago dei,* have been responsible for attributing to this Judaic heritage a kind of piety that interpreted the covenant relationship as implying not an encounter between authentic centers of dignity, as in the I-Thou, but an impassive obeisance which left no room for human protest or assertiveness, except as an act of sin. Theologians have got around this somewhat, as in Reformation doctrine, where the perfectionist emphasis has been deleted, and man is dealt with frankly as being inescapably a sinner if he is to be himself, if he is to be human. The dignity of his humanity demands it. Then the injunction to "sin bravely" becomes a forthright recognition of this human predicament in a context of grace which recalls the terms of the covenant as being a relationship with the righteous, but gracious, God. This, no doubt, is better than letting piety tyrannize over the human spirit; but there is a better way. That is to recognize frankly the limited character of the human structure simultaneously with acknowledging its authenticity as a concrete, innovating center of witness. I am drawing here upon Whitehead's valuation of every concrete event as having a primacy proportionate to its unique occurrence as an individuated event, even as it is gathered into the community of created events, prehending, with varying degrees of relevance, every other created event, including God.[6]

## V

The thematic structure of faith is not complete until the theme of the Suffering Servant is noted. This theme, in effect, is a concealed intimation of God's faithfulness at work in the covenant relationship, taking on the anguish and burden of the relationship, both in its duration and in its brokenness. This deeper import of the theme was to become explicit in the New Testament rendering of the work of Christ as God taking on the form of man and reconciling the world to himself. Here the motif of the divine initiative as a gracious, redemptive act through full identification with sinful, suffering, broken humanity becomes dominant. It is the drama of redemption entering its climactic phase.

Here, too, the meaning of God goes beyond that of creativity to a participating role of sensitivity and negotiability. It is interesting to note that metaphysical renderings of the Christian story tend to subsume the whole of the redemptive story under the notion of creativity. Whitehead's philosophy is expressive of this effort. This procedure is implicit also in the writings of Wieman and Hartshorne; in Schubert Ogden's *Christ without Myth* it is made explicit by way of demythologizing the Christ-event. In my earlier writings, particularly in *Seeds of Redemption* and *The Reawakening of Christian Faith,* I tended to follow this

6. Alfred North Whitehead, *Process and Reality* (New York: Macmillan, 1929), pp. 334 ff.; *Adventures of Ideas* (New York: Macmillan, 1933), pp. 295 ff. See also Dorothy Emmet's discussion of Whitehead's "Doctrine of Prehensions," *The Nature of Metaphysical Thinking* (London: Macmillan & Co., Ltd., 1945), pp. 228–34.

procedure, making of creativity itself a highly sensitive and redemptive occurrence. I am not willing to forgo that tendency altogether for in process thought creativity and the redemptive act do convey common qualities of tenderness and negotiability. And, adequately understood, redemption always takes the form of "a new creation." Yet, the redemptive act, it must be seen, partakes as well of a new dimension of renewal and hope. For, as Tillich has noted, in speaking of the creation of man, there is in this drama a persisting innocence that presents idealizing tones of expectancy concerning possible fulfillments of what has been created. The redemptive act, too, abounds in tones of expectancy, yet not so much as a fulfillment of what had been created as an individuated entity, but as a possession or repossession of the energies of grace now available in the structured relations of other human beings and of God which, in Wieman's words, "can do for us what we cannot do for ourselves." Innocency and the expectations consonant with it are now replaced with grim realization of limited potentialities insofar as individuation in and of itself is contemplated. The individuated self, with all its hoped-for possibilities and failures, its pride and pretensions, must find access to the deeper reality of its individuated existence in the communal ground of God and other human beings, in relationships that offer grace and sustaining love. The sense of individuality in community must take hold of one as a lived experience in which a good not one's own can be received and assimilated to one's individuated existence. And the capacity to receive the grace that is given out of such relationships must awaken within the sense of rapport that may ensue.

The motif of the Suffering Servant conveys also the note of forgiveness as being of a piece with the response of faithfulness in the covenant relationships. Faithfulness in the covenant relationship is more commonly understood in the Old Testament as implying obedience to God and his law. This is the prevailing view of the priestly tradition of the temple. Yet there runs through the prophetic literature and the psalms a kind of summoning of this legalistic view of the covenant relation to take account of the more sensitive aspect as it applies to God in his relations with his people, expressed in the act of forgiveness. Law and forgiveness thus tend to become contradictory modes of interpreting the covenant relationship, and eventually are set up as antitheses between Old Testament and New Testament ways of viewing the relationship, as expressed in the phrase "law and gospel," contrasting Judaism and Christianity.

Careful students of the Old Testament have resisted this easy resolution, insisting that law in the Old Testament is not that rigid; nor is the note of forgiveness that absent from the Judaic literaure. And, on the other hand, careful Christian theologians have resisted so ready an either-or dichotomy between law and love, insisting that love, forgiveness, and gospel, when isolated from the disciplining demands implied in the notion of faithfulness under the law, degenerate into sheer sentimentalism, turning Christian faith into a slovenly piety that disavows all structure and discipline. This is no easy problem. And it has had few satisfactory treatments. One valiant effort to address the issue in recent theological literature is Tillich's *Love, Power, and Justice.*[7] In confronting this issue we are thrust back again to the problem of "forms and the breaking of forms,"[8] structure and the dynamics of the living spirit.

The climactic theme of the Christian rendering of the drama of redemption is the Easter story of the resurrection. If this theme is given simply the connotation of an afterlife, following upon the event of death, it loses much of its import as related to the structure of faith in the Judaic-Christian legacy. Its structural meaning is an affirming note beyond tragedy, a living forward in trust, despite the immediacies of anguish and defeat. It is a final declaration of hope in the relational ground of the covenant, namely, that our life is in God, and, to the Jew as well as to the Christian, it has given a sense of openness and expectancy transcending the closures and despairs of experience and history.

7. Paul Tillich, *Love, Power and Justice* (New York: Oxford University Press, 1954).
8. Alfred North Whitehead, *Modes of Thought* (New York: Macmillan, 1938), p. 119.

Chapter Eight

# Mythos and Logos

The word "mythos" is important to the mode of theological inquiry being projected here; hence some clarification of its meaning is indicated. This word is not to be equated with myth, though obviously it is related to the mode of apprehension that is implied in myth and partakes of the discourse that emerges out of the mythical structures of a people. In *Faith and Culture* I described "mythos" as "the pattern of meaning and valuations arising from within the structured experience of a people which has been imaginatively projected through drama or metaphor, expressing the perceptive truths of the historical experience of a people bearing upon man's ultimate nature and destiny."[1]  I think I should now add the words "as these perceptive truths of experience express themselves within the culture as psychic energy in the form of hopes, expectations, attitudes of trust or apprehension, or even determination; or in the form of human responses to circumstances joyous or tragic, promising or threatening, and similar historical occurrences affecting the stance in meeting human situations."

In now pairing together the terms logos and mythos it would seem that I am associating two incomparables; while logos, in its historical usage, has connoted an ontological notion, mythos, as I now propose to use it, suggests more of an historical and cultural concept, connoting a living structure of meaning.  What justifies such an association of terms is the fact that, in their present usage, both terms partake of cultural as well as ontological connotations, and thus represent, in a way, two modes of awareness which relate to one another.  Logos implies the level of

1. Bernard E. Meland, *Faith and Culture* (New York: Oxford University Press, 1953), pp. 20–21.

rationality implicit in experience which is available through an overt inquiry into conscious experience; while mythos, on the other hand, addresses a depth of awareness which, while available to conscious experience, functions in the main as a noncognitive mode of meaning and motivation in the living structure of experience of any people or culture. In contemporary discussions, therefore, the two terms do actually represent different dimensions as well as different modes of meaning conveyed by experience: experience as thought and experience as lived.

The seriousness with which we have come to consider the lived character of experience, in contrast to the conceptualized report of it, or reflection upon it, would seem to suggest that we mean to attribute to its mode of meaning something more than a psychological or cultural phenomenon. In point of fact we are meaning to designate a depth in cultural experience which partakes of the Creative Passage with greater intimacy and less differentiation than can be assigned to conscious experience and its conceptualizations. Mythos, then, while it partakes of the cultural idiom in any period of history, conveys a mode of meaning at its level of participation in lived experience which conveys ontological as well as cultural judgments about the structure of experience.

The word "mythos" is a less familiar term in theological history and in systematic discussions of doctrine than the word "logos." In fact, as far as I know, the word itself is not commonly in use, although what is pertinent to its meaning is employed to a limited degree and in varying contexts. For mythos in a general way can be said to apply to dimensions of existing and knowing which exceed or elude the rational grasp of mind and experience, but which nevertheless persist as a depth or heightening of the immediacies of knowing and experiencing and in that sense are integral to them. References to "immediate access to the Holy Spirit" in traditional theologies, and later to appeals to religious experience in liberal theologies can be said to have pointed obliquely to what is in focus in speaking of the mythos, although in each of these earlier modes of speaking theologically no sense of the context of meaning or of a persisting corporate reality consonant with an inherent rationality was conveyed. Spirit implied a transcendent working that somehow reached and evoked a responsiveness in the individual person, and religious experience was likewise assumed to be an individual attestation to intimations of reality beyond what reason could convey.

The word logos was appropriated early in Christian thinking pre-eminently from Greek sources, exemplifying a mode of theological thinking that presupposed a basic rationality in all existence and in the cosmic order. The acknowledgment of this basic assumption about life and nature put upon the theologian the necessity of conveying this underlying coherence as it became evident in Christian thinking and living. An alternative to this stance was to accept the assumption of an inherent rationality as applied to natural existence, yet to insist upon the transcendence of the life of the spirit, and to demonstrate their correlation or interrelationship. A third procedure was to dissociate Christian thinking altogether from any assumption of an inherent rationality and to interpret the gospel as the witness to the Spirit transcending and countering all forms of human thought and natural existence. This mode of Christian thinking came to be designated "pneumatic," implying a dynamic of redemptive power beyond the coherences of common existence. Here the basis was laid for regarding all concern with reason, intelligibility, and coherence in Christian thinking as suspect, and as being alien to Christian thought. The persisting issue between certain historic expressions of church theology and philosophical theology roots in this ancient controversy. An historical account of the controversy would reveal that the issue was sharpened by the fact that certain strands of Christian thought were beholden to Greek philosophies, while others assimilated influences from one or more of the mystery cults of the Greco-Roman world.

Variations upon this pneumatic mode appeared among medieval thinkers, such as Jacob Boehme, and various mystical writers intent upon becoming aware of ways to be responsive to this that supervened our natural structures. The numinous theology of Schleiermacher represented an important reassertion of this tendency within the context of a critical philosophy. Kant had provided the essential distinction between types of thinking as applied to moral and scientific domains of experience; but Schleiermacher chose to press beyond Kant's type of critical philosophy to designate the peculiarly religious quality of reflection which, in effect, implied responding concretely and continuously to the God-consciousness. This, in Schleiermacher's view, was a dimension of thinking transcending rational and moral categories. It was Rudolf Otto's concern in *The Idea of the Holy* to give this numinous mode of thinking greater precision and productiveness by relating Schleier-

macher's numinous dimension to the aesthetic notion of *"ahnung,"* as
it had been developed by the philosopher Jacob Friedrick Fries, who, in
decisive ways, had been Otto's own philosophical mentor in earlier days.
Paul Tillich continued this concern with the numinous mode of apprehending Christian meanings, but with the help of Schelling's philosophy
and the theology of Julius Müller, especially his *Christian Doctrine of Sin,*
he sought to correlate this concern with the dynamic and noumenal
dimension of religious phenomena with carefully defined philosophical
categories developed within a system of neophenomenology.

In all of these instances of pneumatic thought, even when correlated
with logos motifs, as in Tillich's theology, the Platonic imagery of a
spirit life "casting its shadow" or its illumination upon natural structures, giving to them a transcendent glow of spirituality, seems to have
persisted.

My use of the term mythos clearly is motivated by a concern comparable to that found in numinous theology, and more particularly that
in which numinous and logos dimensions are correlated; yet it partakes
of a wholly different context of meaning. For what is presupposed in
empirical realism is not that reality casts its shadow or transcendent light
upon natural structures, giving them the appearance of spirituality, or
fleeting encounters with it, but that these immediacies of concrete
experience actually participate in the depth of the Creative Passage in
which the human structure of sensory life is integrally related to other
structures, and to what is genuinely ultimate as a dynamic of creativity.
Each individuated human structure or personality is thought to prehend,
with varying degrees of relevance, as Whitehead has expressed it, what
is ultimate in the reality of things.

Insofar as the history of natural structures is taken seriously within
the perspective of emergent thinking, something of the dimensional
thinking that characterizes numinous thought obtains,[2] though with

2. The affinity between these two modes of thought is emphasized by the fact that early in
the century, before he wrote his *Naturalism and Religion,* Rudolf Otto had been attentive
to emergent thinkers such as C. Lloyd Morgan, and appears actually to have considered
emergence as a way of expressing the numinous quality more precisely than had been done
in German thought; but he was to turn away from it as being less fruitful than the philosopher Fries's notion of *ahnung.* Interestingly enough, in one of his latest works, *Reich-
gottes und Menschensohn,* published in English translation in 1938, one year after his
death, as *The Kingdom of God and the Son of Man,* Otto speaks in a way that strongly
concurs with emergent insights and imagery. It may be pertinent here to acknowledge my
own deep interest in Otto's work in my earlier years, following a year of study at the University of Marburg, Germany, as his student. I had first been alerted to Otto's work by
Gerald Birney Smith who, while he differed from Otto's method, felt the force of his

structural differences. But process thought, in incorporating the structural differentiation of emergent thinking, moves beyond the earlier mode of immanence to what I have called in *Faith and Culture* "a reconstructed immanence," implying structural limitations at all levels of life, thereby precluding any simple projection of the description of the human structure of mind or personality to a depiction of ultimate reality, or the character and mind of God.

Numinous thinking, precisely because it implies individual awareness of the Spirit as an occasional act of tuning in on, or of being "grasped" by the Spirit, in the tradition of mysticism, tends to conceive of the numinous qualiy of experience as being a special, transcendent mode of spirituality to which individual minds are awakened or alerted, as in moments of ecstasy, in prophetic insight, or in the kind of brooding awareness in which outer stimuli are suppressed, as the inmost emissaries of contemplation are given full and uninterrupted attention. The process-emergent mode of thinking also is concerned with this individual access to "invasions of the spirit," or to that sensitive mode of awareness that is perceptive and appreciative beyond the usual responses of one immersed in the practical routines of living. Bergson was to go so far, in his *Two Sources of Religion and Ethics,* as to differentiate between the general mass of common humanity and especially evolved individuals whose capacity for sensitive awareness had been extraordinarily developed; and he actually spoke of such individuals as being of a different level of humanity. The fact of this differentiation is not to be denied. How to understand it, or even more important, how to designate these

---

numinous insights. In a similar way, I, too, found his *Idea of the Holy* and his *Religious Essays* illuminating and compelling. The extent of his influence on me I find difficult to gauge or assess; nevertheless I came to see his numinous theology as a mode of thought attentive to the same underlying concerns as my own, yet as pursuing a different path of inquiry, and in a philosophical context quite different from my own.

On the one hand, process thinking within an emergent perspective is more insistent upon designating the limits of the human structure, though it is assumed that even within each structure so limited, there is at work a nucleus of creativity, a *"nisus* toward deity," as S. Alexander called it, implying an incipient, though inherent thrust toward something more than what has become actualized within these structural limits. This prescient quality is what heightens and deepens the potential, qualitative outreach of man. The qualitative outreach is implicit in every human structure, though it may not be attributed to personality as such, or made the basis for equating the human mind or the human structure with the mind of God, or of attributing to God, what is distinctive of man as a natural structure. In other words, what is representative of man as a natural structure must be taken seriously as being limited in range and sensitivity of awareness. The potentiality beyond that limited structural existence is simply a plus in man's particular concretion which, in effect, disturbs, heightens, quickens and impels man toward an awareness of the creatural depth of his being. The mystery of existing is thus compounded beyond that of his origin to awaken him to a sense of his destiny and ultimate meaning as a creature of the creative process.

qualities of extraordinariness, and to assess them, is the really trouble-some question. Along this path one readily gets into a stratification of the human community that can be insidious in its claims and implica-tions. I have persistently resisted Bergson's account of this dimension discerned in sensitive human beings in the effort to understand its specific bearing upon the human structure as such. To ascribe it totally to rare individuals, I wrote in *Faith and Culture*, "is to individualize the occurrence to the point of dismissing the really precious operations of grace which are at work in all men, however rigid or habituated their modes of life may become."[3]

A parallel path of inquiry of equal importance to understanding what is involved in the life of the spirit within the human community is that of being attentive to what William James initially spoke of as the per-ceptive track of meaning which underlies and provides depth to our conceptualizations. In our time we are able to say more than James was able to say within the limited psychological and philosophical perspec-tive then available to him. For what has developed out of James's own seminal insights in relation to those of Bergson is awareness of life and existence as an ongoing stream of occurrences in which our human history participates simultaneously in a selective, regional, or cultural fabric of meaning, and a depth of structured reality only vaguely appre-hended and articulated in our human structure of meaning, but which nevertheless cradles, sustains, and ultimately receives these historic immediacies into whatever duration of reality survives and subsumes this present reality. This structured reality, both cultural and cosmic, con-ceived within an historic stream of occurrences, provides the ground for addressing the import of the mythos as a corollary of logos in Chris-tian thought.

And this brings us to a further point of differentiation between what I mean to convey in speaking of mythos and the pneumatic or numinous modes of thought. It is assumed in the empirical realism I seek to con-vey that all experience within the various individual life-spans, and in succeeding stages of any cultural history, partakes of this persistent inter-play and creative interchange between the various structural levels of existence and the Creative Passage in its ultimate dimension. This is what gives to existence itself its depth and mystery along with its ambiguity and wonder, its communal character along with its indi-

3. Meland, *Faith and Culture*, p. 188.

viduated mode of awareness and being. No creature is singular or wholly individuated; yet none is assimilable without remainder to the communal life of culture, nature, or, for that matter, to the depth of the Creative Passage as expressed in the reality of God. Conversely, no communal history of concrete occurrences in concourse with the Creative Passage is assimilable wholly and without remainder to specific, concrete events that come into being and perish, certainly not as these are identified with specific clusters of fallible and perishable human beings.

The story of any culture is given only in part in the history of its people. And most histories, insofar as they record only the overt acts of men and women, their wars and their creative labors, the formal decisions of bodies invested with authority and power, and the artifacts that remain as inert, yet meaningful, pointers to the life of a people, tell only what can be gleaned from such visible counters of these historic remains. The depth of motivation, acts, and intentions, along with their persistent interweaving in the rise and fall of generations, provides, as it were, a persisting psychical structure of lived experience that has a way of leaping beyond the dissolution of specific artifacts, individuals, and periods of history to give to any cultural history in the long span of its duration a character and quality expressive through persisting and recurring patterns of meaning, sensibility, hopes, and expectations. These characteristics of the physical structure are what differentiate any one cultural history from cultural histories of a different complex of events and their historic shaping.

The mythos of the culture is this deeply persistent shaping of the culture's pattern of meaning and valuation that arises from within the structured experience of a people. It is conveyed or expressed in limited ways, to be sure, in what is imaginatively projected through drama and metaphor expressive of the judgments, valuations, and perceptive truths of the historical experience of a people. And these judgments, valuations, and perceptive truths are often but the sophisticated version of the culture's psychical energy, expressed more elementally in the form of hopes, expectations, attitudes of trust, or even determinations, or in the form of instinctive, human responses to events or circumstances, joyous or tragic, promising or threatening, fulfilling or defeating. Faith and fortitude, upheavals of dissent and despair, the release of latent powers in a burst of creative achievement—these are all expressive of this accumulative energy of the spirit as it finds outlet in individual or corporate acts.

Such energy of the Spirit in any culture is not to be measured solely by these overt expressions of hope and discontent, for the psychic force of a people works on more hiddenly as a legacy prescient of new life and power, or, conversely, of demonic zeal and destructiveness.

The mythos, then, is this persistent reservoir of psychical energy and sensitivity, laden with intentions and hopes of its own cultural shaping and expressive through the dynamics of individual creativity, or the interaction within communal groups.

In pairing together mythos and logos, and then differentiating them, I mean to suggest that they are inseparable categories of human experience and speak to divergent aspects of our human condition as well as of the stream of experience in which our lives are lived. Logos, in its initial usage in the West, particularly among the Greek philosophers and theologians, implied an ontological premise which, in turn, took on cosmological proportions and implications. That premise held to the inherent rationality of all existence and of the vast cosmos as a whole containing and sustaining man's existence. Moreover, it assumed that man, being a participant in the cosmic structure, participated in this inherent rationality with varying degrees of success and perfection, though deterrents to rational existence plagued man continuously because of his mode of existing, and the passional or sensory intrusions that obstructed or distorted his vision of himself in his ultimate being. This historic portrayal of an inherent rationality at the heart of things stubbornly persisted throughout Western thought though it has been resisted periodically in the name of a divinity beyond rationality, as we have said. The main thrust of the philosophical legacy of the West, however, stemming from Greek origins, has been to identify and to explicate this underlying logos of human existence including all of nature, and to lift it up as its ultimate source and cosmic end. Variations upon this theme appear in the writings of the Thomists, the Cambridge Platonists, and other Rationalists of the seventeenth century, and can be detected with modifications in modern forms of idealism, including personalism, and even in certain present-day cosmologies in which the sciences are made the informative source of its understanding.

This legacy of an inherent coherence persists in Whitehead, though with a perceptive distrust of making it controlling to the point of obscuring or diminishing or frustrating the role of form and of the orderly occurrences in nature. When this subtle break with the tradition of an inherent and persisting rationality is ignored or overlooked in Whitehead, the process mode of thought derived from his writings tends to revert to an all-out commitment to coherence as the underlying and ultimate principle of giving meaning to existence. When this occurs, process thought takes on rational overtones reminiscent of Hegelianism, against which the radical empiricism of James and Bergson protested so vehemently.

It is common to set the Judaic heritage over against this conception of a pervading logos at the heart of things, and to employ it as a fulcrum from which to counter the Greek theme of rationality. While a case for such a polemic can be made, it is somewhat distorting of the prevailing Judaic mode of understanding man and existence, for the law in later Judaism as in early Hebrew thought served as an ethical ordering of the life of man in much the same way that the logos of Greek thought and successive renderings of rationality in the West gave structure to existence. The differences in these two cultural orientations of thought and experience are marked indeed; but the contrast is exaggerated when it is made to imply commitment to form and structure in the one instance, and an indifference to form and structure in the other. The law in Judaism was more than a social institution; it was an underlying mode of rationality stemming from the covenant between man and God, thus providing the backdrop to man's ordered existence.

The contrast between the two modes of rationality is to be seen to stem from a difference in the orientation of the underlying structure. In the Greek, and its subsequent philosophical renderings in the West, it was clearly cosmological. In the Judaic heritage the orientation was unfailingly historical, set in the dramatic mode of the human encounter with the utterances of God through the prophets and seers among the people. This contrast in the orientations of structure in the Judaic and Greek heritage has set the stage for insisting theologically, especially in Protestant history, upon a distinction between understanding man's existence as a personal encounter with a transcendent Deity and man's life as an exemplification of cosmic rationality. What is distilled from this contrast is often that the Greek legacy, with its stress upon cosmic rationality, excludes what is basic to Christian faith, namely, the spontaneity of the Spirit in its communication with persons; hence it is assumed that a kind of determinism accompanies all philosophical formulations of the faith amounting to a denial of renascent and redemptive themes. While the law of Judaic history is seen by many Protestants to be antecedent to the redemptive theme of Christianity, and thus incomplete in and of itself, there are nevertheless possibilities of correlating law and gospel; whereas, with rationality as a given of ultimate reality, the traditional Protestant response in representative form has been quite otherwise. For, in that context, so it has been felt, determinism in overt or subtle form replaces the spontaneity of the work of the Spirit and subjects the individual witness of religious experience to subpersonal grounds of interpreting human existence.

The impasse between these two modes of formulating our religious legacy has been well nigh complete; hence it follows in theological circles that either one opts for commitment to the rationality of experience in the tradition of the Greek mode and Western philosophy, or one commits oneself to a nonrational view of the working of the Spirit as a spontaneous and structureless manifestation of the Spirit, expressive of a divinity transcending form and structure.

In stressing mythos along with logos, I mean to point to a modern corrective of this historic impasse between Spirit and rationality, spontaneity and form, by insisting that both spontaneity or creativity and form are native to this mystery of existing; that both aspects of concrete experience are indispensable, however antithetical they may seem to have been represented in Western thought. The degree or extent of rationality that is discernible in reality or existence, however, is itself a moot point in contemporary discussions. Yet, where the limitations of natural structures are critically observed, such assumption of rationality is frankly acknowledged to be a tool of thought, not a presupposition concerning the ultimate state of things. This tends to imply that rationality is a form which we tentatively bring to the flux of experience by way of wresting from such lived experience some distillation of meaning. Logos, in other words, in the newer context tends to be a conceptual approach to this lived reality, rather than a substantive explication of it.

It does not follow from this assumption that reality itself is structureless. That seems to have been implied in the Kantian *Critiques,* or at least inferred from them by theologians responsive to Kant. In empirical realism, at least, structure is somehow given in the reality experienced. The apprehension of that structure, however, is what presses for clarification. How may such discernment of structure be assured without incurring the risk of simply transmitting or imposing the forms of thought to the reality being experienced? One supposition is that theology and philosophy may have to be content with assuming an experimental attitude and may have to undertake inquiry in the tentative way that describes modern scientific method in its present mode, where Order is assumed not as a condition to describe or explicate in the nineteenth century sense of scientific method, but as a condition of inquiry taken on faith, as it were, by which realities are explored, and somehow experienced and employed for human ends.

Now mythos, being less conceptually oriented to reality, and closer to the feeling context of lived experience, tends to be expressive of what is deeper than, even elusive of, the conceptual grasp of reality as lived.

The outcome of this present-day tendency to ascribe to rationality a tentativeness appropriate to conceptualization, and to see in lived experience a depth of reality that exceeds and often eludes such conceptualization, is to call in question all presuppositions of an underlying coherence as a given of reality which may answer to our studied and carefully devised formulations. Coherence as such is not denied, or ignored; but it is sought in a context of inquiry in which acknowledgment is made of a self-evident condition of dissonance between what man's own structure of experience can report and affirm and what may in fact be true of existence as a total phenomenal fact, or as ultimate reality.

In this redefined estimate of our human experience within the cosmic situation, mythos and logos appear to be indispensable to each other, expressing both the depth of experience exceeding and eluding the conceptual grasp of events and the occasions of an intelligible grasp of experience accomplished within the limited powers of our structured existence. For this reason, neither are expendable; nor are they readily correlated in any easy reconciliation of this seemingly irreconcilable situation of dissonance and coherence.

The word mythos, then, is not to be equated with myth or with mythology, though obviously it is related to the mode of response that has given rise to both in various cultures during the early periods of their history. I am inclined to associate myth with mythos more readily than mythology for myth tends to represent elemental and, one might say, spontaneous and innocent responses to what is deeply at work in the life of a people. Myth is thus an elemental ingredient of the mythos, though less durable and pervasive in the culture as a whole. Mythology, on the other hand, I have come to see as a secondary level of imaginative reflection within the mythical mode which often carries with it certain didactic and speculative intentions. When Hegel, for example, put forth metaphysics as the sophisticated alternative to myth, he was really intending by myth what I have described as mythology—a more didactic and speculative reflection upon the poetry of myth.

By mythos I mean something more than a particular mode of reflectiveness or poetry. The mythos encompasses these responses, but it includes them along with other more visceral and imaginative assertions of the psychical thrust of a people, fashioning them into a structured reality within experiences in a given cultural history, and carrying them forward as a subliminal depth of perception and feeling within the lived experience, shaping the sensibilities, apprehensions, expectations, intentions, and valuations of a people. Insofar as it is expressed at the conscious level, it may be said to surface in the mode of an appreciative awareness or an appreciative consciousness, for the latter represents the conscious life of man responding out of the depth of its relationships in contrast to the kind of critical or observational reason that is selective and sharply focused for definitive, even practical ends.

It has been suggested that what I am describing here approaches what the psychologist Carl Jung designated "the collective unconscious." I have not been conversant enough with Jung to evaluate this observation, and have not drawn upon his thought in developing the notion of mythos. It may be helpful to some, however, as John Spencer has observed, to relate the two notions by way of getting a preliminary grasp on what is here being presented. Professor Tillich's familiar phrases "gestalts of feeling" and "gestalts of grace," speaking within the idiom of Gestalt psychology, similarly, is suggestive of what is being intended here. Neither of these terms, however, gathers in all that I mean to convey by the word mythos, for I am speaking not only of the unconscious mind, or any other psychological construct, but of a structure of experience within the *gestalts* of any given cultural history. Thus the notion of mythos partakes of the stream of experience as well as of the stream of thought. And it gathers in as well inert, though symbolically significant, precedents and practices which body forth, as it were, what the phenomenologists call the *intentionality* of a people.

Ideas that are basic to the notion of mythos as I use the term are James's notion that "relations are experienceable, and are experienced" and Whitehead's notion of causal efficacy, both of which are intended as a kind of corrective of Hume's insistence that relations are conceptual constructs of the mind attributed to concrete events, but which, in fact, have no empirical reality. Both James and Whitehead were putting forth an organismic mode of empiricism in contrast to the Humean empiricism of the seventeenth century. I concur with James and Whitehead in this respect, and use their notions to elaborate upon the structure of lived experience within the cultural history of any people.

It may be helpful, then, in concluding this discussion of mythos and logos to point out that the term "mythos," which I tend to equate with the structure of faith in relation to the structure of experience, emerged in my own thinking out of the confluence of insights from cultural anthropology and the ontological notions of radical empiricism. For me it conveys the psychic and feeling thrust of a people in the way that logos is expressive of an underlying and persistent rationality. Cultural anthropology looks upon culture as being a specific kind of emergent within natural structures, giving rise to various configurations of human growth (cf. Kroeber and Clyde Kluckhohn, *Culture*). Radical empiricism sees the *stream of experience* within any society or individual lifespan forming an internal intention or track of meaning, contributing to a proneness to act in accordance with what has been habitually found rewarding empirically as a resolution of felt tensions, judgments, and demands. What is important to derive from these sources is the notion of an internal structuring or shaping of experience that goes on at considerable depth in a people, much of which remains subliminal as lived experience—history that is lived, though not necessarily thought, but which nevertheless carries weight and formative power in shaping the life history and spiritual outreach of a people. If one is not sensitive to this deeper shaping of human thought and experience, or is impatient with its claims upon conscious experience, preferring rather to confine critical attention to the more manageable, conceptual level of any religious history, the route of inquiry indicated here in coming to theological judgments will be of little interest. It may, in fact, be unavailable.

It may be pertinent to counter at this point the assumption that what is pursued here as religious inquiry into the internal shaping of a cultural experience is but a variation upon mysticism, since the concern of mysticism also is with the internal ordering of experience and reflection, as contrasted with overt, rational thought. In responding to such an assumption, I would point out that mysticism is essentially a disavowal of the conceptual mode of religious expression as being wholly external, and thus dissipating what is internally apprehended or perceived. In the mode of thought I mean to convey in appealing to the mythos, the concern for intelligibility in faith remains central; yet the kind of intelligibility that is sought is one that coheres with the internal ordering of experience which inheres and periodically erupts in experience as a vital immediacy too full for thought. This sense of the fullness of being and existing is itself a datum of reflection that is not to be lost to our conceptualizations. This means that thought which is appropriate and proportionate to lived experience must be content with marginal glimpses of cognitive meaning and periodic resolutions of tensions in thought and experience.

Intelligibility within this context, following within the radical empirical mode, implies a fringed event; that is, an occurrence of knowing that sees the intelligible focus of meaning within a context of unfocused, yet intimately associated, experience. Intelligibility is marginal to the vast fringe of existing meaning, just as the fringe of consciousness will always appear marginal to what is clearly in focus. This is a basic presupposition of empiricism when it partakes of a radical, realistic ontology and epistemology. This means that knowing always occurs within a context of unknowing; but the knowing, however marginal, is a crucial occurrence. It is what provides anchorage to conscious experience, and precludes a mindless immersion in the stream of experience, or a reveling in the fantasies of feeling.

On the other hand, when the act of knowing is unmindful of this context of unknowing—this fringe that is not brought into focus—it tends to lose sight of the marginal character of all conscious experience. Being unmindful of or indifferent toward the marginal character of experience, one then tends to inflate the vision of the mind to encompass the whole of experience on the assumption that a generalization of this empirical aperture of meaning yields total knowledge. To the radical empiricist, this abstract, or abstract generalization, is always undertaken at great risk, and more than likely issues in dubious results.

Taking the concrete context seriously in the act of knowing impels one, then, to be apprehensive, both about being excessively mystifying to the point of internalizing all knowing, and about being unrestrainedly intellectualizing, externalizing all knowing. Such an effort requires a

particular kind of precision in addressing oneself to events or occurrences. The precision employed here is in the assessment of the knowing
experience and in the care with which intelligible notions are established
for usage. When an idea or notion is so established, it is on the basis of
having assured oneself that there is an empirical anchorage for it, that
it brings into sharpened focus an area of concrete experience that gives
gold backing, as it were, to the verbal currency employed.

To return, then, to the deeper shaping of thought and experience to
which we have applied the term mythos, it is important to note that a
careful reading of any cultural history will reveal several varying *gestalts,*
as it were, some of them actually contending against one another. And
increasingly, as cultures mature, a pluralism of persistent modes of intentionality tend to appear. Yet, even in a pluralistic society, this variation
within the cultural mythos tends to give rise to some central thrust of
the prevailing intentionality of a people in a way that identifies the culture
in basically historical respects with one historic sequence of valuations,
against which, or in terms of which, rival religious histories contend.
Thus, in India, it is clearly the Hindu mythos that prevails, though not
without serious conflict and interchange with Moslem, Buddhist, Christian, and other mythical modes. Similarly in other areas of Southeast
Asia and the Far East, and the Middle East, some one mythos tends to
be dominant amidst rival modes: Buddhism in Burma, Thailand, and
Japan; Islam in Pakistan and the Middle East. In the West, as
Easterners and Near Easterners look upon Europe and America, the
Judaic-Christian mythos is in dominance, though enough dissociation
from its prevailing mode of valuation and meaning within the cultural
experience persists to justify speaking of the West as being pluralistic.
In recent years, with the rise of the sciences and the accompanying
developments in technology, secularization as an aggressive and creative
force appears to be on the rise, if not actually in dominance, in the West.

The issue here is not so readily resolved as many would seem to
assume; for when the issue is discussed, it is generally with overt, conceptual meanings and acts that are brought into focus. What is persistently ignored is that the stream of experience among any people
carries much more in the way of formative influences, if only as a
reservoir of potential meaning, than is ever brought into focus in any
given period of history. The range of historical experience in focus in
any one generation is shockingly slight. Often what is vividly and

aggressively to the fore as a wave of protest or cultural resistance is meager in historical sensibilities. Yet the very upheaval following from such protest and resistance may prove to be a means of awakening or reactivating a vast portion of inherited sensibilities to give to the people in protest power and effectiveness within their time beyond their own awareness of the meaning of their acts. It may also, however, be rendered stillborn by its very indifference to what is persistent in the structure of experience. The import of this structural continuity as a persisting dimension of the lived experience, attending and to a degree shaping every instance of historical experience within any culture, may not be denied. And this is what is meant to be conveyed in the notion of mythos.

Part Three

Chapter Nine

# Directives
# for Theological Method

On the basis of explorations in previous chapters, I wish now to suggest some directives for theological method within the perspective of process thought as modified by an empirical realism. Since the mode of inquiry is that of constructive theology, as contrasted with the systematic study of doctrine or dogmatics, the concern in focus is that of attending the problem of faith within the contemporary culture and within the lived experiences of people as they participate simultaneously in the culture and in the legacy of faith that persists within these experiences. So described, the method of constructive theology has often been characterized as one that begins with an analysis of culture as a way of getting at the primal witness of faith. This characterization, while it points up an important aspect of the procedure I find necessary to pursue, does not express the method adequately. At best, the analysis of culture in this procedure can be but one strand of the inquiry. Nevertheless, it must be acknowledged that the method of constructive theology pursued within the perspective of empirical realism takes the immediacies of experience seriously as bearing depths of reality expressive simultaneously of an historical stream and of an ontological present, to which response and interpretation must be given. For that reason, what is undertaken in this context is of necessity a theology of culture even as it explores dimensions of the witness of faith which relate to the historical legacy transmitted through the church and to the accumulative thrust of the mythos.

## I

All human existence takes place within a particularized orbit of meaning. An orbit of meaning is determined by the cultural history of a specific people. Interchanges with alien and rival orbits occur from time to time; hence syncretization and secularization are intermittently present. Yet, historically speaking, initial, primordial drives within a culture achieve sufficient focus, in the form of sensibilities, modes of awareness, and reflection, to generate both a characteristic mind-set and a persistent thrust of the psyche. One has only to look around or to move about among the various well-defined culture-groups of East and West to get some intimation of this historical development. The human response, therefore, is hedged about by two kinds of limitations: (1) the limitation of finitude, of creatureliness that applies to all men; (2) the limitation of the cultural orbit of meaning which prepares the human mind and psyche within a given area of human association to receive and to react to occurrences in specific and characteristic ways.

The tendency of every people is to employ the terms of their orbit of meaning universally, i.e., to speak for every man. The effect of this tendency has been to impel each cultural faith to conceive of its faith and perspective as being singularly significant, if not absolute, and thus to resist alien forms of religious witness. A first step, as a prologomenon to theological method, is thus to attain self-understanding as a participant in a culturally conditioned faith, and to acknowledge as well as to accept the limitations of its historical witness.

The assumption that the cultural conditioning of faith in the case of Christian faith can be circumscribed, or transcended, cannot, in my judgment, be critically sustained. Any effort to dissociate Christian faith from the historical complex of influences or shaping noted in other religious histories by cultural anthropologists and historians of religion can only be characterized as a judgment prompted by confessional bias, and can have no status as a disciplined observation. What can be sustained is an insistence that the witness of faith, as it is faithfully and expertly pursued within the cultus, achieves in some instances a refinement of insight which can provide a cutting edge in conveying or interpreting the historic legacy. It has also happened that such specialized concern with the Judaic-Christian legacy has had the effect of simply narrowing the intent or the import of the faith, restricting its meaning to doctrinal terms that have served more to support the cultic claims of the institutional church than to impart or to interpret the realities of faith inhering within the lived experiences of a people in any given period of its history.

A second step, however, is to take adequate measure of the relative situation in which each cultural witness stands. Empirical realism as a metaphysical interpretation of human existence lifts up the simultaneous presence of an ultimate dimension of reality and the humanly available immediacies *within the stream of existence.* Life for every man is thus seen to be ambiguous: expressive of our human capacities and limitations, yet at the same time borne forth by, and in its momentary passage bearing forth, an ultimate depth of reality. In this respect, no cultural witness, however limited, is devoid of an ultimate reference which simultaneously speaks forth and stands in judgment of the articulate cultural witness. For this reason cultural relativity does not imply sheer religious pluralism. Each bears some relevance to the truth of actuality, though its witness is partial and limited.

A third step is to get an adequate understanding of the phenomenon of myth in any culture, and of the mythos that shapes its orbit of meaning. Myth is the elemental response of a people to what is ever present as an ultimate demand and measure upon human existence (sense of destiny, *sensus numinis,* idea of the holy, ultimate concern, etc.). However transitory specific myths may be, or the mythologies that arise as explications of what is discerned or apprehended in myth, the shaping of the human psyche by the mythical response, generating sensibilities, modes of apprehension, expectations and their consequent reflections, is more enduring. Thus the outgrowing of specifically formulated myths and mythologies does not imply necessarily a relinquishment of the mythos, which is the deep-lying orbit of meaning, giving structure and direction, both at the level of the human psyche and within the realm of imaginative and cognitive experience. Insofar as a people remain elemental in some respect, which is simply to be responsive to what is ultimate in man's existence, they participate in this deep-lying mythos of the culture. But even in becoming sophisticated to an extent, which often impels them to disavow or to ignore this elemental response, they will not wholly relinquish the mythos; for their disavowals, and possibly their alternative, secular affirmations, will partake of or be defined against (and thus to some extent defined in terms of) what has once been elementally embraced. The reasons for this persistence of the mythical forms of sensibility and cognition are subtle and devious, for they have to do with the shaping of the human psyche at a subconscious level, both individually and collectively. Simply dealing with the problem at the level of conscious meaning will not reach the formative influence of *lived experiences,* or of history as it has been lived.

A fourth step is to take note of the various forms of participation in the mythos within any culture. These forms are not always differentiated, nor have they always been so in our Western experience. Looking at the situation in more recent history we would recognize at least three fairly distinct forms: (1) the cultus, (2) individual experience, and (3) the wider, so-called secular domain of experience within the culture. These three forms of participation overlap, even intermesh; yet one can detect boundaries between them at certain points and in certain respects. The fact that there are issues between individual Christians and the faith of the church, for example, or between the church and society, not to speak of tensions between individuals and society on the grounds of conscience or belief, is evidence of the differentiation of which we speak. This degree of differentiation has not always been present in Western culture. For in its earliest history, Western and Middle Eastern life did not acknowledge individuality in the modern sense of that term. Personality meant "corporate personality"—the corporate mind and sensibility speaking through persons. Individuality, understood as a person dissociated from or differentiated from the group mind and its sanctions, was an abnormality not to be recognized or tolerated. Similarly, one can find instances when the cultus and the culture were conceived as being one and the same. This was interrupted by events centering around the history of Israel which were to continue through the early years of Christian history. Medieval Roman Catholicism was an effort to reestablish a church-controlled culture and a conforming mind among its believers. Protestantism created a breach in this pattern of conformity, though with initial qualifications, as expressed in the rise of the nationally established churches. The Separatist movement marked the completion of the breach, issuing in clear demarcations between individual believer and the tradition of church and the state. Liberalism implied an elevation of individual experience and a redefinition of theological norms in terms of the appeal to religious experience. A consensus could be tolerated in this context, but not conformity. So much, then, for these three forms of participation. I shall have occasion to speak further of them as vortices of revelation when we come to a more specific statement of methodology.

II

The critical problem arising from a reaction against liberal theology has been the repossession of the communal context of faith and inquiry and a reassessment of the relation between the individual experience of faith and the communal witness of an institutionalized faith, the church. By way of cutting through the interminable discussion that could ensue, were this age-old tension in Protestantism between individual believer and the faith of the church to come under review, contemporary theologians have defined themselves against both modernism and orthodoxy, seeking to engage theological thinking afresh in the live encounter with revelatory experience in which "God addresses man" (Barth, Brunner), or "grasps man and turns him about" (Tillich), or "transforms man as he cannot transform himself" (Wieman). Insofar as these theologians conceived of their theologies as being something other than a relapse into fundamentalism or a return to some form of orthodoxy in defiance of modern culture, they were clearly drawing upon the resources of intelligibility made available through innovations in the imagery of disciplined thought. And they did so whether their statement of method acknowledged this to be so or not.

The point at which contemporary theologians appear to have exercised an unwarranted tour de force is in their appeal to Scripture or to biblical faith. On examination one will find more explicit justification of this procedure than is commonly acknowledged. Again, this implies making use of the general consensus among contemporary disciplines concerning modes of thought relating to depths of reality which can be approached only symbolically or by way of an internal track of meaning within experience that is lived. Kierkegaard gave some intimation of this procedure in speaking of the truth of subjectivity. James and Bergson made the distinction between "knowledge about and knowledge of" a primary emphasis in their radical empiricism. In Bergson this internal track of knowing was given the value of intuition and was interpreted as such. The philosophy of phenomenology has provided an alternative justification, taking the effects in phenomena as visible signs of realities which can reach us only in this symbolic way. Here the epistemological question which had long haunted philosophical and theological inquiry is circumvented by relinquishing the concern with literal meaning and settling for holding this ultimate reference in focus by recourse to a symbolic discourse.

It is immediately recognized that contemporary theologians have availed themselves of both resources with varying degrees of emphasis in coming to a solution of their methodological problem regarding the use of Scripture in theology. All of them, we might say, have acknowledged the mytho-poetical character of biblical statements, though, contrary to customary interpretations in orthodox circles, they have represented biblical myths as having significance only as signs attesting to depths of meaning in human existence. All historical or temporal reference in such notions as creation, the fall, sin, and redemption, has been dis-avowed. In this respect, the "truth in myth" is considered to be wholly intuitional (as in the Niebuhrs), or phenomenological (Barth, Brunner, Tillich, et al.), pointing beyond itself to what is ultimate in the immediacies of existence.

The appeal to Scripture thus rests back upon a repossession of the language of myth together with a reconception of myth in terms familiar either to radical empiricism or to phenomenology. But this explains only *how* the Bible is to be used in theology. There still remains some unfinished business in this appeal to Scripture. Even after one has justified a way of using the language of biblical myth, the question still persists, why turn to the Bible in this present age? What is there about the Bible or any ancient myth that impels one to be concerned with it as a modern person in modern times? I do not see that any of the major theologians of our time adequately answered that question. Simply to say that it is "the source of the Word of God," or "the primary document upon which the church rests" (assuming this to be true), is not enough to justify the appeal to Scripture within the modern ethos, unless, of course, one conceives of theology solely as a cultic discipline.

This is where some of the bugs in this theological business begin to crawl into view. On the one hand, some will insist upon conceiving of theology as being a discipline of the church, answerable only to the demands of its witness, and, on the other hand, they will defend theology's right to be conceived of as a university discipline—as a science along with other sciences, though in some respects a distinctive science. One cannot have it both ways. Either theology is a cultic discipline, applicable only to what pertains to the internal demands of the church, or it is a cultural discipline along with being a cultic concern. It represents a way of understanding the culture as well as the cultus. And it does so because it sees the culture as having organic relations with the concerns of the cultus. In short, the mythos that has remained in focus in the cultus is persistent, however obscured or ignored, within the cultural fabric of meaning; in historic ways it can be seen to have shaped the orbit of meaning within which the present cultural discourse moves and has its being.

Our analysis has now come full circle: we have now come back to the point with which we started, namely, that all human existence takes place within a particularized orbit of meaning. One is made aware within our culture that the Bible is the repository of the very root-metaphors which have given rise to concrete and relational notions that have gone into the forming of our Western and Middle Eastern orbit of meaning. It is therefore more than a primary document of the church; it is the primal document of the culture as well, however remote from it our present discourse may appear, or our present mores and sensibilities may in fact be. Becoming aware of this fact contributes something of importance to all contemporary theologies based on a repossession of the appeal to Scripture as a mytho-poetic witness.

When the appeal to Scripture is made on these grounds, it is made consonant with the method implied in justifying the concern with revelatory experience. In both instances, acknowledgment is made that the sensibilities of thought as well as the imagery of thought made available by contemporary refinements in human inquiry have opened our eyes to depths of meaning in human existence, thereby enabling us to take some account of the mystery that has cradled us and which presently envelops and sustains us. And this raises the question as to how the witness of faith can be more than a mythical response. I do not say *whether* it should be more than myth, for I am persuaded that modern man cannot live by myth alone. His conscious mind is too sharply differentiated, as was true of earlier Christian thinkers in the history of our culture; hence what is addressed to him as a Word beyond his own human words and meanings will either ride over him as being meaninglessly remote, or it will plague him as a thorn until he comes to terms with it within his own intelligible discourse. This is the problem to which we now turn.

## III

The fact that contemporary theology rests precariously upon a repossession and reconception of myth has led some of our colleagues to challenge any appeal to the biblical witness that has not first addressed itself to the dilemma in which this appeal to myth involves the theologian in modern times. For some, as we know, there is no way out short of demythologizing the New Testament. Without going into the intricacies of that issue, we may note that the end result of this proposal is to move beyond mythical language to analogical statements within a contemporary idiom with a view to setting forth in intelligible and logically defensible terms the redemptive word to which the biblical witness of faith attests.[1] Here we come upon the problem of how we may employ our reason in addressing ourselves to ultimate dimensions of reality. The question as to how reason is to be understood is crucial here; hence, some clarification on this point is indicated.

Reason is not one thing among other things, one faculty or organ among others; rather, it is the total organism acting in a specific way under certain conditions, that is, with a specific focus, following from being attentive to something, in response to something, or intent upon something. Reason is the human organism when it is luminous with thought and inquiry. And the human organism is that kind of structure that can fluctuate between a highly attentive state in which, as we say, reason is alert and active, and a near indolent state in which consciousness appears barely to exist. But one is not to assume that reason is active only in this highly attentive state of the organism; for to the degree that selected impressions have been reflected upon, assimilated and judged, they tend to be stored away, as it were, kept dormant, but ready to be activated internally as a memory recalled, or as an internal stimulus to further reflection. Thus what appears to be indolence is often either reverie or a vibrant internalizing of thought, sustained by this inner stimulus of recall and its reflective response.

1. Cf. Rudolf Bultmann, *Theology of the New Testament* (New York: Charles Scribner's Sons, 1952); H. W. Bartsch, ed., *Kerygma and Myth* (New York: Harper Torchbooks, 1961); John Macquarrie, *The Scope of Demythologizing* (New York: Harper and Row, 1961); Schubert Ogden, *Christ without Myth* (New York: Harper and Row, 1961).

This understanding of reason rests back upon what is understood to be the limitation of creatureliness as it applies to man. Our limitations of creatureliness can be defined more precisely as the structure of organic existence characteristic and defining of the human being. The human organism, which forms the organic base of personality, stands high in the sequence of organic development commonly spoken of as the growth of natural structures. One may not assume, however, that this human structure is definitive of reality beyond its own level of emergence, or even indicative of what is ultimate. The practice of employing human personality or the human body pictorially or analogically for extending the range of existence is understandable as a mytho-poetic way of speaking or thinking. However, to the extent to which it presumes to be a serious undertaking in logical construction, it becomes a dubious venture. For then what is metaphorically imagined is given the weight of literal meaning, and the literal and imaginative elements then become so intermingled as to produce a new mythology. The fact that one does not acknowledge this effort to be mythological makes it all the more dubious, for one then assumes that one is really speaking logically in every respect, when as a matter of fact, one is simply marshaling an intricate system of logical arguments behind a mytho-poetic assumption. The enterprise as a whole rests upon a mythical apprehension.

Now the response to mythical awareness is legitimate when it becomes a way of expressing wonder, apprehension, gratitude, praise, or even anxiety before the mystery that holds us in existence. This is the elemental response in man that is always appropriate, if not imperative. And it is quite possible that, given man's structural limitations, he cannot respond in any way other than that which employs terms analogous to his own world of experience and meaning. But whenever the response takes on the semblance of literal understanding, fortified by meticulous logical argument, it becomes illegitimate as religious or theological speech precisely on the grounds that it is no longer simply pointing or reaching toward realities that form the depths of existence, but is presuming to define, describe, or characterize them in logical terms. This is patently to overreach the human structure of conscious existence, and thus to impress upon these realities the restrictive image of this limited human structure.

Apart from being an illegitimate extension of the human structure, this kind of procedure tends to preclude the possibility of a more sensitive encounter with realities at the edge of our being and instead to enclose our understanding within the recognizable bounds of our own structure of meaning.

It has seemed to me that the ventures in theological method presently being pursued, both within the perspective of existentialist philosophies and of process thought, must come to terms with this kind of critique of analogical thinking. What Professor Ian Ramsey[2] has said concerning both scientific and religious language applies even more forcibly to theological language, namely, that they can no longer justify employing "picture models" in any form of inquiry bearing upon ultimate issues or concerns. What alone are available are what he calls "disclosure models," models which presuppose a distance between humanly formed notions or analogies and the realities toward which inquiry is being directed. In this mode of address, the terms familiarly in use, when applied in theological inquiry, or in the making of theological statements, are not made defining or descriptive in any categorical or doctrinal sense, but they are simply suggestive in an explorative effort to find a way in which the reality apprehended can be thought about or made marginally intelligible within our commonly accepted disciplined discourse.

Maintaining a sense of distance between imagery and reality in the use of disclosure models can be accomplished far more readily when one is employing such models simply to demonstrate the fact that religious language already in use is meaningful, as Ramsey does; he works mainly with the language of the Prayer Book. When, however, one presumes to use such a model, calling it an analogy, to see what a biblical or theological assertion does in fact mean as a normative statement, such as the statement, "God was in Christ," or "God acted in history," the tendency to assign definitive meaning to analogical statements, and thus to close the gap between imagery and reality, is inescapable. Likewise, to attribute to what is distilled from the philosophical framework definitive truth concerning the infinite structure amounts to specifying the structure of reality which again is to close the distance between imagery and reality. The framework and what issues from it in the way of a model are clearly a human formulation having the value only of a venture in intelligibility. The truth is not given by the framework. The

2. Ian Ramsey, *Religious Language* (London: SCM Press, 1957); and *Models and Mystery* (London: Oxford University Press, 1964).

truth is a truth of actuality (revelation), received from the witness of faith, or out of the depths of experience. Presumably one can live in the truth of this event, be transformed or shaped by it, yet have no vivid glimpse or grasp of its structure or meaning. One may, on the other hand, bring the resources of the mind to bear to some extent upon this witness of faith or upon the experience of judgment, confronting the act or event with an analogy out of the humanly formed framework, in which case, a margin of intelligibility may ensue. The concurrence of the act and the illumination of the analogy may thereby be sufficient to commend the truth of this actuality to the mind's vision. And in this way, the mind, with this margin of intelligibility at hand, can affirm what faith and experience have conveyed as a lived and living truth.

Attaining intelligibility in our thoughts of this work of grace and judgment is not to be equated with seizing upon the truth of this reality in the sense of assimilating it completely (without remainder) to a philosophical framework. It is more a matter of momentary recognition that alleviates "the mind's allegiance to despair" as it strains to conceive beyond its bounds. It is an effort, summoning our perceptions to a vision of the mind that can serve to illumine the context in which this mystery occurs, such that we can receive and respond to its visitation, or, to speak more properly, to the depth of its occurrence. Thought so employed is instrumental to effecting a human response to what is given as a depth of reality beyond our own structure and form, in a spirit of waiting and wonder anticipating the more that may be apprehended or given as awareness deepens, and is made sensitive, or as the fullness of disclosure can become available to our structured existence.

There is more involved here than assessment of the powers of reason in relation to faith; it implies also an assessment of the mythical response which expresses itself through the act of faith. Since so much of the discussion of faith and reason has taken place in the context of conscious experience, resulting no doubt from the dominance of idealism, faith has been given the meaning simply of a subjective response, or inner experience. Thus, in contrast to the more public and verifiable exchange at the level of reason, the report of faith has seemed unreliable and dubious. In associating the act of faith with the mythical response, I mean to break away from this subjective connotation and to represent it as a holistic response to this depth of reality in experience which is not readily available to conscious scrutiny, yet ever-present and efficacious in experience as it is lived. Faith as mythical response is more elemental than reason, not in the sense merely that it is less critical, less sophisticated; but in the sense that it is more basic in its creatural integration with this depth of reality, more innocently responsive to what is unmanageable and commanding in the exigencies of existence. Reason offers each individual person freedom, independence, and an assertiveness expressive of one's individuated existence. Left to itself it can be divisive and alienating; but when it is responsive and integrative with faith, it can be illuminating. It can be emancipating without dissipating this elemental response to the depth of experience.

IV

I should like now to consider more specifically how the theologian may appropriately employ philosophy in pursuing his task. One's view on this matter may determine other matters bearing upon theological method.

As a preliminary observation, I would say that a theologian, insofar as he is a disciplined mind, will exemplify a critical handling of his material without necessarily calling attention to, or even being self-conscious about, the specific aspects or bases of his critical procedure. In this respect I would argue for some indifference toward what shapes one's intellectual bent of mind in theological inquiry *at the time one is engaging in it*. This is not to say that one will be indifferent to the problem as to what makes for disciplined theological inquiry. I am speaking here solely of the creative or constructive effort in expressing theological judgments or in venturing interpretations. Here all that has previously entered into one's experience and preparation is suffused into a sharply focused act of attentive inquiry and reflection to yield disciplined decisions. At the moment of inquiry and decison, for better or worse, we are what we are as a holistic being as a result of what we have been becoming. Furthermore, during the act of theologizing, one's disciplined effort in thought in this creative or constructive act cannot readily be reduced to a simple ideology or a particular school of thought. Usually it is a very subtle blend of many disciplining influences, ranging from humanistic studies, including philosophy and literature, to various kinds of sciences. The act of disciplined thinking in theology is thus like the matured effort of a disciplined artist: it has been chastened and perfected through technical study; yet, in the performance itself, technique does not protrude. It subtly, yet faithfully, serves the theologian, as it does the musician, the artist, in carrying forward his disciplined act of inquiry.

On examination, following his effort at theologizing, a theologian should be able to be self-conscious to some extent about what has entered into his critical decisions and formulation, and be able to state his basic presuppositions; but he may not be fully aware of all that has given discipline and authority to his mode of speaking.

But now we move to a further aspect of the problem; and here I go beyond the kerygmatic theologian to affirm some degree of conscious effort in bringing intelligibility to theological statements. Yet I would want to do so in a way that stops short of translating mythical apprehensions or statements of faith into explicit metaphysical or ontological propositions. What I understand theologians to be doing when they propose translating myth into ontological statements "without remainder," strikes me as being an overreaching of the philosophical concern in theology. What is permissible, as I see it, over and above the implicit use, say, of process or phenomenological thought integral to one's disciplined act of theologizing, is to employ selected ways of speaking derived from such modes of thinking, or suggestive notions consonant with their imagery by way of suggesting how a mythical symbol of apprehension could be made understandable within a contemporary idiom of thought. This is to introduce a margin of intelligibility into one's theological explication without seeming to enclose all meaning attested to in the witness of faith within a philosophical framework. The philosophical vision is thus made to illumine the witness of faith and its theological explication. Neither the witness of faith nor the theological explication is reduced "without remainder" to the philosophical notion itself, or to the philosophical system.

To illustrate what I mean, I would say that it is helpful within the process idiom to employ the notion of emergence by way of understanding what it means to have an innovating mystery break forth from a given structure of existence. But I would regard it as an act of overreaching simply to equate "revelation" with "emergence." In the one instance one is availing oneself of a helpful image within an intelligible discourse to grasp at a mystery that evades one's discourse. In the other instance one would be incorporating the mystery into the accepted framework of meaning and thus reducing it to an intelligible notion "without remainder."

To the question How may one employ a philosophical framework in the theological task?, I would argue along this line: A theologian must distinguish between having his own theological thinking shaped by a particular philosophical system, and the act of assimilating or accommodating every theological statement or statement of faith to that system. A philosophical system is a rigorous and comprehensive characterization of the whole of reality as the human mind can envision it within the laws of thought formally accepted within this sphere of thinking. Its principles of logic designate the rules of responsible reflection within the human frame of meaning. It is avowedly a look at the world as a disciplined human mind can envision it. Now if the limitations of creatureliness or of the human structure are ignored, one will assume that what the human mind thus envisions can be taken to be reality as it really is. Any misgiving about the disparity between reality and our human vision, however disciplined, will open the way for acknowledging some distance between what the mind envisions and what really is. On this basis, process philosophy, in speaking of its own basic notions as metaphors, has intended to be faithful to this acknowledgment. At the base of its system, therefore, there is the recognition of a distance between imagery and reality.

Now it is possible that the process theologian may assume that, because there is this acknowledgment at the base of process metaphysics, he is free to assimilate theological statements and statements of faith to this framework without committing any misrepresentation of the witness of faith, or the ultimate reality to which it points. However, even if this practice were legitimate, it is made such a cumbersome procedure that the sensibility of thought necessary to maintain this distance between imagery and reality is dissipated. For in order not to misrepresent the theological explication on the metaphysical level as saying more than one intends to say, the philosophical theologian would have to remind himself and his listeners periodically with the caution, "Understand, I am speaking analogically, not logically in a literal sense." The fact that this procedure is cumbersome means that the process thinker tends to fall into the habit of assuming that what he expresses at this ontological level is, in fact, not only intelligible but true in a definitive and adequate sense of that term. And because of the seductive nature of this habit of mind, one will soon speak theologically within this framework as if the framework itself were normative of meaning for ultimate reality itself. This is indicated by the readiness with which the process theologian will repeat the metaphysical dictum, "God is not an exception to the metaphysical principles, but their exemplification." Now I would say that this statement is appropriate as a philosophical statement, for presumably the process philosopher is aware of the fact that he is speaking within a human framework, and means to give only a full report of reality as it looks from within this rigorously defined human perspective.

To say in this context that God is no exception to the principles, but their exemplification, means that insofar as one attempts to speak of God philosophically within the human framework he must be faithful to the limitations which that framework imposes. The statement appropriately put, then, should read: "Philosophically speaking, we can say no more than that concerning our understanding of the notion of 'God.' " To be sure, the philosopher, in falling into the habit of taking his principles as being more than analogical, may himself imply by this assertion that there is in fact nothing more one may say of God; in which case the human formulation is made normative of the ultimate reality. And this is what I have called overreaching, whether it occurs within philosophical speech or within theological speech.

However, one who is sensitive to the limits of the human structure, and therefore the limitations of human reason, will be content to view this work of reason as a vision of the mind which may be tentatively and experimentally employed, say as a model of disclosure or in any case as a defensible way of speaking intelligibly within the limits of this human structure. The degree of congruence between this vision of the mind and reality remains at best a hypothesis or a venture of hope. In this approach to reality, the metaphysician will be exhibiting the same degree of reticence and sensibility in the use of his formulations that the relativity physicist displays in his use of mathematical formulae. I have understood Whitehead to have philosophized in this manner. In this context, to say that God is not an exception to the principles, but their exemplification, should be taken to imply not a definitive and exclusive statement concerning the reality to God, but a caution as to what one is entitled to say definitively when one presumes to be speaking within this humanly formulated vision of reality. Were it to imply anything more, particularly if it were to mean that God is declared to be nothing more than the principles express him to be, the language of philosophy would not be analogical, but literal, definitive, and thus exclusive of any judgment beyond this rational formulation.

Theology can be served helpfully and imaginatively by an appeal to philosophy, then, only if this distinction between ways of speaking is observed. What I am implying, of course, is that when one speaks as a philosopher, one is speaking rigorously within the accepted limits of a categorical system. A theologian, by reason of the fact that, admittedly, he undertakes a less manageable task, namely, that of attending to the witness of faith and bringing to it the refinement of critical and disciplined thinking, must assume a more difficult and precarious stance with regard to the disclosure of meaning. When, as a theologian, one employs a philosophical notion for tentatively offering some possible meaning to the mystery to which the act of faith bears witness, one is borrowing reflected light from this framework of intelligible discourse. The model so employed reflects meaning from the system only indirectly. It insinuates meaning. It suggests what this reality could mean, not what it does in fact mean. Even after this philosophical notion has been brought into the service of the theological task one continues to look at this depth of meaning as through a glass darkly, yet with a margin of transparency; enough at least to enable one to receive this mystery at a minimum level of intelligibility. And this may be enough to let the mind be efficaciously addressed by, or be related to, this depth of meaning.

To be sure, there will be more than insinuation of meaning taking place in such an employment of philosophical notions. The philosophers we are will unwittingly say more philosophically through our theological interpretation than we intend to intrude, or than we consciously undertake to say. And this may be good or bad. But this is why one must be wary of every theologian's speaking and insist upon looking for his veiled presuppositions. But the conscious use of philosophical notions is something else again. Here we need to be aware of the proprieties of theological speech, as distinguished from the demands of philosophical reasoning when one is speaking as a philosopher within a philosophical system.

Let me say a brief word about theological speech. Theological speech, as well as philosophical speech, is a human form of speaking, and therefore subject to the limitations of the human structure. However, the object of theological speech differs from that of philosophical speech. The philosopher attends to the world of meaning which can arise within conscious awareness from whatever point he may wish to start; his speech is pursued within the rules of an accepted logic. The theologian, on the other hand, must attend to the intimations of an ultimate reality which, presumably, persistently sustains existence, but which intermittently arrests his attention as a work of grace and judgment. The theologian is thus compelled, as it were, to live on a frontier continually bordering his clearly formed structure of existence with an unmanageable depth of grace and freedom that opens into a relational ground exceeding his conceptual reach. The language appropriate to this mode of inquiry and speaking is not the language of philosophy or of any discursive discourse. And when the idiom of philosophical speech is drawn upon, as it frequently is in theology, it must be summoned to a precarious role which of necessity strains its conceptual meaning to the utmost, even as it responds to the incursion of innovating depths of meaning in the act of attending to what is other than the human structure.

This places a burden upon the philosophical theologian which is not readily clarified or relieved. What seems clear is that the philosophical theologian is not justified in simply translating the narrative vision of faith and experience, or even theological judgments, into explicit terms of the philosophical overview. The latter, as an "adventure of ideas," is a mode of illuminating concrete, historical experiences, offering intelligible possibilities of meaning appropriate to the outreach of faith. If one is committed to an empirically realistic stance, the adventure of ideas and the concretely lived experiences will be continually, or at least frequently, in concourse with one another by way of probing or reassessing the validity and fruitfulness of either claim. This may raise questions concerning the way process theologians currently appeal to the philosophies of Whitehead and Hartshorne. To be sure, all of them would not concur with the restrictive procedure I am projecting here. However, it becomes clear that, in responding to the stimulus of these mentors, or in reemploying their modes of thought, something of their own sensibilities of thought stemming from their sense of speaking out of a community of faith, or a legacy of faith, impels or shapes their use of these resources. Thus these theologians venture formulations on their own, or reconceptions of insights offered as a philosophical resource, in expressing theological judgments. In the interplay of reflection evident here the very encounter between narrative vision and overview, or between philosophical vision and theological judgment, may be at work. The question here turns on whether the interplay is in fact such an interchange between modes of discourse, between judgments generated by responsiveness to the lived experience and the judgments of an abstractive overview, or simply an exchange of philosophical judgments at the abstractive level.

Where metaphysical or empirical inquiry is employed to assure literal certainty in religious belief or affirmation the problem of appropriateness, or even validity, intensifies. Here we come into an area of process thinking that is most difficult to address; feelings run high in the advocacy or defense of whatever position is embraced. For many years, for example, Professor Wieman persisted in sharpening the criteria by which the reality within experience worthy of our ultimate commitment might be designated. As one who grew up intellectually under the shadow of that vigorous intellectual pursuit, and who shared for a time in the excitement of exploring it, I cannot speak critically of this effort without acknowledging at the same time profound respect both for the magnitude of the effort and for the utter candor and persistence with which it was pursued through the years. At the time that it was initially projected, one could see the force and relevance of such an inquiry, for it came at that juncture in liberal Protestant history when, as it were, liberal theology had become virtually emptied of any theistic motivation and seemed helpless to resist the humanistic tide that was steadily mounting. Wieman's formula for religious inquiry came as a shock in that context; the simplicity of its wording in itself seemed to dispel argument, and to invite serious consideration. Said Wieman,

> Whatever else the word God may mean, it is a term used to designate that Something upon which human life is most dependent for its security, welfare, and increasing abundance. That there is such a Something cannot be doubted. The mere fact that human life happens and continues to happen, proves that this Something, however unknown, does certainly exist.[3]

Unless one had anguished through years of responding to the question posed by Gerald Birney Smith, by way of disarming humanistic argument, "Is theism essential to religion?", I doubt that the force of

3. Henry N. Wieman, *Religious Experience and Scientific Method* (New York: Macmillan, 1926; paperback, Carbondale, Ill.: Southern Illinois University Press, 1971), p. 9.

Wieman's simple, yet arresting utterance could have the effect that it registered among many of us during the mid-twenties. As a plug in the dike, it was a dramatic reprieve, and the spell of it lingered far beyond the point that had occasioned the surprise of it. The formula was to produce a succession of tentative formulations by Wieman, designating that Something worthy of ultimate commitment, culminating in the fourfold event which was to be given the more concise rendering of "creative interchange."[4] With this culmination as a theory of value, or even as a summary response to that initial, dramatic query, "What is that Something upon which human life is most dependent for its security, welfare, and increasing abundance," I find ample accord. Yet, in retrospect, it appears to me now to be inadequate for theological inquiry, both because of the motive for inquiry and the mode of inquiry involved.

In the way Wieman stated his formula for inquiry, it appeared in that context to be a direct and persuasive corrective of the appeal to human ideals, which had reached the peak of absurdity in personalism. And Wieman was consciously combating that form of idealizing the human structure, pointing, so it seemed, to a good not our own, "which could do for us what we cannot do for ourselves." And in that vein, it was of a piece with the new realism that was on the rise both in philosophy and theology. Yet, in the final formulation, "the good not our own" became the fruition of "the conditions we provide" in the relations we set up, and in the responses we make to those conditions. There is a clue here to what human devotion can eventuate in; but, as set forth, it presumes an idealizing function of human imagination, valuation, and action in the imagery of John Dewey's *A Common Faith*. And it is my impression that, in recent years, Wieman readily acknowledged that his thought had converged toward that of Dewey's more than toward any other contemporary thinker. In Wieman, however, the lure of certainty was more pronounced than in Dewey; thus his intensity in affirming the ultimacy of what he had disclosed in his criteria was greatly accentuated in contrast to the procedure of Dewey for whom projection of the imaginative capacity in man toward yet unrealized good was always in the spirit of a tentative venture with no foreseeable closure, except to employ what was distilled as recognizable attainment in envisaging the good for necessary purposes at hand. In Wieman it was more than a venture in attaining tentative horizons of human good.

4. Cf. Henry N. Wieman, *The Source of Human Good* (Chicago: University of Chicago Press, 1946).

Initially it was a definitive effort to achieve certainty in affirming God. In his recent writings the theological intent of his inquiry seemed less in focus, as he addressed urgent problems of the human community within the context of sociological and psychological concerns. However, insofar as these concerns assumed the gravity of an *ultimate commitment,* the theological intent of his efforts persisted. In that sense I believe Daniel Day Williams was justified in assessing Wieman's work as being theological.[5] And it is on those grounds that I have had misgivings as to the appropriateness of his procedure.

While process theologians in recent years have appealed to the philosophy of Charles Hartshorne in formulating their own judgments and ways of responding to Christian doctrine, it cannot be said that Hartshorne conceives of himself as a theologian, or as doing theological work. He conceives of his role as being that of a metaphysician. In his metaphysical work, Hartshorne's rigorous pursuit of *the logic of perfection,* seeking to arrive at the most competent and adequate way possible of speaking about ontological questions within his philosophical framework, would seem wholly justified as a methodological procedure. The question that I find persisting as I contemplate his impressive efforts in relation to process theology is, does Hartshorne project his efforts as an *adventure of ideas* in the spirit of attaining a provisional overview? Or does he employ analogical thinking in such a way as to close the gap between imagery and reality? Is the intent, in other words, more definitive in producing certainty of belief than such an adventure implies or affords?

I must confess that I have had serious misgivings in these respects. Hartshorne's frequent appeal to Leibniz and his complaint that other ontologists have not read Leibniz enough would seem to suggest affinity with the view that presupposes a large measure of harmony between our human imagery and reality, and, therefore, that logically clear and defensible statements can be assumed to be explicitly true to the reality apprehended. Hartshorne, in other words, would appear to be bent on precision and perfection of conceptual statements in the sense in which "picture-models" can be presumed to provide descriptive clarity in an ultimate, rather than a provisional sense. In this respect, if I have not done injustice to his intent and procedure, the mark of rationalism

5. Daniel Day Williams, *The Empirical Theology of Henry Nelson Wieman,* ed. Robert W. Bretall (New York: Macmillan, 1963), pp. 73 ff.

appears to be more in evidence in Hartshorne's language and program of inquiry than in any of the other formative process thinkers such as Wieman, Whitehead, James, or Bergson.

When applied to theological discourse, the issue here becomes even more arresting; the import of this strong, rationalistic bent of mind is to presume more security and certainty in religious belief than human judgment is entitled to affirm. And this may encourage the process theologian to take his theological assertions as well as the philosophical notions underlying them more literally than his discourse can justify.

I would insist that, theologically, neither the ontological security to which this rationalistic effort aspires, nor the degree of empirical certainty which Professor Wieman sought to establish through the years, is available to us. Both efforts seem to me to draw upon intellectual assumptions, or upon assumptions concerning the status of our intellectual powers which our present imagery of thought will not sustain. I would acknowledge that what Wieman and Hartshorne have provided, each in his own way, in their precise rendering of what is apprehended when we speak of God, are as parables concerning this ultimate reality discerned in the Creative Passage. As such they contribute mightily to our awareness of what conceivably is beyond our comprehension, but which, nevertheless, is ever present in the immediacies of existence as each of us meets with its mystery and efficacy, as resources of grace and judgment. At best, through the most disciplined and persistent efforts, with adequate sensibility as to what is beyond comprehension, conceivably beyond our apprehension, we may aspire to a degree of intelligibility and encouragement to persist in the act of faith in a mood of trust and openness to such intimations of insight beyond the assured sense of intelligibility as these lived experiences may yield. Our disciplined efforts may alleviate conditions impelling "allegiance to despair"; but they cannot forever rout them.

To insist upon achieving certainty beyond that degree of intelligibility and trust is to encourage, if not to incur, illusions at the rational level which can be as imperiling to the sanity and proportion of faith as excessive claims of religious assurance tend to be when they have only zeal and pious sentiment to support them. On the surface these two modes of response, the rational and the sentimental, seem poles apart; as modes of response, they appear to be the inverse of one another. Yet, in their common zeal to achieve or to express certainty of belief, they give voice to a common demand of piety which impels an over-reaching of the human spirit. In either case, the lure of certainty is destined to create false gods.

## V

But my quarrel with such rational or empirical zeal, as it relates to the theological task, goes more deeply than this matter of our present facilities of thought. It touches upon what is basically involved in the concern to bring to modern man, or to restore to him, the religious option which, presumably, for many reasons, has been lost to modern life. To put it bluntly, it is not simply a matter of putting into the hands of modern men a theological or ontological formula that will speak to their sophisticated minds, and thus enable them to participate, at least at an intellectual level, in the demands of the Christian story. Rather, it is a matter also of challenging this sophistication of modernity, of breaking through this pose of human self-sufficiency and its facade of intellectualism or aestheticism or scientism which has enabled modern man for more than three hundred years to stand off from, or to appear superior to, the elemental stance of man as creature.

Cultural anthropology and the history of religions have led me to have profound respect for this response of elemental man. All of the contemporary disciplines to some extent, for that matter, seem to be striking at the root of this modern pose, and to be recalling us to look at every man more elementally, and in Schleiermacher's terms, as being ultimately dependent, a condition that allies man with all creatures of God. This is to call us back to what, in the nature of things, in the nature of ourselves and our human history, can evoke this deeper, more elemental response in us. The procedure to be encouraged, in other words, is not to intensify reliance upon the intellectual formulation of meanings as such, as if these were the modern man's alternative to encountering the realities of faith; but, rather, to take seriously this fresh awareness of the depth and complexity of the sheer act of living and dying, the tragedy, pathos, and hope of mere existence, and thus to seize upon the degree of elementalism that is offered us out of the historical situation that is upon us. It will then devolve upon us to bring our disciplined speech and modes of thought to terms with this fresh awareness of realities as well as to bring our disciplined thought to bear upon them, in the hope of wresting from such awareness a measure of intelligibility and discernment.

This is the reverse of demythologizing. It is recovering what the liberal era forfeited: namely, a vivid sense of this shaping and redemptive force to which the life of faith bears witness as an elemental, creatural response. This, in my judgment, is not going back of liberalism, but through it and beyond it, repossessing on critical grounds what liberal disciplines helped to establish, the witness of faith expressive of the mythos which persists with efficacy, informing and motivating our structure of experience. But it is also to go beyond conventional and traditional modes of piety which tend to assume that, in embracing this elemental stance of creaturehood, human beings must become docile to the point of disowning, or even dissipating, their critical powers and appreciative capacities expressive of their own emergent structure. The fact that this stance would seem to cut a path between these two modes of response, the critical and the elemental, is not to be interpreted to mean that it offers a reconciling position between them. Obviously, it partakes more of the philosophical orientation that seeks intelligibility and critical awareness in theological expression than it does of any elemental piety that would eschew all critical reflections and inquiry.

My concern in these remarks has been to retain within the critical perspective a methodological concern for the kind of awareness in critical theological reflection that keeps in focus the degree of elementalism that pertains to all human wonder and inquiry, however sophisticated or critical, given our level of emergence. This would argue for the kind of sensibility in critical reflection that relates inquiry to our elemental stance as creatures, not one that would depreciate such reflection or inquiry in deference to that creatural stance.

## VI

What this analysis comes to in the form of directives for theological method can be summarized as follows:

1. The relation between reality and human reason is simultaneously that of continuity and discontinuity. The extent to which continuity or discontinuity is stressed will determine the degree to which rationality is made relevant in pursuing ultimate questions. On the basis of my own understanding of the development of natural structures and the

experimental evidence of modern physics in the use of its reconstructed models, I am led to assert as an ontological judgment that our human structure both participates in, and to a decisive degree is in tenuous continuity with, if not in certain respects discontinuous with, the ultimate structure of reality. This is simply a way of acknowledging the creatural limits of the human structure of consciousness without disavowing altogether its creatural participation in that ultimate structure. Human reason is not directly, or wholly, consonant with the ultimate structure of order; yet it bears witness to it, and in marginal ways is expressive of it.

2. Because intelligence is marginal and ambiguous in relation to the ultimate structure of reality, intelligibility can be only marginal. Any effort to make it more than that, or to extend it to proportions of an all-inclusive rationality must be regarded as an overreaching of the human structure, and a willful retreat to an ideational illusion.

The reality of our situation thus presents us as moving ambiguously and in tension on a frontier of awareness between our human structure and the infinite structure of the Creative Passage.

3. Now to speak more explicitly of the theological task as I envision it, and of the procedure by which this task is pursued: One who takes the cultural history of the West seriously as being integral to Christian history will be encouraged to see theological method as a comprehensive dialectic between its primal source of ultimate valuation in the Bible and the contemporary forms of witness to this depth. This may prove to be more complex than the dialectic between kerygma and proclamation, but the pattern and movement are comparable. The latter is a church dogmatics and presupposes a single strand of witness issuing from the preaching of the Word in the churches.

The procedure I mean to convey presents a theological texture with diversified, yet interwoven strands of witness, with the faith of the church forming the central strand of the vertebrae. Historically, one would see the structure of Christian faith forming out of the movement from the primal myth of Scripture through the Christ-event, which then issues in the notion of the living Christ. When one traces this movement symbolically it takes the form of a supervening work of judgment and grace which is intermittently known and experienced sacramentally or ceremonially through the forms of the church. A method of empirical realism would see this sacramental expression as one strand of the Christian witness, bodying forth the living Christ. And beyond this sacramental and ceremonial witness it sees other vortices, or centers of witness: (1) the culture, both insofar as it retains formative influences within its orbit of meaning expressive of the mythos and in the sense that it exemplifies the fate and folly, along with the glory and creativity, of the human structure in its participation in the infinite structure of the Creative Passage; (2) the individual experiences of men and women insofar as they bear a distinctive witness of response and decision.

4. These diversified, yet interwoven, strands of witness within the culture constitute the articulate aspect of the Judaic-Christian mythos. What persists as a shaping force at the level of sensibilities and perceptions conveys the mythos as unconscious motivation. But the living Christ is encountered more concretely as energies of grace and judgment in the exigencies of living, which may or may not be known for what they are by all who experience them throughout the culture. In this sense men and women participate in the stream of experience more deeply than they know. To the extent that we are made aware theologically of what this concrete encounter implies, we will be led to respond to them consciously as one participating in the Judaic-Christian mythos. Thus it will be seen that there is a conceptual or symbolic level of witness of the living Christ as well as a concrete level of participation in the energies of grace and judgment. In some instances the latter is vividly known as concrete experience with little or no knowledge of their symbolic reference. In other instances the symbolic level of meaning may be readily acknowledged and verbalized without a vivid sense of the empirical realities of Spirit as these are concretely encountered.

The method of empirical realism means to be attentive to both levels of witness in its dialectic. Thus we are concerned to say that each of these vortices or dynamic centers of witness points beyond itself to the continuing work of the New Creation, revealing the Infinite Structure in each generation of history. Together they point back to the primal witness in Scripture which, for reasons of symbolic force and historical primacy, has been acknowledged to be the theological norm for Christian faith. But one can make an even stronger case for this biblical norm; not only are all the root-metaphors of the Judaic-Christian mythos to be found in Scripture, but the structure of the Christ-event is vividly set forth in that portion of the New Testament called the *kerygma*.

However one views this luminous center (the Christ-event), one cannot ignore its controlling force in theological construction. It is the fulcrum which gives leverage to every other doctrine. Hence, in the last analysis, one can say that the structural character and temper of a Christian theology turn on the strength and character of its Christology. A firm Christology will give focus and clarity to the Christian themes. An indecisive one will leave a theology without clear directives. Or again, an inclusive Christology that draws all men and things into its luminous center will disclose this revelation in Christ as a unifying and transforming event, literally a New Creation. An exclusive Christology, on the other hand, that dissociates the Christian witness from every thing other than itself will disclose this revelation as a restrictive and judgmental word to man and culture, thus turning the redemptive life that is thereby revealed into a radical disavowal of what was given in Creation.

Lacking a Christology, one will be disposed to turn to a theory of value, to an empirical criterion of God's working in history, or to some other normative measure by which a selective view of good and evil, grace and judgment in existence can be established. I have always considered Wieman's concern with an empirical criterion of God's working in his earlier writings to be his alternative to Christology. In his later works he associated the Creative Event with the Christ-event, which he carefully delineated in *The Source of Human Good*. Similarly, one might see in Whitehead and Hartshorne philosophical notions of God being qualified by his goodness as a philosophical way of pointing to what is basic to a Christology.

Now I regard it as important to strive toward a firm understanding of this focal Event and of the primal witness in Scripture, both antecedent and subsequent to the Christ-event; but it is also important to be aware of this Event as a continuing revelation, or a recurring innovation of grace and judgment through these vortices of witness in man's existence. Thus theology as a constructive discipline must be a sensitive and imaginative effort to keep the lines of communication open between these dynamic vortices of witness within the contemporary culture and the witness of Scripture. To lose sight of this dynamic of faith as a causal efficacy within the structure of experience is to miss the deep-lying mythos which unifies the Judaic-Christian witness. And this can be a serious loss. For it is this mythos which conveys to contemporary history its sense of a depth of past valuations in the present as a living Word, opening up to individual man and his culture the relational ground which has become redemptive through what Scripture and the Christian witness in doctrine and confessional acts have designated the New Creation in Jesus Christ.

We should observe, in passing, that the Christian mythos is in the idiom of the dramatic event, "the story of our lives," as H. Richard Niebuhr has phrased it. It is a drama of redemption that transpires within the context of Creation and the New Creation. A theology that is faithfully pursued within that idiom would keep this note of narrative and dramatic event to the fore, and thus benefit from its method of indirection. But the fear that this would present the Christian witness as mere play-acting has impelled theologians and churchmen to speak more prosaically, and to press for more literal meaning in the statements which both theologian and churchman make. It is this drive toward literalism and the status ascribed to literal propositions that has plagued theological inquiry, and has tended to drive theologians away from their distinctive task and mode of speaking. But more of this in a moment.

One will see, then, that speaking of my method simply as an analysis of culture does not express it adequately, or even focally, unless one means to begin with the mythical response in its primal context. Since I use the term "mythical response" interchangeably with the witness of faith, as the elemental response to what is ever-present as an ultimate demand and resource in the immediacies of existence, focusing upon the mythical response leads me to the Bible as the primal document of Christian faith. Everything relevant to theological inquiry, formally speaking, fans out from that focal document, and becomes an historical and empirical commentary upon it. But I am concerned to point out that materially, the Bible may not be the starting point for every Christian, or for that matter, for every theologian.

In our contemporary experiences it takes a bit of doing to get back to the Bible methodologically with integrity of meaning and purpose. Thus it may be that one will start where the problems are thickest and more acute—that is, with a specific area of individual experience where faith and belief are in crisis; with poignant reports of the human story in modern literature and the arts; with the tragic cleavage between human groups within society; with the struggle for unity and identity within the contemporary Christian church; with human anxiety as such as it tears men and women apart in their loneliness and growing sense of life's meaninglessness. All of these represent vortices of human experience where the realities of existence come vividly and critically into play; where, in a word, ultimacy and immediacies traffic together. These vortices of witness will not be made the source of theological method, but they may be the occasions, even the beginning of what prompts one to turn, or to return, to Christian faith in its more structured form, to "the story of our lives" as it has been written into events and decisions previously recorded.

What constructive theology seeks to do, then, is to atune our listening to the realities of faith beyond, yet intimately involving our structural existence. And its task is simultaneously that of conveying this witness through, yet differentiating it from, the limited and ambiguous cultural forms, which are the only forms we have through which to become self-conscious and articulate. The tension is always between form and realities.

To state the method of empirical realism succinctly, then, one may say (1) that theology begins as a critical response to what is conveyed through the three vortices of the Christian witness within the contemporary period: the cultus (or church), individual experience, and the culture. This critical response consists in attending to that witness in the light of the disciplines available for studying the phenomena of man's elemental response to what is ultimate in existence. (2) On the basis of this critical appraisal, the theologian must determine whether what is given in the witness of faith is available only to one who stands within the community of faith, that is, whether it is clearly a cultic statement of faith made on the basis of a volitional act of acceptance, irrespective of the mind's resistance or despair, or available to everyone within the cultural orbit of meaning who is open to receiving this witness as pointing to a depth of grace and judgment in every man's existence. It will be clear that I have moved in the latter direction. (3) Although the tendency of the impatient modern mind will be to try to find a swift and convenient way of taking hold of this insight into the depth of our existence through recourse to psychology, philosophy of religion, or some similar medium, the theologian will insist upon understanding this insight in the context of the nurturing matrix which has kept this witness of faith alive and efficacious through many centuries of our cultural history.

(4) The nurturing matrix is the Judaic-Christian mythos and the

cultural forms that have bodied it forth. Whether or not even the notion of such a matrix is available to the modern mind turns upon the question of whether one who is responsive to the imagery of thought that is formative within the disciplined thinking of our time finds it possible to embrace this dimension of man's elemental response to ultimacy. I have argued that this possibility is available to the modern mind. And it is possible (a) because a relational mode of thinking, along with the imagery of depth in experience, makes such notions as revelation, grace, and judgment, as well as their relation to man's freedom, conceivable and employable on the basis of analogical thinking; and (b) because the mythical response as a holistic phenomenon can be given credence within the contemporary idiom.

(5) It is on the basis of this contemporary repossession of the notion of myth as a legitimate and persistent human response to ultimacy in existence that the modern mind finds its way back to its primal beginnings, and in this return, recovers the significance of the Bible as a primal document.

(6) At this point one is made ready to attend to the witness of faith in its primal historic form, the Word of Scripture, which comes to a sharpened focus in the kerygma and its witness to the Christ-event as the New Creation.

(7) There then follows the crucial matter of receiving this witness of faith, of being addressed by that to which it points concerning the Infinite Structure in God. It is here that one confronts the options whether (a) to demythologize the witness of faith "without remainder"; or (b) to retain the mythos as being itself the elemental response to ultimacy appropriate to every man who is sensitive to the limits and depths of his existence, yet concerned to attain what margin of intelligibility is possible under the circumstances of our limitations.

The movement of the method thus completes the circle in that it begins with the empirical witness in the present, moves to the primal source and norm of the mythos, and returns to the present demand for intelligibility in Christian faith.

Chapter Ten

# Culture as a Source for Theology

The import of what I have just set forth as directives for theological method is to say that the witness of faith in any culture, and of
the Christian witness in our own culture, pervades the whole history of
any people, even though a sharpened focus of its theological history and
meaning is to be discerned principally in the cultus or the life of the
church. This raises the question, then, as to whether culture itself is a
source for theology, and if so, in what sense. One is not to assume from
this observation that I am speaking of a cultural faith or civic religion
as opposed to or in lieu of the cultic faith of the churches. That is a
theme that has received considerable attention in recent years, especially
among sociologists and religious groups dissociated from the Judaic-
Christian legacy. The methodology I have put forth means to be
attentive to such phenomena as exhibiting in remote ways distillations
from that legacy, radically reconceived and even set in opposition to the
historic witness of faith. Yet, in speaking of the cultural dimension or
manifestation of the legacy, I am viewing it within the total context of
the cultural history that embraces all dimensions of the historic mythos,
including as a focal source, the witness of faith within temple, synagogue,
and church.

A second observation to note is that the theological method here employed, following from its orientation within a mode of process thought
described as empirical realism, presents existence in this twofold manner,
as embracing simultaneously dimensions of immediacy and ultimacy.
On its subjective side, I see existence as a stream of experience; in its
objective aspect, as a Creative Passage. I use the term "Creative Passage"
as an ultimate reference in the way traditional metaphysics employed

150

the term "Being" or "ground of Being." Back in the nineteen thirties I found it useful to point up this radical empirical note of existence as a stream by setting the notion of "Becoming" over against "Being,"[1] and thus spoke of my thought as a philosophy of becoming. I still hold to this essential contrast in the main, though I have come to see that, on the one hand, there is no becoming that is without something that is persisting, giving to every moment of becoming its identity; and, on the other hand, that, except as one absolutizes the notion of becoming in the modernistic sense of indefinite and uninterrupted progress, one must acknowledge that there are periodic plateaus and even critical instances of regression and defeat within this stream of experience. Thus I came to see that to speak of existence as being simply an event of becoming seemed sanguine, or at least unrealistic. Yet the stress upon the notion of becoming, I would hold, is justified, certainly as a process among other processes, or even by way of pointing to a prevailing tendency among those complex occurrences of incessant "coming into being and perishing" which make up our daily existence. As a way of settling upon a more neutral term, therefore, taking account of both being and becoming and of their interplay, thus acknowledging persistence and creative change, I have come to think of the Creative Passage as being the most basic characterization of existence as it applies to all life, to all people, to all cultures.

Furthermore, I have come to see the reality of God as being of a piece with the Creative Passage. For reasons which may become clear, I have recoiled from trying to envisage or to define God in any complete, metaphysical or ontological sense, preferring instead to confine attention to such empirical notions as *the creative act of God* and *the redemptive work of God in history.* Much of the meaning we appear to find in life, we bring to it, as Kant observed, through our own forms of sensibility and understanding. But, as James and Bergson were later to remark, countering the stance of Kant and Hume in one basic respect, the nexus of relationships that forms our existence is not projected, it is given. We do not create these relationships; we experience them, being given with existence. And from this matrix come resources of grace that can carry us beyond the meanings of our own making, and alert us to goodness that is not of our own willing or defining. This goodness in existence which we do not create, but which creates and saves us,

1. Bernard E. Meland, "Growth Toward Order," *Personalist* (1940), pp. 257–66.

is the datum to which I mean to attend. It is literally a work of judgment and grace, a primordial and provident goodness, the efficacy of which may be discerned in every event of creativity, sensitivity, and negotiability. Thus I am led empirically to speak of God as the Ultimate Efficacy within relationships.

I

One may wish to go beyond this empirical line of inquiry to enlarge upon or to give further intelligibility to the claims that are made for it. Such a metaphysical vision can be justified to the degree that it has some empirical basis: that is, if its primal perceptions can be said to have a basis in experience or in history. A metaphysics that is purely a work of the imagination, however valid it may be internally as an exercise in logic, has seemed to me to be a floating vision having only the value of wishful thinking or of a reverie as an aesthetic creation. But where a sense of ultimate persuasion arises in experience, or out of events in history, as a serious estimate of the character of events that are daily encountered, one's judgments can be said to be empirically anchored in the realities of existence. Such apprehensions may be taken seriously as interpreting experience to some degree, however vaguely or ambiguously they may have been gleaned. One may thereupon seek further intelligibility by extending the vision of the mind, cautiously moving out from these basic apprehensions imaginatively and speculatively, but always with a restraint consonant with empirical demands and with the limitations of our human powers of inquiry.

On this basis I have ventured to enlarge upon this empirical persuasion by projecting it into a metaphysical vision, albeit a modest one. It is understandable, perhaps, that I should have availed myself of the stimulating imagination of Alfred North Whitehead in this undertaking, since he took it upon himself, as he said, to complete the task begun in radical empiricism by William James and Henri Bergson. But my response to Whitehead with regard to this crucial empirical datum has been qualified by preferences of my own. For example, Whitehead, in considering where one might begin in one's metaphysical explication of the creative act of God, pondered the primal alternatives which Western history offered, namely, the Hebraic and the Platonic myths. Whitehead decided that the Hebraic myth of creation was too primitive for modern metaphysical speculation and thus chose to build upon the Platonic myth. I have chosen otherwise, not on philosophical grounds, but on grounds indicated by hints from cultural anthropology. The Hebraic myth, I would hold, is not only more basic to Western forms of thought and sensibility than the Greek myths, but it has been more pervasive in its influence in shaping the human psyche of the West as well as its religious institutions. The Platonic myth has been influential at the level of philosophical reflection, but in other areas of cultural expression its influence has been marginal and intermittent. It is true that Christian theologians have assimilated Platonic imagery in certain areas of their thought, but in dealing with what might be called the basic theological formula, the *imago dei,* by which the Christian understanding of man and of his relation to God have been explicated, they have resorted to imagery that roots in the metaphor of the covenant and in the biblical story of creation.[2]

Within the Creative Passage there occurs the passage of history, not as a single stream, but as diverse cultural currents, each of which has its own dynamic structure, integrating through memory, precedent, custom, and much more the sequence of events and actualities that have constituted its living stream. The dynamic passage of events within each culture has given form to a *structure of experience* which can be said to be the enduring structural residue of the cultural history within its particular orbit of meaning, as seen from within the perspective of every present moment of that history. The structure of experience is thus the present immediacy within the total and inclusive Creative Passage. The distinction between these terms is somewhat comparable to the distinction implied in the contrast between "essence" and "existence," though the context here is the culture, rather than individual man.

Within each structure of experience there is to be found a persisting, elemental myth, giving shape to its cultural mythos, expressive of the hard-earned, endurable modes of response, subliminal for the most part, which have formed within that orbit of meaning. It reaches to the level of the creaturely stance which a people will assume in speaking of their

2. In earlier works, notably in *Faith and Culture* and *The Realities of Faith,* as well as *Seeds of Redemption* and *The Reawakening of Christian Faith,* I sought to bring emergent and organismic insights to bear upon our religious history as this cultural and religious history takes its rise out of the Judaic-Christian myth of primal beginnings. It would be accurate to say that my efforts parallel Whitehead's metaphysical vision and, at certain crucial points, partake of it; but they do not stem directly from it, as one can see from the qualifications I have just cited.

existence.  It affects and shapes not only language, the mode of thinking and speaking, but sensibilities of thought, psychical orientation, and thus psychical expectations.  In our more sophisticated and technical theological speech, this cultural élan is often expressed in universal terms as the response of the individual, for example, *sensus numinis,* "sense of destiny," "idea of the holy," "ultimate concern," etc.  In using such terms one may intend to transcend the cultural myth, or one may simply mean to point to a quality of response implied in all myths which can be legitimately assimilated by modern man and correlated with his use of reason.  As a way of evoking general acceptance of this elemental response within the modern ethos, these terms serve a purpose, but they do not do justice to what is culturally expressive of this élan.  In fact, in employing such terms, modern theologies have tended to emulate the Enlightenment in individualizing, and then universalizing, the religious response.  The concreteness of the response within its cultural history is thereby dissolved, and thus the efficacy of the response as a persisting psychical orientation of thought and experience within that cultural history is readily overlooked, if not ignored.  It is in recognition of this fact that I have argued for retaining a concern with the mytho-poetic mode of thought and awareness in modern cultures, and with the kind of elemental outreach which it conveys.  This, in my judgment, is consonant with retaining the psychical depth of the cultural response.  And I urge this as an accompaniment of, rather than as an alternative to, efforts to rationalize experience.

The Judaic-Christian mythos underlies and is formative of the sensibilities and psychic outlook of our Western culture.  The Christian expression of this *mythos* bears witness to a specific occurrence in our history in which the saving work of God became manifest as a New Creation; that is, the creative work of God assumed a new and decisive degree of concreteness.  This, I am inclined to believe, was made possible by the emergence of a sensitivity and qualitative response within the human structure, enabling the Creative Passage to assume a new degree of concreteness in human history.  Nothing ontologically new occurred in this New Creation; that is, nothing new ontologically occurred in God's character.  But something quite new as a social energy was released into history, giving rise not only to new expectations, new hopes and possibilities within existence, but to new understanding of the movement of goodness and grace within relationships that form and hold us in existence. A vivid sense of the energies of grace and judgment being ever-present as a resource beyond our own energies and efforts came into human lives, opening them to the depth of their creative ground or matrix wherein relationships were made redemptive and recreative.

It is this New Creation as a redemptive goodness in the relationships of history to which the Christian mythos bears witness, either explicitly or implicitly, and in this sense it is the deepest vein of our structure of experience.

Now there are various forms of participation in the *mythos* within any culture. And here, as I have noted, I come to a distinctive emphasis in my own theological method, namely, those distinctions of the witness of faith as expressed through the culture, the cultus, and individual experience.

## II

Since the terms "culture," "cult" or "cultus," and "individual experience" are important to my presentation, let me try to make clear what I mean by them. Culture, as I use the term, connotes the total complex of human growth that has occurred within any clearly defined orbit of human association, expressing its prevailing sentiments, style, and way of life. This is a shorthand way of saying what I have written in *The Realities of Faith,* where I defined culture as being

> the human flowering of existing structures and facilities, becoming manifest as an ordered way of life in the imaginative activities and creations of a people, their arts and crafts, their architecture, their furniture and furnishings, their costumes and designs, their literature, their public and private ceremonies, both religious and political. It is in their formative ideas, giving direction to their educational efforts and customs, as well as to their religious notions and practices, their social graces and manners; in their habits of eating and body care; in their modes of livelihood and the social organization that follows from them.[3]

Culture, then, is any society seen in terms of its total human expression, wherein the accumulative qualities of *lived history and experience* are made vivid and distinctive. To be sure, spatial demarcations in the history of peoples are by no means fixed or enduring; yet there has been sufficient durability of large and small blocks of human society

3. Bernard E. Meland, *The Realities of Faith* (New York: Oxford University Press, 1962), p. 212.

throughout the world's history to enable one to say that there have existed "clearly defined orbits of human association" in which distinctive and pervading qualities of experience have developed. Mobile and unstable as these demarcations have been, they suffice for speaking in a general way of varying human cultures, distinctive clusters of human growth evincing a particular structure of experience. Thus, in speaking of man, of people or the human community, we deal in abstractions until we conceive of these people or communities within historical orbits of association that have yielded distinctive cultures.

The cult, or the cultus, is generally defined as a particular system of worship, including its body of belief, its organization, as well as its ceremonial. Often the cult exists as a culture within culture. That is to say, the cult becomes so effective in redefining an orbit of spatial existence for its devotees within the culture as to exclude much that is expressive of human growth outside its restrictive orbit, thereby rendering it nonexistent for its own defined purposes. Yet this exclusion is never totally effective; for even under the tightest controls, certain minimum lines of communication between cult and culture are made necessary, even if they have to be underground and clandestine.

The history of our Western experience presents considerable variety in the relations between cult and culture, ranging from the secretive encounters of the catacombs to the quasi-secularized religious societies of recent liberal vintage. To whatever extent religious organizations and culture may have coalesced, however, each of them has nevertheless continued to be in some sense a particular focus of religious witness and practice.

Now in Western society there has emerged a third distinctive focus of the religious witness, namely, the individual, or the individual experience. In the earliest stages of Near Eastern and Western experience, individuality was virtually nonexistent. Personality, insofar as the term existed, was understood to mean corporate personality, expressing the mentality or spirit of a people through individual representatives. Even throughout early Christian history this sense of conformity to the corporate image persisted, within both religious and political societies. Individuality as such appears to have accompanied the rise of the city-states in Greece and Rome and the consequent dissipation of corporate control or even of corporate ties. Nonconformity in religious and political spheres was by no means an innovation peculiar to that period of our history; but nonconformity as an expression of individual experience, rivaling both cult and culture, was. In subsequent years, say from the eleventh century on, this particular form of religious witness, rising from and resting upon the authenticity of individual experience, was to become increasingly formidable in challenging, and at times radically altering, the religious witness of both cult and culture.

Now I mean to argue that the Christian witness, rather than being contained, as it were, within the community of believers commonly identified with the formal organization of the church, has been exercised, with varying degrees of definitiveness, throughout Western history, acquiring a distinctive focus, with varying degrees of intensity, in these three areas or vortices of experience—culture, cult, and individual experience.

This way of looking at the witness of faith presupposes, as I have said, the concreteness of God's working at the level of the Creative Passage in each moment of historical time and a symbolical (or cognitive) participation in the mythos arising from the witness to the living Christ. In some instances, the former may be vividly known as concrete experience, with little or no knowledge of its symbolic reference. In other instances, the symbolic level of its meaning may be readily acknowledged and verbalized without experiencing a vivid sense of the empirical realities of Spirit as these are concretely encountered. I am trying to be attentive to both levels, to the empirical as well as to the symbolical. I am concerned to say that responding to the revelatory event in Jesus Christ is not just a matter of perpetuating the recollection and psychical shaping of an historical event through memory and tradition, but of experiencing a work of judgment and grace concretely in the depth of present events and relationships. Participation in the mythos provides the first, and gives illumination to these occurrences and encounters; actual response to the efficacy of judgment and grace, as these come to us in events and relationships, provides the second, giving concreteness and reality to what is borne forth as a witness of faith.

With that explanation in mind, it will become clear why, in formulating a theological method, I choose to speak of correlating three vortices of the Christian witness. One who takes the cultural history of the West seriously as being integral to Christian history, and who envisages both of them as occurring within the Creative Passage, will be encouraged to see theological method as a comprehensive dialectic between its primal source in the biblical witness to the New Creation and present participation in the efficacy of Spirit, along with the contemporary forms of witness to this depth in our historical experience and existence. This method may seem somewhat reminiscent of Schleiermacher's appeal to the religious consciousness. It is, however, more inclusive in what it considers to be relevant to the witness of faith. And further, the method I employ is more organismic, more contextual in its understanding of the dynamics of faith, regarding it, not just as a teleology within consciousness, but as a dynamic nexus of formative relations within the culture itself. Again, the pattern and movement of the method I have outlined may seem to have affinities with that of dialectical theology; but on examination, or perhaps on the face of it, it will prove to be more complex than the dialectic between kerygma and proclamation. The latter is a church dogmatics, and presupposes a single strand of witness issuing from the preaching of the Word in the churches. My own method presents a theological texture with diversified yet interwoven strands of witness, with the faith of the church forming the initiating and active strand of the vertebrae.

Even as I emphasize the importance of culture as one vortex of Christian witness, I recoil from speaking of it as a *source* for theology lest this way of expressing it should seem to say more than I intend. It is a source of data for theology in the sense that the religious consciousness was such a source in Schleiermacher's theology. Yet the data of theology, whether gleaned from culture, the church, or individual experience, point us to deeper realities which speak through these data. Thus I am concerned to say that each of these vortices points beyond itself to the living Christ as a continuing work of the New Creation, revealing the Infinite Structure of grace and judgment in each generation of history. Together they point as well to the primal witness in Scripture wherein the legacy inhering in the Christ-event as a defining datum is available to Christian faith. However one views this luminous center, one cannot ignore its controlling force in theological construction. It is the fulcrum which gives leverage to every other doctrine. Everything relevant to Christian theological inquiry, formally speaking, fans out from that focal event. If the phrase "source for theology" is applicable to any datum, it would seem to apply to this revelatory event.

Having said this, however, we should note again that, materially, this formal center, the Christ-event, may not be the starting point for every

Christian, or for every theologian. That which prompts one to be theologically reflective or inquiring may be some specific occurrence in one's experience, some situation of impasse or crisis, of release or heightening. Such reflection may arise from one's awareness of critical issues arising within society, itself, stemming from a conflict of judgment over human rights, or inhumane circumstances or acts that threaten or violate the integrity of human relationships, whatever the circumstances. In all such instances the cultural scene, itself, provides the living context in which issues of the Spirit erupt and evoke response. Such instances, in fact, suggest how volcanic these lived experiences really are, how ever-present the energies of judgment and grace are, how concretely real the life of the Spirit is within these concrete circumstances, and why it cannot be contained within institutional forms of man's own making.

It is this underlying conviction about the freedom of the Spirit as it arises out of the Creative Passage, and as it emanates from the New Creation that was discerned in Jesus Christ, that impels me to look beyond ecclesiastical forms for these acts of witnessing, even as I try to give full attention to the proclamations of the kerygma within the community of the church. Yet, in speaking of the freedom of the Spirit, I would not wish to be understood as saying that these energies of grace and judgment appear and do their work without benefit of structure or human form. On the contrary, they occur within the relationships, and not just certain *sanctified* relationships; that is, relationships set apart in this community or that. "The Spirit bloweth where it listeth." And in this sense the entire culture in which the Word is proclaimed, wherein the primal mythos is conveyed, shared, and participated in, is made resonant with varying degrees of relevance to the focal event of the Christian story.

## III

Now that I have made the point that the source for theology, substantively speaking, is the dimension of ultimacy within history and within present immediacies, and that this Ultimate Efficacy of Spirit is received within our structured experience, I can proceed to point up the way in which culture plays a role in shaping our encounter with its realities, and in giving verbal or symbolic response to such encounters.

In the first place there is simply the matter of language itself, forms of speech, characteristic modes of thought, facilities for inquiry and the imagery of thought that is employed in any given period of history in carrying on the verbal and intellectual business of theology. This was a major emphasis of the early Chicago school under Shailer Mathews, who argued that the social mind of every age was formative both of the problems that arose, precipitating theological discussions, and of the analogies and social patterns by which solutions to problems were sought and found. I have added my emphasis to this effort, pointing out in addition that the imagery of thought in any period of history within a culture tends simultaneously to offer new opportunities not only for seeing into problems and issues, but for seeing realities afresh, even for repossessing what has been lost to previous generations by reason of restrictions which its imagery of thought imposed, and to enclose the new generation within the frames of meaning that are particularly appealing and illumining to it. I have pressed this point sufficiently, perhaps, in my other writings, so I shall not belabor it further. What I shall do instead is argue that the culture makes a concrete contribution to theological understanding and thus, in a way, suggest that the culture may be more substantive as a source for theology than I have acknowledged.

I shall begin by pointing out what has been lost to theological under-standing because of the tendency to conceive of the witness of faith too narrowly and exclusively. The formal accounting of Christian theological history, say between the fourth and the seventeenth centuries, has ad-hered rather rigidly to the doctrinal history of the cultus. Our theolog-ical history, therefore, in large measure is the story of the Christian consensus. It records the line of Christian thinking emanating from the victory of the majority or the party in power in church councils over competing views and viewpoints, with some marginal reference to minority groups or individuals who provided some opposition to this Christian consensus. As a history of dogma, that is, as a history of Christian belief that became controlling and mandatory, this accounting is fairly reliable. As a history of the Christian witness, however, it is highly selective, consciously biased, and apologetically inadequate. Ex-cept for isolated instances of this Christian witness beyond the firm line of conformity within the church, much of the nonconformist expression of the Christian witness has probably been permanently lost. Thus we have come to know the Christian story and the Christian witness within this vast ancient and medieval period largely through the authoritative, doctrinal deliverances of the established church.

One large exception to this statement can be made. This exception points up one important bit of evidence for the thesis for which I have implicitly pleaded in my writings on Christian theology, namely, that the culture provides an important supplement to the church's formal witness to the faith. The exception is that intermittent shafts of reflected light from the environing culture filter through these cultic discussions sufficiently to give hint of divergent views and voices. For an accounting of this cultural witness we have been largely indebted to church historians.

Incidentally, I should like to say that one of the important reasons for having rich offerings in church history, in addition to historical theology, is that church historians are more likely to do justice to this witness of faith within the culture beyond that of the formal cultus than historians of theology. Church historians are the true secularists of theological seminaries. They mingle with literary and political historians, with architects, dramatists, and art collectors. They even visit bawdy houses, dives, and beer cellars, looking for artifacts that will fill in their story.

The church historian, when he has been imaginative, resourceful, and enterprising, has provided us with our best accounts of this witness of faith issuing from the culture; though often he has done so with a sense of guilt inasmuch as he conceived himself to be a *church* historian, and as such, so he thought, should confine himself to more recognizable church activity and functions. But I would argue otherwise. What has been expressive through the culture, say within the medieval period, and captured in church history, is not just a pale reflection of that found in the formal cultus, nor a spillover from it; rather it is the gospel story re-enacted and communicated with the subtlety and sensitivity of the creative talent within art forms: in the medieval miracle plays, in the cantos of a *Divine Comedy,* in wood carvings, in painting, or even in the floor plan of a cathedral. It is this story that is amplified or exemplified in the disciplined speech of philosophers, publicists, statesmen, or poets. It is this story critically confronted and countered, yet with an integrity of mind and heart that lends fiber to its presentation. Christianity so conveyed may or may not speak through the churches. Often it has not. Furthermore, artists and scholars are a crafty lot. At times they speak out of the independence of genius, however much they may be sponsored or seemingly controlled by conformist thinking. The hidden nuance or emphasis, if it must be hidden, can be a carrier of new overtones of meaning and intention. Orthodoxies have been satirized, taunted, and eventually undermined by the subtle innovations of a creative talent. What is present in any period of history as a force bent on creativity within disciplined and imaginative minds, or the skill of craftsmen, can loom as a tidal wave of renascence and reform, with power to overthrow the established church and to break asunder its consensus of belief and practice. One should bear in mind that, before the dams of conformity began to break in the fourteenth to the sixteenth centuries, much that was brewing as intimations of renascence and reform was issuing from this cultural witness of faith.

But I should not want to convey the impression that these sensitive and creative voices of the culture had value only as a dissonant and disruptive force, countering the dogmatic consensus. On the contrary, one should take account of the fact that such voices arose within the church, and in large measure concurred with the historic consensus to which orthodoxy was committed. Yet, in being zealous participants in the culture of the period as well, they were able to bring to this established line of dogma fresh insight and nuances of thought that saved the orthodox confessions from becoming inflexible stereotypes. They were able to do this principally because, as participants in some restive or creative area of the culture, they had assimilated into their thinking and feeling some of the creative ferment of the period that was either pertinent to the idiom in which the witness could be significantly conveyed, or expressive of the truth of the faith within an idiom that was relevant to the period. Significant figures both in Roman Catholic and Protestant history can be cited to illustrate this point. Some of them were known as renaissance men, others as reformers; but whether reformers or renaissance men, they were ambiguously involved both in the church and in culture.

Once the historic cleavage came in Christendom, setting culture and cultus apart from each other more vividly, say in the seventeenth century, their interrelation became more self-conscious, more strained, and possibly more tenuous, yet no less inescapable. By this I mean that, even after the seventeenth century, cult and culture in the West were held within a common orbit of meaning by reason of the historical interweaving of the common strands of experience. What issued from this organic complex was a contextual outcome of historical occasions that could not readily be set aside by conscious decision or by indecision. Nevertheless, we must acknowledge that the modern period of Western culture has presented a different and more perplexing picture with regard to the cultural witness of faith. The very fact that the church's authority over culture and over the arts and sciences of society had broken left cultural activities and the various disciplines of learning to pursue a more forthright and thus a more vigorous course along independent lines of inquiry and interest. In time this was to have the effect of causing the formal church to retrench in its public activity and of causing those activities within culture outside the church to loom as a more formidable and cohesive organization of life, set over against the churches. It became possible, under these circumstances, to conceive of the church as being the sole embodiment of what persisted as the Christian witness and to view the culture as a secular force in the face of which Christianity and the church were at bay.

The growth of lay Christianity within the free churches in the seventeenth century and following was to alleviate this situation temporarily as demarcations between church and culture among them became less pronounced; but it was to become apparent that, even under these circumstances, the issue between the two could not be ignored or set aside. However, with the free churches having accepted the "right of private judgment" in matters of faith and belief as a guiding principle in the conduct of church affairs, this issue tended to take the form of setting the religious conscience of individuals over against the tyranny of power exercised by political sovereignty. Later, within the American experience, the reverse of that situation was to occur when it became necessary in forming the federal government to restrict the expression of partisan voices in the churches with regard to the affairs of the state through the First Amendment, providing for the separation of church and state.

Yet the most serious threat to the Christian witness within the modern period was to come from another source; namely, in the emergence within Western culture of sciences, philosophies, and other creative disciplines, along with social institutions that were to rival, and then challenge, the church and its ethos. Since the appearance of this more explicit form of secular knowledge and activity within Western culture, the sense of its continuity with the Christian *mythos* has become difficult to sustain. Roman Catholic scholars and churchmen have forthrightly declared the modern period of the West to be a post-Christian era in culture.[4] And the implication of their characterization has been that

4. Christopher Dawson, *The Historic Reality of Christian Culture* (New York: Harper and Row, 1960).

only in the authoritative institution of the Roman Catholic Church is the witness of faith to be found and acknowledged. The orthodox line among Protestants has simulated this ecclesiastical judgment; thus theology in this context has meant specifically *church theology*.

The free church tradition in Protestantism, and later liberal Protestantism, has, in general, veered from this orthodox line only in insisting upon an appeal to the right of private judgment, which in liberalism became an appeal to religious experience or to a judgment of fact. Out of this free church and liberal heritage has come a form of theologizing which has often eschewed the formal traditions of church doctrine, combining in its stead a selected body of Scripture with present-day claims based upon individual experience and judgment. Among nonliberal Protestants of the free churches, the culture has tended to be more and more excluded from their concerns, leading finally to a dissociation of theology and culture more explicitly and decisively than in orthodox traditions. These nonliberal Protestant free churches have adopted a policy of "Christ against culture"[5] which has implied even more disavowal of any cultural influence in theology than in orthodoxy.

Liberal Protestantism has taken a different stand on this issue. Along with its concern to give credence to the witness of individual experience, liberal Protestantism has sought to avail itself of the guidance and control of the cultural disciplines in the interest not only of achieving relevance in its interpretation of Christian faith but of bringing integrity and intelligibility to its formulations within the modern idiom.

Now my efforts must be seen in relation to these several established procedures. I have argued that theology cannot adequately convey the witness of Christian faith by conceiving of its task solely within the bounds of the institutional church. I have argued further that it cannot do so by undertaking to express it simply in terms of individual experience or judgment, as clarified and tested by contemporary cultural disciplines. What I seek to add to these, even within the modern period, is the data which comes from the witness of the culture within which both church and individual have achieved their historical experience.

Now you will readily see that to argue that the culture in our modern Western experience is or can be the bearer of the Judaic-Christian witness, despite all that has happened in Western history, takes a bit of doing. Neither orthodox nor liberal theologians are ready to concur with

5. Cf. H. Richard Niebuhr, *Christ and Culture* (New York: Harper, 1951).

such an argument. This means that neither the approach to Christian history within traditional categories nor the understanding of the Christian experience within historical liberal categories can provide the structural basis for enlarging the scope of the Christian witness to include culture as its third vortex. In this respect, I find myself moving into a post-liberal methodology.

My method, I am inclined to believe, rests precariously upon the assumption that our culture cannot extricate itself from the Judaic-Christian mythos, any more than any existent event can relinquish its past as it lives on in the shaping of its present structure and dynamics; or, to speak of human events, as one lives on in the present shaping of one's individuated psyche and structure of experience. One can modify and discipline the emotions attending these past valuations, one can summon them, insofar as they are articulate within one's conscious experience, to confront the demands of new occurrences and new knowledge. Thus, in part, this primordial shaping can be altered; but, in part, it cannot be altered. To the extent that its shaping goes deeper than man's conscious awareness, it tends to elude the conscious efforts modern men may employ to advance their sophistication, with indifference to elemental demands. And in this I mean to take issue with modernism as such, as we have come to know it in the West.

But I seek to rest my case not simply upon the persistence of this elemental shaping of our structure of experience, but on the soundness of what is implied in this elemental dimension of existence, however much its historical working out in Western culture may have proven offensive to sophisticated and disciplined minds of the modern period. By the elemental dimension of existence I mean simply living with an awareness of the fact of birth and death, confronting man's existence, its range of opportunity for human fulfillment, not only within these acknowledged limits defined by birth and death, but with creaturely feelings appropriate to them. Simply living within these limits on a sophisticated level, shunting off emotions, anxieties, and inquiries evoked by an appropriate elemental depth of our nature, is the usual commonplace pose of sophisticated modernity. It is a pose that was given intellectual credence a generation ago by the pseudoscientific dictum "all beginnings and endings are lost in mystery," thus seeming to release the modern, informed mind to be attentive only to this span of existence between beginnings and endings, as if no mystery or ultimacy attended these years in between. While this cleared the board for a more simplified and controllable form of intellectual inquiry, it condemned it to shallowness, however refined and precise its disciplines might become. Elementalism, I would hold, is simply a capacity to acknowledge humbly and humanly this fact of existential limitations, defined and symbolized by the events of birth and death, and to experience creaturely feelings appropriate to such limitation and dependence.

Now there can follow all grades of response to this inescapable fact, expressing such feelings in many different modes. But, however expressed, as long as the elemental dimension of existence is alive and assertive in modern experience, it. will be continuous with what is primordial as a mythical response.

Thus, while I understand what can be implied historically in speaking of modern culture as being post-Judaic-Christian, namely, that disavowals and estrangements exist between secularized segments of our society and the practicing cultus of Jews and Christians, I do not acknowledge that this modern culture, by its disavowals and alienations, has extricated itself from the primordial mythos of the culture that has shaped the dynamics of the human psyche and its ethos within its orbit of meaning. Its very secularization, in its peculiar way, bears a kind of witness to the faith it disavows.

If one argues that this is indeed a pale and hollow form of witness, more negative in its implications than the assertion that our doubts are of a piece with our faith, I would reply that it is in fact quite otherwise. And it may be this very fact that lends force to the various proposals that are being made these days advocating a "religionless Christianity" (cf. *Honest to God* by John A. T. Robinson). Undoubtedly the effort to achieve a new Christian worldliness, or to "secularize the gospel" is motivated in a variety of ways: in some instances it appears to be prompted by a dubious concern to attain intellectual and cultural respectability for religion, reminiscent of the modernistic zeal of the twenties; in other instances it appears to be favored because it promises to be an astute way of carrying on the apologetic task in the modern world among "its cultured despisers." For the most part, however, this new mood among us seems to be embraced simply out of weariness with formal Christianity, a kind of modern-day recurrence of the lay Christianity that has periodically burst forth throughout Christian history as a revolt from within, bent on "cleansing the inward parts."

It is quite possible, however, that these present-day efforts to bring the Christian witness incognito into secularized centers of the culture will yield some unexpected results. Committed Christians may discover amidst these so-called secularists resources of judgment as well as of grace that will radically transform and possibly deepen their own understanding of the Christian gospel. Anxiety, alienation, and despair, when humanly confronted as stark realities, can have a dimension of meaning, and possibly an impact, that eludes their liturgical or theological rendering. Experiencing gross indifference to human sensibilities, the raw exercise of power, and contempt for human sentiments of every kind can alert one to the hardness of heart in humanity as few sermons and scriptural homilies can convey. And, conversely, under other circumstances, encountering the human goodness of people outside the churches, sensing the quality of their discernment, judgment, and discipline of spirit, despite their seemingly secularized ways of living and thinking, may put to shame the churches' stereotyped estimates of human nature.

What I am insinuating by these oblique remarks is that there are resources within the culture that lend a sense of reality to this gospel of grace and judgment to which the church bears witness, but to which, the church as *church,* and Christians as *Christians,* may be but vaguely attuned. To apprehend the realities of faith as energies of grace and judgment concretely at work in culture, in human relationships, in the crises and triumphs of human enterprise, is no small or insignificant theological achievement. And a theology that is quickened to discern this dimension of the Christian witness has access to the very realities that speak forth through the Scriptures when they say, "Behold, and see!"

Faith, we may then discover anew as church people, is not a memory merely, recalled in creed and litany, not just the story of our lives reenacted in pageantry and ritual, not a will to believe despite all evidence to the contrary. Faith partakes of all these acts of reminiscence and decision, we will affirm; but we will discover that it is this and more. And this *more* of faith, we will find, issues from the realization that what we read about in Scripture, celebrate in sacrament, and proclaim through the Word, is a truth of immediate experience, a truth that transpires within every epochal occasion to visit upon every nexus of relationships, its offering of grace and judgment. Our faith, we may be startled to find, is not just a faith in the scriptural memory of the Christ-event, not just a symbolic transfer from an ancient to a modern idiom, but faith in the reality of a New Creation that meets us in every event of betrayal or blessedness, in every experience of sin and forgiveness, in every encounter with defeat and despair, and in the joys of the resurrected life that follows again and again upon this experience of judgment and grace as we mingle with our fellows, of whatever confession, or of no confession, and as we stumble into or out of the stark, tragedy-laden events of these harrowing experiences of present-day history.

I have done my best in these pages to declare a truth about the Christian faith that will not let me go, and which motivates my every word in formulating a Christian theology. That truth is that the realities of this faith are living, vital energies in the immediacies of experience. As such they are no respecters of persons or situations, or forms or institutions, though they exist and transpire through forms and institutions. But the forms we provide will not contain them—neither intellectual, aesthetic, moral, or institutional forms. For the Christian gospel leaps beyond the sanctuary into common places, like a fire that is no respecter of structures, particularly of those that would enclose or contain its flames. So, too, with these energies of grace and judgment of which the gospel speaks.

This does not imply, I would argue, that the forms, institutions, and structures which we create in order to express, convey, or clarify this life of the Spirit are of no avail. They are of the utmost importance when we are dealing with the problem of our own understanding of these realities, or with our own efforts at disciplining our capacities to receive and to respond to them. Every conscientious concern to achieve intelligibility in apprehending the Christian faith speaks out of an integrity of mind that carries its own justification. Every caution to preserve a sense of dignity and restraint in our approach to what is holy attests to the depth of our witness of faith, and to a humility that is proportionate to it. Every intimation of sensitivity in act or expression in bearing witness to our faith gives evidence of the disciplining to which we have submitted in restraining egoistic passions and feelings, thus summoning them to a more discerning level of wonder in worship. In each of these ways, let us confess, we do go astray, making idols of our human forms of sensibilities, our categories, our codes of conduct; yet through each of them we open ourselves to the chastening effects of a human grace that is akin to the sensitivity that is in God. We do not become divine by becoming more human; but neither do we attain spirituality by denying our humanity! Yet, when we pursue these human capacities and sensitivities under the judgment of grace, which is a good not our own, they can become the disciplined instrument of devotion and inquiry despite the fact that, as human forms, they present a possible threat as barriers to what is real and good beyond our human measure.

I must add a footnote to these concluding remarks. I am confident that some readers will feel that I have exaggerated the role of culture in theology, even falsifying its relation to the church. You may wish to criticize what I have presented, saying, "But don't you recognize that Christians themselves are people of the culture? The culture is in the churches, even as the churches are within the culture. The distinctions you make here are arbitrary and misleading."

In reply I must say: to be sure, Christians are people of the culture, and to that extent the culture is in the churches, even as the churches are within culture. In our modern society the lines of cleavage or demarcation are not sharply drawn. Nevertheless, they exist because there are distinctions between the people of culture who are within the church and the people of culture who are without it. In this respect, Christians, who are also people of the culture, do not fully embrace or express the culture in all its dimensions of human goodness and evil.

Let me put the matter bluntly and boldly: I mean to express a conviction that neither the glory of the human spirit nor its degradation in major key appears within the community of the committed. You can qualify that in whatever way you wish. It does require qualification in order to be reasonably accurate. But face the extreme assertion of this conviction first: there is something about church Christianity that depresses the creativities of men, that foreshortens their imaginative and critical powers and impels them to suspect concern with qualitative attainment, thus lulling them into or even summoning them to a preference for mediocrity. We should now qualify this assertion by saying that neither the glory of the human spirit nor its degradation in major key appears *readily* within the churches. By this I mean to acknowledge that there are to be found within the churches those for whom these human creativities mean much and who in themselves express this qualitative outreach of the human spirit. But they are lone voices, crying in a wilderness. It is true that they who speak in this way are lone voices crying in the wilderness of modern culture as well; but the fact remains that when they appear, they appear as a more formidable expression of this dimension of our humanity. And thus, simply on the pragmatic basis of turning to where they are, I tend to urge that theology, in order to be attentive to the meaning of man in terms of his human creativities, and the glory that is visited upon his structure of existence by reason of them, needs to have access to the resources of the cultural witness.

In a similar way, I would argue that church Christianity has little access to the depths of human degradation; thus, while Christian preachers and theologians speak freely of human sin and moral evil, their encounter with it tends to be circumscribed. Often it tends to be more formal than material. Do not misunderstand me. I am fully aware that church people, themselves, are sinners. Whether we are speaking in Niebuhr's terms of the sin of pride and arrogance that issues from men's so-called higher natures, or the shabby instances of clandestine sexuality in church circles that periodically break into the open in scandal sheets, there is no lack of human degradation among people of the churches. What is less available to the religious consciousness that is confined to its circles, however, is a concrete awareness of such human evil in its massive, persistent, and organized expression, such as appears in the workaday world of the culture, where evil, as a surd of insensitivity, perverseness, and violence, appears in demonic form. Our awareness as theologians of this dimension of the human spirit and its structured existence tends to be remote, meager, and secondhand. Thus our knowledge of man is partial, truncated, symbolic. If we venture to reach beyond our contained Christian outlook, we speak abstractly or obliquely about these surmised depths of human evil without really knowing the context in which they occur, without noting the ambiguities that attend such human evil in the *lived experiences* of men.

All I mean to say here is that the church theologian who presumes to speak out of a witness of faith concerning the human situation that has been insulated from that situation as it actually occurs in the teeming life of culture must admit to being deprived of material resources for his discipline. His theological critique, like his sermons and homilies, must, in the nature of the case, be "sicklied o'er with the pale cast of thought" peculiar to one who remains remote from the realities of which he speaks.

Now I am giving the impression, no doubt, that I mean to argue for immersing the theologian in the hubbub and hovels of culture, when actually I mean no such thing. Many theologians who have become awakened to this cultural dimension of the Christian witness and to the resources it brings to the theological task will readily follow this course and find identification in their own experiences with the problems to which they address themselves. I concur in this provided one recognizes the limits to which one can go in pursuing this course profitably as a disciplined inquirer. But being receptive to the resources of culture in pursuing one's theological task is more a state of mind than a state of life, implying a readiness to receive the life of culture freely into one's own life as one's own history and experience and to think and participate in it as being of a piece with its depths of reality. It then becomes a way of conceiving the revelation of God in Christ, as well as of understanding the plight and possibilities of men's souls. One for whom the gospel and culture must be segregated moves within a theology of containment, wherein the demarcations between spiritual and the secular, the sacred and the profane, are sharp and unyielding. And in that containment neither the full meaning of the gospel nor the full meaning of the culture, nor for that matter the full meaning of man as man, can be known or understood.

The life of the Spirit, as it appears within the structures of history, is a vast movement of grace and judgment, treaching the whole of a people's life. There are distinctions and specializations of practice and performance within this historical pageant of creativity and redemption, giving rise to different vortices of witness, bodying forth our human response to this life in God. But no one of these vortices, no one of these specialized functions, can exhaust or fully contain what is given in this good not our own, as it issues forth from our life in God.

Chapter Eleven

# The Christian Legacy
# and Our Cultural Identity

My intention in this chapter is neither to counter the claim that
Western culture has become secularized and thus post-Christian[1] nor to
aid and abet the effort to demonstrate that we are a Christian culture.[2]
Neither do I mean to join the chorus of moralistic voices urging us to
become more Christian. I share some of the concerns and judgments
implicit in each of these efforts; but I have misgivings about each of
them as well. I must confess also to a bias against the assumption that,
by increasing our moral effort and purpose to be more Christian, we
will necessarily improve matters humanly, politically, and every other
way in Western experience. Paraphrasing a statement William Ernest
Hocking once made concerning religion, Christianity throughout Western history has been "a huge potency of ambiguous meaning and
value." Some manifestations of it, to be sure, have been neither
ambiguous nor potent. Some have been unambiguously evil; and some,
while they may be reckoned unambiguously good, have lacked potency
and effect. Yet, it would commend no one to be unambiguously for or
against things Christian, any more than it would enhance one's judgment to be for or against religion *per se*. Compassion and concern in
registering such misgivings and judgments are imperative, however, in

1. Cf. Gabriel Vahanian, *The Death of God:* The Culture of Our Post-Christian Era (New
York: George Braziller, 1957); Mircea Eliade, *The Sacred and the Profane* (New York:
Harper, 1957); Harvey Cox, *The Secular City* (New York: Macmillan, 1965); Bernard
E. Meland, *The Secularization of Modern Cultures* (New York: Oxford University Press,
1966).
2. Cf. Christopher Dawson, *Religion and the Rise of Western Culture* (London: Sheed and
Ward, 1950); *The Historic Reality of Christian Culture* (New York: Harper, 1960); T. S.
Eliot, *The Idea of a Christian Society* (New York: Harcourt, Brace & Co., 1939).

both instances lest one be seduced into assuming he is critically minded when, in fact, he may simply be embittered and biased. Yet compassion need not give way to uncritical approval of whatever presumes to be religious or Christian.

I

What I am concerned to assert is that our identity as a people of this Western experience partakes of the Christian legacy in ways that go deeper than the ideography of our art and architecture, or than the various conceptual formulations conveyed in systems of Christian doctrine and philosophies that have appeared during the several centuries of our history. For its identity is indicated not simply in these symbolic and conceptual forms, but in the structure of experience at the level of feeling and sensibilities, expressed through our hopes and expectations as well as through our cultural élan. The identity of any people coheres with the orbit of meaning in which their historical experiences take place. By orbit of meaning in this context I refer to the cycle of responses giving rise to a complex of symbols and signs, expressed or anticipated, which contribute to a sense of orientation and familiarity in one's mode of existence. Such orientation carries with it a degree of ready recognition of the intentions and expectations expressed within the routines of the lived experience, and of the complex of feeling that is forming or has formed within that context of culture. There are, to be sure, orbits within orbits, as one contemplates the historical formations of cultures: regional and racial peculiarities, amidst a wider, communal, national, or continental consensus; radical shifts in sensibilities and judgment as the generations move in upon one another. Yet one comes to recognize encompassing, yet defining limits to the various inter-orbits of meaning that have formed through historical periods of time to give rise to discernible cultural areas within which a recognizable path of characteristic human responses, expressions, and behavior transpires. Cultures in this sense are historical growths with a specifiable space-time continuum, and as such, convey a kind of duration peculiar to their temporal-spatial history. Within every such orbit of meaning an historical sequence of reflection, decision, and action has emerged to give a characteristic outlook and style of expression to the cultural experience of the historically conditioned stream of events.

It should not be assumed that, in speaking of cultures in this historically temporal and spatial sense, one is necessarily compressing the
mode of life within the geographical and occupational bounds of that
experience. That, I think, was a limitation of early environmental
studies such as W. G. Sumner's *Folkways* and Emile Durkheim's *Les
Formes Élémentaires de la Vie Religieuse,* which succeeded fairly well
in translating all symbolic references and ritual expressing outreach and
wonder into dramatic simulations of occupation and environment. Even
though these prosaic features of occupation and environment provided
the format and script of ritualistic action, the ritualistic response itself,
or the very dramatization of occupational routines as ritual, conveyed
an assumption that this round of prosaic activities opened into a penumbra of cosmic and trans-functional meaning, or in some sense
acknowledged such a dimension as being integral with what was
familiarly encountered in experiences, yet carrying overtones of a wider
sphere of reference, however designated.

That ultimacy as a dimension of experience beyond our knowable efforts
or awareness transpires to give depth of meaning to the human situation
as immediately discerned within our structured existence need not be
disavowed. Conceivably, all lived experience participates in a context
of relations and resources that exceed and even elude our perceptual
experiences, not to mention our cognitive formulations. One does not
need to relapse into supernaturalism, or even some mode of neo-
supernaturalism, to take account of this fact. The new physics has
already assumed this stance in its experimentations and mode of
inquiry. And recognition of the definitive, and thereby limited, character of all natural structures at any stage of evolvement led emergent
thinkers in science and philosophy a generation ago to presuppose intimations of relations and prescient occurrences attending the *field,* or
creative nexus, of all lived experience. Like William James before them,
these emergent thinkers thus sought to be attentive to a horizon of
expectancy as a resource of potential insight, or as a source of judgment,
for each percipient event. That this that extends our range of apprehension is "more than we can think" or perceive need not, therefore,
imply transcendence in a supernatural sense but, rather, a depth or range
in the natural habitat itself that simply exceeds our manageability as
creatures, as natural structures that have attained a given level of
emergence.

Applying this observation to our awareness of any cultural history, we may be led to surmise that apprehending meanings and expectations within the various cultures that extend the scope and significance of immediate occasions in the sense of participating in depths of ultimacy as they loom within the immediacies of man's manageably structured and more discernible existence, may simply be the most natural response of discerning and sensitive human beings. Insofar as this that is so apprehended or attended is not catapulted into some absolutizing or finalizing revelation, routing all sensitive, empirical inquiry, such awareness could enhance, rather than distort, what is clearly perceived and structurally formulated.

All peoples' cultural experiences speak, then, one may assume, within the limits of their structured existence, yet speak in terms that reach or extend beyond that recognizable structure of experience. What is acknowledged, affirmed, and communicated as a witness of faith attests, with varying degrees of accuracy and relevance, to what has happened within that cultural history, yet not in the sense of conveying the full dimension of its lived experience. The witness points simultaneously to what has been a recognizable and communicable sequence of events, and to what is beyond comprehension, designation, or communication, or even beyond what one can think. This penumbra of a undesignatable and seemingly incommunicable fringe of meaning will find its way into various modes of creative and imaginative discourse where the intention is not designation, but expressiveness, a way of holding in focus or of pointing to whatever evokes or attends the "More" of experience conveying the wider field or dimension of living.

When myth and poetry, music and the dramatic arts, that attend every religious culture are understood on these terms they become exceedingly important as indices of "the rich fullness" of events that has been discerned and lived with throughout its history. To be sure they give evidence as well of the imaginative and expressive power of a people under duress or stimulus, as well as their power of restraint or lack of it in being expressive. In any event, the responsiveness of a people, both to the functional needs that concern survival and nurture and to their wider awareness of intimations of meaning that add to the surplusage of experience, is what gives style and character to the culture that has evolved within that history. And this style and character, hard-earned and persistent, provides a culture, in turn, with marks of its identity.

The style or character of a people is never one thing, though it may persist as one prevailing thing among many competing strands of influence and interest. No culture, except possibly among primitive peoples, where uniformity and conformity are more readily manageable, has succeeded in adhering continuously to a single line of development. And were one to become more attuned to the subtleties of exchange between people of primitive societies, one might find variations and cycles among competing themes of identity even among them.

## II

The Judaic-Christian legacy as a heritage shaping our cultural identity is not simply a legacy of doctrine and belief. In fact, I would argue that doctrine and belief have been the most expendable aspects of this legacy. Doctrines and beliefs have undergone considerable attrition, revision, even rejection. Nor has any specific ethic, moral code, or set of ideals persisted from age to age as the definitive statement of the Christian witness or measure of life, though particular groups or sects within that tradition have held persistently to their own historic formulations as being definitive for them. What have been enduring and efficacious have been the *primal themes or motifs of the faith,* conveyed through the *mythos* of our culture within a *structure of experience* that defines and has given character to our Western experience as a people—a structure, not so much designed by any single generation, as distilled from the persisting modes of feeling and decision within that lived experience. It may be helpful to comment on each of these terms.

### *Themes (or Motifs) of the Faith*

In Chapter Seven, the motifs of the Judaic-Christian faith were presented as themes relating to the drama of redemption which had emerged initially in early Hebrew history as recorded in the chronicle of events, poetry, and literature. Eulogies of the Suffering Servant, to be followed by explicit expectations of the Messiah, assumed more definitive form as a Christian drama of hope and renascence in the kerygma of the New Testament, attesting to the resurrected Christ and the Christian community that took form in response to that witness to the "New Creation." These motifs of the faith, expressive of hope and new life in the face of dire events presaging almost certain defeat, convey a sustained élan of trust and expectancy; first with regard to the historical process, itself, in Judaism; then, in Christian writings, with regard to the ultimate outcome of history, the *eschaton,* in the Kingdom of God.

## Mythos

This word functions as a persisting pattern of meaning and valuation arising within the structured experience of a people, and imaginatively projected through metaphor and drama, conveys the perceptive truths of the historical experiences bearing upon man's destiny. These perceptive truths of experience express themselves within the culture in the form of hopes, expectations, attitudes of trust, or even determination; or in the form of human responses to circumstances affecting the stance in meeting commonplace as well as significant human situations, much of which gets recorded in the reflective and poetic literature of a people. Yet, by mythos I mean something more than a particular mode of reflectiveness or poetry. The mythos encompasses these responses, but it includes them in the context of more visceral and imaginative assertions of the psychical thrust of a people, fashioning them into a structured reality as a continuous cultural history, and carrying forward as a subliminal depth of perception and feeling that which gives shaping to the sensibilities, apprehensions, expectations, intentions, and valuations of a people.

Insofar as the mythos becomes expressive at the conscious level, it may be said to surface in the mode of an appreciative awareness, or a questing sense of wonder. For in this mode, consciousness responds out of the depth of its relationships, in contrast to that kind of critical and observational reason that is selective and sharply focused for definitive or practical ends. The mythos partakes of the stream of experience as well as the stream of thought. And it gathers in as well inert, though symbolically significant, precedents and practices which body forth, as it were, what the phenomenologists have called the *intentionality* of a people.

## Structure of Experience

Mythos and structure of experience tend to merge in our speaking in such a way as to seem to come to the same thing; yet they connote different representations of the historical experience, and point up different characterizations of it. Mythos is the psychical thrust issuing from an orientation which any orbit of meaning and its primal motifs bequeath to experience. And in any epoch of that historical experience it is the complex of feeling expressive of sentiments and sensibilities informing decisions, action, and expectation. The structure of experience, on the other hand, is the dynamic, living residue of historic acts and decisions, manifest in the immediacy of every individuated and communal experience of a people or culture. The mythos presupposes some continuity of historic motivation, giving rise to hopes and expectations; the structure of experience registers such continuity as lived fact and circumstance, a distillation of the historical experience as lived, and thus as a stark given of every immediate moment of history.

In *Faith and Culture* I tried to convey some sense of this stark given of the immediate moment of history, saying:

> To trace the routes by which the valuations of the culture are mediated to each emerging generation would be an enormous undertaking; but it could be done with some success. The full delineation of these routes, however, would be only a partial portrayal of the emerging structure of experience; for there is much that is gathered into the depths of the moving moment of history that cannot be brought to light or designated.
>
> What the historian cannot bring to light is the accumulative wisdom and concern that works at the feeling level of men's consciousness, unbeknown to them, but with a shaping that is unmistakable in retrospect. The historian looking back can recount the visible features in contrast to other moving edges of history; thus he can know that this deeper shaping was at work. But this internal wisdom of existence, by which the structure of experience is communicated to each living person, can only be appropriated and, as it were, unwittingly disclosed, as in the more intimate, personal histories of people.[3]

## The Three Foci of the Christian Witness

What has been said in characterizing the three basic notions—motifs, mythos, and structure of experience—was aimed at giving substance to the conception of faith as psychic and social energy. We now advance to a further stage in the argument in recalling that the witness of faith in any culture, but preeminently in the culture of the West in which the Christian legacy has been formative, proceeds from at least three sources.

3. Bernard E. Meland, *Faith and Culture* (New York: Oxford University Press, 1953; paperback edition: Carbondale, Ill.: Southern Illinois University Press, 1972), pp. 103–4.

Thus we must speak of three foci of the Christian witness, three centers from which response to the themes of the legacy has been conveyed in Western history: (a) the cultus (church); (b) individual, often dissonant strands of nonconformity (saints, mystics, and other minority voices); and (c) the culture, itself, notably the cultural arts and music, but even the philosophic lore and sciences as they relate to the primal themes of the legacy, not to speak of industry and the political sphere.

In my judgment, the historical witness of faith or experience of faith in Western history has generally been conceived in too restrictive a way as being wholly church-centered. Thus, in the last analysis, the Christian legacy has been looked upon essentially as a cultic legacy which somehow managed to survive within Western history, thereby taking on Western cultural forms of the various periods, and later being transmitted to other cultures of the world with varying degrees of success and failure. In contrast to that assumption I suggest that the Judaic-Christian legacy is more than a cultic witness of faith and that it was never otherwise. However much its origin may be traceable to developments leading to the establishing of the church, once it was given impetus and carrying power, the witness fanned out, into broader streams of influence and motivation, generating modes of incentive and creative expression which could only indirectly be related to the cultus. These broader streams of influence, following from the fanning out of its witness, are to be discerned in the very early stages of Western history, even when Christendom was at its height. For throughout this period are to be found instances in remote areas of the culture of creative art and expression, not authorized or sponsored by the church, partaking of the motifs of the Christian legacy, and, in their manner, bearing witness to that legacy in ways that could not be accounted consistent with the church's rendering of it. This would include not only the so-called heretical forms of thought and experimentation that were detected and summarily dealt with by the church, but nuclei of piety groups and mystics, craftsmen and artists and other simple folk among fishermen and farmers, whose deviant practices, expressive in their own way of the legacy of faith, did not come to public notice sufficiently to be apprehended by the hierarchy. What was covert throughout the ancient and early modern period of Western history became overt and explicitly expressed, once the control of church authority subsided.

It is common to designate the modern period of Western history, beginning with the mid-seventeenth century, as a time when the cultural arts and sciences, along with industry, won their freedom from ecclesiastical control, and thus set forth upon independent routes of secularization. This, for example, is Arnold Toynbee's judgment in *An Historian's Approach to Religion.* If "church-control" is made the criterion of the continuing role and shaping of the Christian legacy within Western culture, then clearly the freeing of the arts and learning, along with industry, in the seventeenth century and after marks a time in Western history when the shaping of Western culture by the Christian legacy came to an end. The secularist is content to settle for this judgment of events. Indeed, many people of the modern world who continue to consider themselves Christian in matters of personal faith are persuaded that the secularization of the culture must follow, as an inevitable consequence, following the collapse of the church-control of culture. This means, in effect, that attentiveness to the Christian legacy is purely a matter of personal choice and interest. And its continuance within Western culture rests upon individual preference and decision in supporting and participating in the cultic activities of the faith.

I find problems not only with the judgment just expressed, but with the assumption that precedes it, namely, that the Christian legacy is to be understood solely as a cultic phenomenon, and thus to be discerned solely within the institutions and practices countenanced by the church, either within the earlier period of Western history in which the church-control of culture was intact, or within the modern period following the collapse of such control. The Christian legacy, I mean to argue, is a more subtle and diversified complex of phenomena than this view of our history presupposes. And as a witness of faith, both as an historical legacy and as a persisting phenomenon within the structure of Western experience, it is a vast and variegated complex of meaning and valuation conveyed through multiple modes of expression, decision, and action.

Faith is not just a response of sentiment, nor is it purely conceptual, as in forms of belief; it is an ingredient of the human psyche which weights heavily our human acts and decisions, as well as the states of mind and bodily feelings with which we come to acts and decisions. Faith is a primal energy of a people and of individuals which is of a piece with the structure of experience that has formed the matrix of their living, and which, in every moment of immediacy, gives context, depth, and relationship to their individuated modes of existence. However inchoate, however intermittently assertive or expressive, faith is the elemental source of our being, active often only at the level of bodily feeling, but always potentially expressive through conscious and assertive acts. In brief, faith points up the character of a people or of individuals, rising out of participation in any given structure of experience. Thus faith as a social energy, conveyed through the mythos and expressive within the structure of experience, is what bequeaths to a people their identity as persons and as historical beings.

But faith has its language and its modes of creative expression. Not all of it is pious or conforming to the demands of cultic proprieties; in fact, not all of it within the church itself simulates its stereotypes. For, when the creative spirit addresses what might otherwise be cultic or conventional, this legacy takes on nuances of meaning and beauty which only the imaginative talent can bequeath to it. Similarly, when a critical, probing mind addresses its themes and its issues, it can assume proportions of meaning not readily discerned in the cultic statements of faith formulated for purposes of piety, preaching, and other practical or didactic disciplines. These critical inquiries may also dissipate the lure of faith and create dissonant reflections that confound one's identity, which is the risk of all inquiry. Yet the health of creative imagination and of critical inquiry, and their power to enhance the witness of faith beyond its cultic expressions, has been demonstrated again and again; and is, in fact, a presupposition of all liberal learning and enlightened culture.

This vast heritage of creative and imaginative rendering of themes or motifs of the Christian faith within and under secular auspices is one of the major dimensions and sources of the cultural witness of Christian faith, and as such, is a resource for enlarging and rendering in subtle and imaginative form, not to speak of disciplined form, the vision and incentives of human experience as these are conveyed within the Christian mythos.

I might say, parenthetically, that our inability, or our reluctance, within our American experience to take readily to discerning this cultural rendering of the themes of our historic faith stems, in part at least, from our mode of studying our religious history. It stems also, of course, from our historic, Protestant posture within the American experience; but that is another story. To put it briefly, the study of Christianity tends to be pursued differently from the study of other religions. We rarely think of the people of other religions or cultures, or of their religious ideas and practices, in isolation from the lived experience within these several cultures. This, no doubt, follows from the fact that the disciplines employed to study these faiths have been the history of religions and cultural anthropology. Yet no historians of religion to my knowledge have delved into the cultural matrix of Christian faith in the way, for example, that they have explored Hinduism, Buddhism, Islam, and other non-Christian religions. And few church historians have addressed themselves seriously to this cultural matrix. Not until Troeltsch's studies and the socio-historical inquiries of the early Chicago school were even environmental studies undertaken. There is some corrective of this lack among church historians today, but the efforts here are still not probing, and they may not be until our historians of religion overcome their reticence to enter their homeland with their disciplined tools of study.

### III

Some beginnings were made in probing the deeper complex of the lived experiences within Christian and Western history by Wilhelm Dilthey in his *Einleitung in die Geisteswissenschaften* (1883), in which he sought to look at "the stream of history" as experienced both in terms of the self and in culture. Much that has since appeared in this vein, especially in the existentialist literature stemming from Heidegger, is indebted to the stimulus of Dilthey's insights. Among recent phenomenologists, the work of the late M. Merleau-Ponty in exploring the "phenomenal field" of perception has been particularly illuminating. The fact that he, more than any other phenomenologist, addressed himself to problems and drew upon resources common to phenomenology and process thought made his work particularly interesting.

In a related way, the efforts of Ernst Troeltsch as well as those of the early Chicago school of Shailer Mathews and Shirley Jackson Case were innovating in exploring the cultural context of the Christian legacy. They were especially effective in pointing up the environmental factor in the rise of Christian doctrine and institutions. One detects echoes of these earlier studies, both concerning the inner stream of history, and the environmental influences, in H. Richard Niebuhr's writings, notably in *The Meaning of Revelation, Christ and Culture,* and *Radical Monotheism and Western Culture.* And, in a different vein,

Sidney Mead's *A Lively Experiment* can be said to employ these modes of analysis in interpreting the American experience.

While the environmental approach to understanding the growth of Christian belief and institutions in Western history, as presented by Troeltsch and the early Chicago school, proved illuminating, it always seemed to fall short of conveying the dynamic of Christian faith as a legacy shaping the culture. And, while "the story of our life" as presented by Richard Niebuhr in *The Meaning of Revelation* succeeded in conveying, and even heightening, one's sense of such a dynamic, the effect of the interpretation was to insulate that inner stream of Christian history from the broad stream of our cultural history. Undoubtedly, what lay back of these restrictions in both cases was the cultic conception of the legacy itself. While the forms in which the historical faith was expressed or conveyed partook of a cultural imagery, the faith, itself, was not to be conceived as being culturally formed or conditioned to such a degree as to be expressive of the cultural élan.

When attention is directed away from the exclusively cultic stance, as well as from the overt, conceptual and institutional level of Christian history in the West, to the emerging and persisting complex of the lived experience of Western peoples, the assumptions commonly associated with such characterizations as "the age of Christendom" in contrast to "a post-Christian era" of the West, appear inadequate, if not misleading. For what is involved as a persisting dimension of the legacy within the lived experience is not to be equated simply with what endures or does not endure in doctrine or any institutional practice, or in the prevailing tone of the cultural mood or style, as expressed in overt language. All of these enterprises fluctuate in response to changing winds of doctrine and precedent, which affect both cultus and culture.

What is less subject to the impact of the interchange of communicable meaning at the level of discourse is the stream of experience that is transmitted as bodily feeling from age to age. Not that the feeling context is consciously conveyed from generation to generation, or that an entire area of the lived experience of a people simulates a unity of sensibility and psychical thrust; there may be striking contrasts between them in that area of response. Rather, it is that a funded resource of expectation and outreach persists, seemingly indolent and inexpressive at times, until tapped by assertive effort, or by the convergence of historical accidents and circumstances disrupting a prevailing consensus, or even by an unmanageable mood of relinquishment under the duress of circumstances that seem unendurable, except as respite is offered, and grace is given. It is then that the tides of inchoate action and reaction assert themselves out of this funded complex of feeling, often to redirect human effort and conscious decision. Such occasions afford contemporary man experiences of the limits of his own conscious designs, and simultaneously awaken him to the More within the Creative Passage in which life is cast, to redirect the venture in living. There is no adequate way of speaking about this depth of passage that attends, and intermittently erupts, within each instance of existing. A minimal way is to say that it carries forward within individuated life experiences and within a total community the vital nexus of inherited bodily feeling in which all alike, basically, within a given orbit of lived experience, share.

Now to cognize this persisting resource of lived experience in which the immediacies of every concrete event share taxes the mind to its limits. And the truth is, we can only cognize the faintest glimpse or momentary awareness of it, enabling us to acknowledge that we live more deeply than we can think, by reason of a past inheritance of contextual relations which, in actuality, we cannot reject bodily, however much we may ignore or repudiate them consciously. Such glimpses in turn may point up a depth of ultimacy within our immediacies which attend every moment of our existence, in which we confront an unmanageable surplusage of experience which functions both as a resource and as a restraint upon our conscious reflections and inquiry. We face here the possibility of having to say that there is no way by which to address ourselves to this unmanageable surplusage of experience. And, in fact, this observation has already been made, encouraging some to pursue its vagaries with zest as a mystical venture, or to acknowledge it as a horizon of all critical human thought, though unmanageable, and to settle for a mode of inquiry that is manageable. All disciplined inquiry, of necessity, must choose the latter course. But then it follows that disciplined inquiry is thereby radically limited, not only in method, but in expectations regarding the outcome of its inquiry. In short, the *reality* of a situation and the *understanding* of it which any disciplined inquiry yields, or is able to disclose, are not to be equated. If this dictum is disregarded, disciplined inquiry is made deceptive and potentially illusory.

Yet, one is made aware of the fact again and again that disciplined inquiry is itself a fluctuating and growing procedure. A science, for example, will persist for a considerable time within a range of pre-suppositions which tend to lend larger scope and application to its find-ings, as did the Newtonian notion of absolute space from the seventeenth century through the close of the nineteenth century, when relativity physics disclosed the illusoriness of such a firm notion of natural order as Newtonian science had presupposed. Similarly, new modes of inquiry in philosophy, psychology, anthropology, and religious studies have altered not only procedures, but suppositions as to what is avail-able to inquiry, thereby either restricting or enlarging its scope. With such changes in procedure and expectation have come also new tools of inquiry which have opened up or lighted up a range of data hitherto not even suspected of being available to inquiry. The disclosure of atomic structure in the new physics, following from discoveries in radiation, is a case in point. The demonstration by William James that relations are experienceable and are experienced[4] is another such innovation, as was Whitehead's formulation of the notion of "causal efficacy."[5] All of these innovations opened the way for attending dynamic relations within the structural immediacies of the lived ex-perience, and indirectly, they provided critical grounds for reexamining and reassessing the persistence of past legacies, notably at the level of feeling and motivation, within the immediacies of experience as conveyed within individuals, communities, and the culture.

Whitehead's formulation of causal efficacy, presupposing both James's innovating view of relations and the dynamic structure of relations as formulated in the new physics, is particularly illuminating as these bear upon the persisting force and character of past legacies within the immediacies of experience. Here are some of his words bearing on this theme:

> For the organic theory, the most primitive perception is "feeling the body as functioning." This is a feeling of the world in the past; it is the in-heritance of the world as a complex of feeling; namely, it is the feeling of derived feelings. The later, sophisticated perception is "feeling the con-temporary world."[6]

4. William James, *Psychology* I (New York: Henry Holt & Co., 1890), pp. 243 ff.; and *Essays in Radical Empiricism* (New York: Longmans Green & Co., 1912), pp. 41 ff.
5. Alfred North Whitehead, *Process and Reality* (New York: Macmillan, 1929), chaps. II, IV, and VIII; and *Symbolism, Its Meaning and Effect* (New York: Macmillan, 1927), chap. II.
6. Whitehead, *Process and Reality*, p. 125.

Perception in (this) primary sense is perception of the settled world in the past as conditioned by its feeling-tones, and as efficacious by reason of those feeling-tones. Perception in this sense of the term will be called "perception in the mode of causal efficacity."[7]

But what is already given for experience can only be derived from that natural potentiality which shapes a particular experience in the guise of causal efficacy. Causal efficacy is that hand of the settled past in the formation of the present.[8]

It is evident that "perception in the mode of causal efficacy" is not that sort of perception which has received chief attention in the philosophical tradition. Philosophers have disdained the information about the universe obtained through these visceral feelings, and have concentrated on visual feelings.[9]

Presentational immediacy is an outgrowth from the complex datum implanted by causal efficacy.[10]

The contrast between the comparative emptiness of Presentational Immediacy and the deep significance disclosed by Causal Efficacy is at the root of the pathos which haunts the world.[11]

Our experience arises out of the past; it enriches with emotion and purpose its presentation of the contemporary world; and it bequeaths its character to the future, in the guise of an effective element forever adding to, or substracting from, the richness of the world. For good or for evil.[12]

There is, in the mode of causal efficacy, a direct perception of those antecedent actual occasions which are causally efficacious both for the percipient and for the relevant events in the presented locus.[13]

The "inheritance of the world as a complex of feeling" points to a deeper and more subtle shaping of the human psyche than is recorded in the history of ideas. To a degree, of course, the history of ideas and doctrines partakes of it, but only in the way that conscious, conceptual meaning can be distilled from the perceptual flux within the lived experience. And it may not be assumed that what is so distilled as conscious and critically controlled meaning is all that is important or relevant in gauging either the potency or the duration of a legacy of

7. Ibid, p. 184.
8. Whitehead, *Symbolism, Its Meaning and Effect*, p. 50.
9. Whitehead, *Process and Reality*, p. 184.
10. Ibid, p. 262.
11. Whitehead, *Symbolism, Its Meaning and Effect*, p. 47.
12. Ibid, pp. 58–59.
13. Whitehead, *Process and Reality*, p. 256.

faith. On the contrary, what inheres in the structure of experience at any given time in history, as a persisting depth of latent impulse and motivation, will always have the potential of vastly enhancing and accelerating the force of critical insight and judgment, or of whelming it beneath a flood of reaction and resistance.

Neither does it follow that critical awareness and decision are always on the side of virtue and value, nor that the potency of this persisting complex of feeling invariably threatens or destroys value. This, I think, is a bias that misleads many who dismiss this latent, primal efficacy, issuing from the complex of feeling, as being primitive, elemental, and thereby inferior in the way that instinct is rendered inferior to reason. To be sure, it is "a huge potency" often "ambiguous in meaning and value"; but it carries in its passage as well depths of the lived experience and nurture which, in their own way, yield wisdom and proportion, sensitivity and awareness, that may season, restrain, or actually nurture the impulse to action, prompted by immediate demands.

The mythos by its persistent shaping of the complex of feeling, along with other precognitive influences, generates a structured reality within experience in any given cultural history. The structure of experience is the most elemental level of meaning in any culture; this is so in contrast to the highly focused level disclosed in critical reflection and inquiry in which cognitive awareness is sharpened to its maximum degree. Yet it is also the most inclusive and, conceivably, mature, insofar as it bodies forth distillations from critical thought which have been assimilated to the lived experience of a community. The structure of experience may thus be seen as a depth of the Creative Passage within culture mediating the shaping of mythos and logos, and bodying forth the interrelated distillations from each dimension, along with the dissonance engendered between them.

The structure of experience is thus simultaneously inclusive and selective. It is inclusive in the sense that, at each point in history, within any culture, it is the distillation of all that has happened as actual event within the lived experience of a people. Yet, being a distillation from the passage of events, what it presents as the lived experience of any culture in any given immediacy of its history is the stark, living residue, shorn of what could not be assimilated to the lived experience.

What is distinctive about the structure of experience, however, is its livingness, and the efficacy afforded it as a causal factor in conveying this distillation of the lived experience to the immediate moment of creativity. To be sure, the immediate moment of present creativity is also selective—so selective, in fact, that, in that instance of time, what is bodied forth as a context of feeling and distilled wisdom can be only marginally appropriated as a conscious event. Its selectivity may not proceed necessarily from an increase in critical awareness, but from a blockage of judgment in regard to the inherited past. In such an instance of resistance, what has immediately preceded will be most firmly rejected, and, in its stead, some earlier context of the historical experience will be imaginatively appropriated. Every renaissance, Toynbee has observed, exemplifies this kind of dialectic. Yet the full burden of opportunity and peril which the structure of experience bodies forth in each immediacy of history is rarely, if ever, discerned. There is an economy of decision and action to be observed in this interchange, based upon the fallibility of man and of each generation of history, which limits the degree to which the assimilation of the structure of experience in any moment of history can be effected, and the character of what is assimilated, appreciated, and acknowledged. Yet what appears unassimilated as conscious event or decision is not thereby rendered inactual. This, I think, points to one of the serious illusions borne by all reform movements and reactions, and by liberating efforts to be done with the tyranny of the past. The fact that any portion of the structure of experience cannot be consciously assimilated to the present, or accepted, may not mean its dissolution, however much rejected. For the rejection is only a conscious act, leaving the psychical, bodily, or structural dimension uncalculated. Thus, what is dismissed from consciousness as an unreality for the present may persist as a bodily and psychical feeling, laden with its own latent, accumulative efficacy.

The argument toward which these statements intend is that an historical legacy persists with a tenacity and subtlety in shaping the lived experience of a people which renders it indispensable to the culture's identity. However rejected, muted, or ignored, the legacy persists as a mode of efficacy.

As I continue to press hard on this insistent theme that our identity as Western peoples stems from its Judaic-Christian heritage, I sense a flood of demurs echoing the protest, "Certainly, Western experience is not simply the bearer of a Judaic-Christian heritage. What of the refractions of Greece and Rome, that of the Moslem era of the Near East as it flooded in upon Europe, notably Spain and France, and through them, a prolonged era of Aristotelian Greece? And what about Marx, Darwin, and Freud, to mention only three dissonant voices?" My comments here may not seem persuasive, but I offer them as supplements to what I have already said by way of correlating these divergent and challenging episodes of Western history with the structure of experience I have described.

One will immediately recognize that the Judaic-Christian pattern of meaning and valuation has undergone periodic translation, even metamorphosis, at various stages of Western history. In each instance the primal themes, in effect, have been summoned to the demands of, say, Greek or Roman, even Moslem, modes of thought and styles of expression, or they have been sharply challenged, even driven underground by them for stretches of time, as in the case of Marxist and Freudian attacks in recent times. This legacy of faith has been summoned as well to release its cultic form of witness from inhibiting restraints which foreclosed interchange with modern science in response to discoveries and new perspectives upon man and his world, as in the Darwinian episodes of reaction and, more recently, in the refashioning of the imagery of thought following upon disclosures in physics concerning relativity and atomic research.

These many historical challenges I have taken to be not rival alternatives to the Christian mythos and structure of experience, though each of them in turn has, in effect, simulated the cultic role. Rather, at times, these deeply dissonant, even heretical, strands of disavowal have often purged the contemporary formulation of faith of debilitating idealizations and illusions, and confronted it with realistic demands of the lived experience insofar as they have been assimilated to the witness of faith. Orthodoxies and fundamentalist expressions of the Christian legacy, sad to say, have followed a consistent method of eluding encounter with any such deviant challenges to their historic formulations. They had only to declare them heresies, meaning innovating or strange doctrines carrying a margin of truth hopelessly mingled with error, and thus basically false doctrine, to exorcise their threat to the faithful. Unfortunately, it was often the margin of truth, pertinent to that occasion in history, that offered serious challenges and corrective to these historic formulations, from which new insight into the faith might possibly be forthcoming. We see this in the Marxist attack upon individualistic modes of idealization and fulfillment to the neglect of the human community, or in the Freudian disclosure of the unconscious as a challenge and supplement to our insulated modes of reflection and inquiry, based on a rigid adherence to *conscious* experience. When Christian theologians and churchmen have simply reacted negatively to these dissonant strands of disavowal, they have forfeited occasions for rigorous appraisal and reform of cultic and cultural perversions of the sustaining faith.

To be sure, these dissonant strands, when they have assumed cultic force and appeal, have been taken to be viable alternatives to the Judaic-Christian legacy. Insofar as this legacy and its survival hinge upon its doctrinal decisions or perspectives, these dissonant cults tend to be just that. But, as I have insisted, the vitality of this Judaic-Christian legacy does not rest exclusively upon the viability of its doctrinal statements. Nothing is more fraught with seasonal judgments, amounting to positive error, than many of our staunchly held *"truths of the faith."*

## IV

Now to move swiftly, and, as it may be, prematurely, to a statement of how I see our cultural identity as being related to the Christian legacy, I must say that I find myself persuaded, as an initial judgment, that the redemptive theme has entered subtly and pervasively into the shaping of our Western experience. It is not the theological rendering of this theme that has been efficacious in this context. Much that has happened in that highly technical sphere of discourse would seem to have eluded the persisting stream of lived experience. Rather, what appears to have been formative of the Western psyche through successive generations of its history is a cultural distillation of this primal motif, conveying, not a doctrinal judgment of belief, or a liturgical act, but a cultural stance toward life. Gamaliel Bradford, a literary figure of a generation or more ago, expressed this cultural stance aptly in his book, *Life and I,* saying, "Life is the triumph of hope over experience." Interestingly enough, this is precisely the turn given to our Western élan by non-Westerners, particularly in Southeast Asia. For, through the years, this openness to the future in Western thinking has stood in sharp contrast to the realistic, if not fatalistic, motif that has characterized and motivated their own mode of life and imagination. Hope springs eternal? Only among a people and in a culture for whom the options are left open, and in which life is lived forward. The redemptive theme, then, translated into a cultural stance, appears to have been made the leitmotif of Western experience, as it was in the primal drama itself.

One could, of course, make a case for saying that the motif of sin wielded considerable influence in Western thinking and sensibilities, not only in shaping its conception of man and the human condition, but in governing, directing, and nurturing the common life of society. An outstanding instance of its prominence is the Puritan epoch in seventeenth century England and colonial America. Each of these Puritan strongholds succeeded in impressing upon the culture at large a radically restrictive and repressive intonation of this theme which had serious repercussions, not only in dissociating the cultic life of faith from the culture, but in shaping the human psyche both within the cultus and in the culture at large. For a time the notion of sin loomed as the focal point of the legacy. Grace and forgiveness and the tenderness of life consonant with the drama of redemption itself were obscured, if not routed, as being overpermissive and weak in motivation. In their place, judgment and punishment loomed as characteristic motifs of the Christian legacy, second only to the doctrine of sin. Apart from the distortion of the legacy that was implied, this reversal of themes paved the way for the opposite reversal in liberal theories of man in which the notion of sin receded, and then, presumably, vanished, as concern with human ideals gave rise to theories idealizing human nature and the possibilities of man simply as man.

One could argue that proportion and adequacy in conceiving of the Christian legacy turn on the degree to which attention is given to the holistic character of the drama of redemption, and in what that purports concerning the intentionality of a people. On this basis, our Protestant heritage, especially in its American mode, gives one cause for reflection. For much of Protestantism is either unmindful of, or indifferent toward, the Christian legacy as a holistic structure, or as it is disclosed in its total impact upon Western experience. For Protestant history has been one of selecting or isolating some one doctrinal strand to the exclusion of others. Often the doctrine so isolated has had but a marginal relation to the dramatic structure of the legacy as expressed in its primal themes, or in the cultic history and in the culture at large. Insofar as the Protestant sects or communion have approximated rapport with the dramatic structure of the legacy, they have done so by elevating the notion of sin in the way we described earlier; this has had repercussions beyond that of restricting and impoverishing their appeal to the legacy. In restricting their appeal to the legacy in this manner, our Protestant forebears paved the way for the strong, moralistic bent of mind that was to sweep away every vestige of religious sensitivity, other than a moral concern, and to double their energy in resisting and, at times, defiantly opposing creative and imaginative expressions of the human spirit and of the Christian legacy as being seductive lures, dissipating or corrupting the moral sense. Among certain sects, intellectual inquiry itself became suspect and openly discouraged or suppressed. In this restrictive and repressive mode, overt expressions of the Christian legacy among Protestant sects became singularly impoverishing. In effect, religion and morals, so conceived, were equated. And, since so vast a proportion of the American experience has been historically shaped by such a restrictive appeal to the Christian legacy, much of the culture remains indifferent, if not hostile, toward appreciative and creative concerns of the human spirit.

Strange to say, the liberal era in Protestantism did not alter this stance significantly, except in their concern with intellectual inquiry. Rendering the witness of faith intellectually defensible and respectable was a high priority in liberal religion, and with it a sharpened concern for ethical sensitivity. In a way their concern with ethical sensitivity was a refinement of the moral bent of evangelical Protestantism. This was a definite advance toward broadening the appeal to the Christian legacy, and toward enhancing the impact of that legacy upon cultural experience. And, insofar as historical and scientific disciplines were made the tools of thought, the rapport between faith and culture among Protestant liberals increased. Yet, the one aspect of our cultural history and of the legacy that remained unattended by Protestant liberals was the appreciative and the imaginative dimension of experience, so basic to the art and poetry of life. Here the liberals remained ardently Protestant, pursuing ethical sensitivity with the zeal to which their forebears had employed their more restrictive moralistic measure. Thus it must be said that the liberal era did not substantially veer from the essentially moralistic bent of mind which has characterized American Protestantism, and which, in large measure, has shaped the style and tone of American culture as well.

Although the cultic history of the Christian legacy within Protestantism conveys a collapse of the dramatic structure of faith, elevating a secondary theme to dominance, it may not be said that the leit-motif, namely, the redemptive theme, subsided altogether as a motivating influence in Western culture at large. And here we see this redemptive theme, being extricated again from its cultic formulation, and set more explicitly in the cultural context. The initial, historical turn of thought which was to effect this transition was not outside the cultus. This, as we said earlier, came about in a subtle transition effected by Puritanism in which primary attention was focused on the secondary theme of the drama, namely, sin. The reversal of this restrictive, Puritan presentation of the legacy in the Romanticist period of liberal history, while it had decisive repercussions in the doctrinal history of the cultus, was a kind of renaissance of Christian piety among literary writers and artists of the eighteenth century who, at the same time, were under the influence of Spinoza. Schleiermacher was among this group, and, in his way, as author of the *Speeches,* must be considered a partner to the effort to transmute the notion of redemption into the more culturally accepted notion of human fulfillment. Even in his *Christian Faith,* wherein emulating or participating in the God-consciousness of Jesus is designated as the means to salvation, something of this notion of fulfilling human possibilities, so expressive of the Romanticist élan, seems to be implied. This theme was given even more encouragement in the writings of Johann Fichte and of George W. F. Hegel. Hegel might well be considered the precursor of much that has followed since the nineteenth century to transmute the redemptive theme into one of human fulfillment. For it can be argued that the pervasive influence of Hegel's absolute idealism had much to do with putting forth the developmental notion as a metaphysical counterpart of or even an alternative to the mythical notion of redemption. Having said this, one needs to recall that all absolute idealism cannot be so characterized, for it was Royce's *The Problem of Christianity* which jolted and sobered liberals into rethinking the import of historic Christian doctrines concerning "the moral burden of the individual," "guilt," and "grace."

There is a basis for arguing also that the philosophy of personalism, which is an American rendering of Lotze's transcendental idealism, advanced this transmutation of the redemptive theme into the notion of human fulfillment; in Borden P. Bowne, the founder of American personalism, human ideals were, in themselves, indices of the divine life of God, and the pursuit of them, the route to human fulfillment consonant with that divine life. But it was Horace Bushnell, a theologian who straddled the two worlds of the nineteenth century, who put the matter succinctly and at a point of crucial importance in saying, in *Christian Nurture,* "A child may grow up to be Christian and never know himself to be otherwise."[14]

Once the developmental theory of human nature gained ascendancy, the twice-born theory of earlier views of sin and redemption were put to rout. This conception of human nature was to be greatly accelerated by the philosophy of John Dewey and made influential as a cultural force when it became the principal source of insight and directives for the progressive education movement in American public schools.

That the notion of human fulfillment can in any way be squared or correlated with the redemptive theme of the Christian legacy, except as a reversal of it, or as a perversion of it, will certainly seem unlikely to most interpreters of the two modes of human destiny. And this judgment follows quite naturally, I think, from a consideration of the contrary methods of human renewal involved. The redemptive theme presupposes the need for resources other than one's own and a candid acknowledgment of human limitations and failings which stand in need of the redemptive act. Human fulfillment, on the other hand, in its initial formulation, seemed to imply that nothing more than the unfolding of an endowment already given was implied, though this was the Greek version of it, which, in effect, the Lotzean and personalist mode of idealism presupposed. The Hegelian philosophy of human fulfillment was more Roman in its sources, as C. C. Webb has observed in *God and Human Personality,* which implied a winning of successively new images of self-reality through social interaction and decision.

Whether such transmutations of the redemptive theme are to be considered reversals of it, or in some sense a carrying forward of it under auspices of a different order of change and renewal, will turn somewhat on the objective being pursued. If clarity in method and procedure is the concern, then clearly the two stand differentiated. If, however, the end result is in focus, positing openness to change, to renewal, and to future realization of what is presently denied, positing hope and expectation, then the redemptive theme and its cultural counterpart,

14. Horace Bushnell, *Christian Nurture* (Hartford, Conn.: Edwin Hunt, 1847), p. 6 (republished New York: Scribners, 1860), p. 10.

expressed through the yearning for fulfillment, have, to say the least, affinities as contrasted with non-Christian Oriental theories of man, which have looked to no such future renewal of man.

Whether or not this kind of correlation between the redemptive theme of the Christian legacy and qualities of the human spirit, discernible in our Western identity, can stand critical scrutiny, the fact remains, I think, that the correlation has been made; if not by us, by non-Westerners who are more sensitive to the impact of our identity upon them than to the logic by which we seek to justify or to criticize it.

And, whether we are Western or non-Western in sensibilities, it is not difficult to see how Westerners have trivialized and exploited this legacy of hope and renewal to make of this Western experience a crass venture in individual enterprise and cultural imperialism. And thus the legacy impelling openness to the future, resilience of spirit, expectancy, zest of mind and heart, has turned us to ruthless efforts, in missions and in industry, and, more recently, within the political maneuvering of our foreign policy, to make other peoples and civilizations over in our image. Bolstered by theories of inevitable progress and limitless resources, this zeal to redeem the world, that is, to make others more democratic, more Christian, more Western, has made us a formidable and menacing power, indeed, "a huge potency of ambiguous meaning and value."

Or again, in our Western experience, this legacy has often bogged down in a sentimental idealism which thrives on a wide range of clichés voicing an airy philosophy of *futurana*. When this legacy of an open future lapses into a commitment to inevitable progress and a pollyanna vision of life with no awareness of the stark realities of the lived experience that nurture and sustain such a stance, or that threaten it, our hopes become our nemesis.

When the redemptive theme is not trivialized, brutalized, or sentimentalized, when it is correlated realistically with seasons of anguish and despair or their possibility, with sober reflection upon man's limitations and failings, and with the disciplining of mind and spirit that can follow from such chastening, then this legacy looms as a resource of the spirit of considerable magnitude. For it then points up the promise of renascence within the very context of depletion and denial. It prepares the mind and spirit to confront loss and deprivation, even the tragedy of death and the dissolution of cherished relationships when these come to one.  For redemption in this context is no vain hope, or illusion of the mind simply to sustain one amidst broken dreams.  On the contrary, it is, in fact, a working of grace within relationships all about us.  It is what happens in the way of organic changes within people and situations, in response to the disciplining of the mind and spirit in confronting and participating in the rigors of deprivation and loss, in coping with frustration and momentary defeat in whatever, in one's heart and judgment, one must do.  This resource of grace is what happens, too, in response to the upwelling of human affection and camaraderie that follows upon experience of loss and despair.

Yet the redemptive theme, when it is soberly and sensitively attended, does more.  It opens up to us vistas of these troubled experiences which can only be characterized as moments of wonder and surprise: glimpses of a good-not-our-own, forever redoing the stubborn, relentless march of events that could otherwise be our undoing.  To be attentive to these vistas of wonder and surprise in the routines of the lived experience is to cultivate awareness of that which is "more than we can think," as a resource for enhancing, judging, and possibly redirecting that upon which we can and do clearly think and act.

V

A legacy may not be adjudged an asset or a liability *per se*.  It is, in fact, both, and ambiguously so.  Hence, it does not follow that, having defined the legacy from which one's cultural identity has derived, one may then flaunt either the legacy or the identity as a necessary virtue.  For each of them serves to characterize both the positive thrust of a people and their inherent limitations as a culture.  And it may be possible, having some awareness of each, to distinguish between what in history has served to enhance the cultural experience in relation to the historical experiences of other people and what has worked in opposing directions.  Self-understanding, whether it be of the individual or of a society of individuals, is a potential advance in human relationships.  Yet, what follows from it may not, in itself, be accounted an assured good.

In a similar manner, it is important to recognize that, coming to the judgment that our cultural identity is inextricably involved, and somewhat continuous, with the Christian legacy, is not to be taken as being necessarily a positive or negative connotation. Because of the ambiguity that pervades all religious legacies, one may not assume that simply being continuous with such a legacy is necessarily a good to be cherished. Being aware of such continuity, however, and of the subtle and persistent shaping of its mythos within the historical structure of experience can inform and enhance self-understanding and understanding of the culture in which one's life is cast.

Conversely, not to be aware of such personal and communal involvement in a persisting structure of experience is to open one to various illusions in regard to one's own stance and the stance of one's culture in relation to other people of the world. The liberal era, including its aftermath in the present period of world history, was rampant with such illusion concerning the role of individuals and of Western culture in world relations. Individuals, awakened to the historical experience of people nurtured by and involved with other religious histories and cultures, sought to identify themselves conceptually and appreciatively with them, often deciding that these other faiths and cultures offered more in the way of human understanding and fulfillment than their own indigenous faith or culture. And in this, they may have been right. Yet their lack of insight into the contextual character of all existence and their exaggerated individualism, along with their singular stress upon personality as an individual, free-floating entity, capable of identifying with any culture or religious experience, led them to assume that a will-to-believe, or not to believe, to be open or closed to another faith, was all that was involved in negotiating one's relations with other faiths and cultures. Their openness to other cultures and their religions was a definite advance upon the closed, introvert societies of Western experience of generations before them; but their zeal for taking up with other faiths and cultures in the free, individualized manner they imagined was sheer romance. In a similar way, and for the same reason, the dream of a universal faith, extricated from cultural inhibitions and historical biases, partook of this romantic vision.

The realism which a contextual and relativistic view of cultural histories and their religious legacies brings to our thinking upon problems of faith and culture radically alters the stance of critical reflection upon these issues. It does not lessen the concern with other faiths and cultures, nor soften our critique of our own religious and cultural history. In fact, it intensifies and accelerates both of them, and adds a further dimension to inquiry.  For the new empirical realism, stemming from the contextual and relativistic stance, has intruded a new measure of value in approaching other religions and cultures, based upon appreciation of the theme of dissonance, as contrasted with that of coherence, or the universalizing of the notion of coherence.  In a world of contextual meaning, dissonance takes on the import of qualitative distinctions which, in themselves, carry values to be cherished and sustained.  Such dissonance can mean a readiness to live together with differences in the interest of retaining, cherishing, and hopefully participating to some degree in the complexity of meaning and value which these cultural and religious differences offer.  Premature concern with coherence or universal agreement can mean the suppression of such qualitative differences as being simply discordant notes in an otherwise universally established, however impoverished, sense of unity and agreement.

A further factor enters in here to enlarge and, to a degree, to enhance this relativistic and dissonant stance in confronting other faiths and cultures.  In the empirical realism from which this presentation proceeds, the contextual and relativistic stance presupposes a depth of ultimacy embracing all faiths and cultures, in which each of them participates with varying degrees of relevance and revelatory power.  Yet no one of them can presume to speak other than as a witness of faith in response to this dimension of ultimacy within its historical immediacies. That each of them does, in fact, elevate its witness to an absolute disclosure of what is ultimate in experience, must be accounted a form of cultic hubris common to the human family when it ignores or overlooks the structural limitations of all human perception and awareness.  To speak humanly is to speak limitedly, yet with varying degrees of appropriateness, relevance, importance, and interestingness in relation, or in response, to the depth of ultimacy that subsumes every moment of immediacy.

Once this juxtaposition of our human limitations and our own participation in what exceeds our limited, structural existence is taken seriously, the qualitative differences among us in bearing witness to these depths of ultimacy within our various immediacies, and the cultural creations and growth consonant with them, take on significance.  The significance, to be sure, is augmented by the fact that each of the witnesses of faith bodies forth as well the limiting character of its own cultural structure of experience.  Yet, as a witness to the dimension of ultimacy apprehended, and the cultural creations that follow from it, each such witness is to be cherished, to some degree attended, appreciated, and received within one's own purview of understanding and faith to whatever degree this may be possible.

Some understanding of one's own cultural identity, and of the religious legacy contributive to it, can prepare a people to be critically and appreciatively responsive to this wider context of human participation in the depths of ultimacy and its consequent cultural creations. More particularly, it can alert a people critically to the immediate import of their own identity, and to the resources as well as the perversions that are implicit in the religious legacy that is consonant with that identity, and contributive to it.

# Index

Abstraction, xii–xiii, 22–28, 41–58, 67, 82, 129–41, 152
Alexander, S., 19, 50, 105
Altizer, Thomas, 17n
Ames, Edward Scribner, 7, 9n, 17n
Appreciative approach, as method in theology, 40–41, 87
Augustine, 90
Authority: biblical, 13, 50; church, 5, 38; challenge to, 64, 70, 73
Awareness: depths of, xiii, 27–33; creatural, 42–45, 53, 105–9; critical, 186–88; appreciative, 28–33, 177. *See also* Wonder

Baker, Herschl, 92
Barth, Karl, 3, 5, 8, 10, 16, 125, 126
Bartsch, H. W., ix, 128
Beardslee, William A., 57n
Belief, security of, xi–xiii, 73–79
Bergson, Henri, 4, 11, 13, 19, 48, 51, 106, 107, 110, 125, 141, 151–52
Bible, 12, 13, 16, 34, 88, 89, 93–101, 125–28, 144–49
Bixler, J. Seelye, 74
Boehme, Jacob, 104
Bonhoeffer, Dietrich, 36
Bowne, Borden P., 17n, 193
Bradford, Gamaliel, 190
Brown, Delwin, 19
Brunner, Emil, 3, 17, 125
Buber, Martin, 4, 21
Buddhism, 7, 30, 38, 48, 71
Bultmann, Rudolf, ix, 12–13, 18, 128

Burtt, Edwin A., ix, 16
Bushnell, Horace, 193

Calvin, John, 10
Calvinism, 91
Case, Shirley Jackson, 7, 17n, 182
Causal efficacy, 114, 185–87
Certainty: lure of, 71–77; illusions of, 141
Chicago, University of, vii, 6, 160
Chillingworth, William, 91
Christ, Jesus, 14, 76–77, 99, 130, 144–47, 164, 171, 176; as revelation in act, 93–95; as New Creation, 158–59. *See also* Christology
Christology, 77–78; in theological method, 145–47
Church, 89, 95, 124–25, 144–45, 147, 160–64; culture within, 167–71, 178–79. *See also* Cultus
Clement of Alexandria, 90
Cobb, John, viii, 19
Coe, George A., 17n
Community: individual in, 80–81, 96; church and, 168–71; style of a, 173–76; subliminal resources of, 183–84
Constructive theology. *See* Theology
Copernicus, Nicolaus, 92
Cousins, Ewert H., 19
Covenant: its restoration in Renaissance thinking, 92; as the root-metaphor of Judaic-Christian drama, 96–99; modes of interpreting, 100
Cox, Harvey, 17n, 172n

202